# TALKING TRAUMA

## PARAMEDICS AND THEIR STORIES

TIMOTHY R. TANGHERLINI

UNIVERSITY PRESS OF MISSISSIPPI
JACKSON

Copyright © 1998 by University Press of Mississippi

Manufactured in the United States of America

01   00   99   98      4   3   2   1

The paper in this book meets the guidelines for permanence and durability
of the Committee on Production Guidelines for Book Longevity of the Council
on Library Resources.

Library of Congress Cataloging-in-Publication Data

Tangherlini, Timothy R.
    Talking trauma : paramedics and their stories / Timothy R.
Tangherlini.
        p.      cm.
    Includes bibliographical references (p.    ).
    ISBN 1-57806-042-7 (cloth : alk. paper). — ISBN 1-57806-043-5
(pbk. : alk. paper)
    1. Emergency medicine.   2. Emergency medical technicians—
California—Alameida County.   3. Storytelling.   I. Title.
RC86.7.T364      1998
362.18—dc21
                                                      97-41468
                                                        CIP

British Library Cataloging-in-Publication data available

To Margaret

In the real dark night of the soul,
it is always three o'clock in the morning.
*F. Scott Fitzgerald*

You always get the weirdest calls at like
three o'clock in the morning.
*Oakland paramedic*

# CONTENTS

# PREFACE

My first exposure to paramedic storytelling came through my younger brother, himself a paramedic and the one who helped me contact the people at Regional Ambulance who could assist me in carrying out this project. After years of asking him not to tell me stories about crazy people, suicides, and automobile accidents, I realized that his storytelling pointed to an intriguing aspect of occupational culture not revealed by the popular representations of the field. The plans for this project were hatched one evening at a party when an acquaintance mentioned that he had noticed my brother and several other medics sitting alone on a back porch swapping work-related stories. Initially, the project was envisioned solely as a video documentary of paramedic storytelling. Once that was completed, it became apparent that, while one can convey certain types of information in a documentary, film is not suited to substantive discussions of wide-ranging topics. So I decided to write a book.

When I started, I felt compelled to record the paramedic stories in the context in which they were most frequently told, namely in the downtime between and after calls. Thus, I needed to ride along with crews during their shifts. Sometimes I would go home from a "strike car" shift at four in the morning, and return to the "barn" to meet up with my next shift a few hours later at seven. One crew would suggest other crews to ride with, and, after several weeks, it became clear who the paramedics considered to be the best storytellers; accordingly, most of the stories presented in this study come from a small group. I did not ride solely with those medics, however, as I wanted to witness a wide range of storytelling styles and explore the numerous storytelling contexts that occur over the course of a shift. Some paramedics were at their best at three in the morning, talking to their partner. Others loved crowds, preferring to present their stories as raucous performances. Different contexts also led to different kinds of storytelling, both in style and content. When I had a choice among several story variants on a particular topic, I decided to present the most engaging one.

Even though I rode along with forty different paramedics (nearly one quarter of the entire Alameda County paramedic force), and collected stories from over sixty, the stories of sixteen medics surface time and again in this study. One is Darryl, a former soldier who rides in the professional rodeo circuit on days off, and is best known in the company for his enthusiastic storytelling and high energy approach to everything. Tom B., his former partner and also an old hand in the company, studies auto mechanics and is contemplating a career change. Derek, Darryl's current partner, is a race car driver on days off and plays straight man to some of Darryl's more outrageous stories. Steve Y. and his partner, Stephanie, are more sedate, and are best known for their dry humor and cynicism. (Taking their partnership to another level, they married soon after I finished my fieldwork.) Lars and Mark G., both athletic and in their mid-twenties, have wry senses of humor, an addiction to caffeine, and a profound distrust of management, a description equally fitting for Patrick and Tony. Bill L. is a quiet man, said to have a "Zen" approach to paramedicine, while his partner, Bill R., is loud, boisterous, and always on the lookout for funny situations. Mary and Kathryn are tough, no-nonsense women who share a passion for country music. Among the most engaging of the storytellers is Bill V., a former member of an air force pararescue team who, because of stress, decided to leave the field and become, to everyone's great surprise, a cosmetologist. Another medic, Lisa, had become a paramedic after deciding against a career in veterinary medicine, while her quieter, yet deeply cynical, partner, Melinda, came from the East Coast seeking a job that would keep her away from "pesky" supervisors. Finally, there is George, a supervisor, who was known to most medics as a "Ricky Rescue," a person far too caught up in the media portrayals of the field.

It would be misleading to suggest that my presence in the ambulance did not affect the storytelling context, since the paramedics knew that I was there to observe and record them. Indeed, given the small size of the ambulance, it was impossible for me to be an unobtrusive observer. On the other hand, not a single paramedic found my request to hear their stories strange—I never had to ask for stories once they heard the reason for my being there. Even during our introductory conversations, the paramedics would begin to tell their stories and I would listen.

I was not prepared for the things I saw, heard and, most notably, smelled while with the paramedics. After the first few shifts, I would find myself lying in bed exhausted yet unable to sleep, replaying in my mind the various patients whom I had encountered that day, the numerous houses I had been in, and the different emergency rooms I had seen. But, as I grew accustomed to the work pace and the environment, the calls started to blend into one another. Soon, I was unable to give an accounting of all the calls my crew had responded to during a given shift. Only calls that had unexpected twists remained in my memory. As might be expected, some of these same calls entered the medics' storytelling, at least for the rest of the summer. And while I had been surprised initially at the laughing that accompanied much of the storytelling, by the end of my fieldwork I found myself amused by many of the situations they described in their stories, even those including graphic descriptions of injuries.

I hope to call attention with this study to the dynamic and rich tradition of paramedic storytelling. I include transcripts of storytelling sessions, and suggest some of the potential meanings the stories have for the paramedics. Often, the stories comment on aspects of the job, and at times the paramedics present conflicting attitudes. Consequently, in my analyses, I attempt to provide numerous perspectives on a given story. I agonized for quite some time over the presentation of these stories in a written text. At first, I experimented with standard systems of transcription, such as Dennis Tedlock's notation, but found them to be awkward.[1] Finally, for the sake of clarity, I decided to edit the stories, removing the overabundance of words and phrases such as "you know" and "like," as well as deleting redundant passages. These changes make the stories far more readable but, as a folklorist, I realize that I have done a certain violence to the texts. Yet, even if the stories were not edited, the simple act of committing them to paper fundamentally alters them. The stories are out of context; one cannot hear the paramedics' intonations nor see nonverbal cues such as gestures. Undoubtedly, my voice, that of the fieldworker and folklorist, makes itself heard along with those of the paramedics. However, I have tried throughout this work to act less as a narrator than as an engaged and interested observer. In addition, the video documentary on paramedic storytelling is available, and I propose that those interested in the rich performative aspects of this tradition—aspects impossible to capture on paper—use that in conjunction with this text.

Folklorists examine who tells what to whom, how and when they tell it, and then try to explain why. In the case of this study, the "who" is limited to a group of paramedics working in Alameda County in California for Regional Ambulance, a private company providing the exclusive 911 coverage for the East Bay counties of Alameda and Contra Costa. Regional Ambulance is a relatively large private ambulance provider, with several hundred employees. Near the end of my fieldwork, the company merged with several others to form the largest ambulance corporation in the country, American Medical Response. Although many paramedics offered skeptical comments on the emergence of this megacompany, and on the move away from the "Mom and Pop" operations that typically provided 911 services before Regional Ambulance secured the contract, others noted that the new configuration offered them advancement opportunities otherwise lacking. In the following pages, the paramedic group is more closely defined, and the "when," "how" and "what" of their storytelling tradition are scrutinized in greater detail. Throughout, I suggest reasons as to why a story might be told by the medic in that specific setting. As a form of shorthand, I often refer to paramedics as "medics." Since medics are prone to use jargon which can be confusing, I have provided a glossary explaining these terms. Finally, I have changed all of the names of the paramedics, their coworkers, and their patients.

Primary fieldwork for this project was carried out in the summer and fall of 1993, with additional fieldwork in the spring and summer of 1994 and the fall and winter of 1995. Many people helped me with the fieldwork, the documentary and, ultimately, this book. The lion's share of the thanks goes to my brother Niels for assisting me in the research. At the ambulance company, I would like to thank all of the executives, managers, and field supervisors who allowed me to do the work. I am also grateful to the officials of the state Emergency Medical Services Administration, the California Highway Patrol, and the Division of Labor Statistics and Research for their assistance with statistical information. Gayle Eads, Paul Ecord, and Jonathan Knight provided me with housing and camaraderie during my time in the Bay Area. At UCLA, Michael Owen Jones motivated me to complete these studies. I would also like to thank my chair, Mary Kay Norseng, for encouraging me to pursue the research and helping me secure much-needed funds for transcribing the many hours of tape. Irina Ozernoy deserves thanks for transcribing the tapes with both patience and alacrity. Bruce McCrimmon and David Hillary helped bring the video documentary portion of this study to completion. I would like to thank Jack Santino and Regina Bendix for their comments on that documentary. JoAnne Prichard, at the University Press of Mississippi, offered both encouragement and good suggestions, and her help has been instrumental in seeing this project through to completion. In addition, I would like to thank John Lindow, Mark Livengood, and my brother Arne Tangherlini for reading and commenting on earlier versions of the manuscript. My wife, Margaret, deserves thanks for unwavering support during the past years when I talked incessantly about medics and their stories of grisly accidents. Finally, I would like to thank all of the paramedics who were so willing to let me into their ambulances and tell me their stories.

# INTRODUCTION

# EVERYBODY'S GOT STORIES

Most people's impressions of the work of emergency medicine come from popular television programs. Among the earliest representations of the paramedic profession is *Emergency!*, a show from the 1970s that many medics jokingly refer to as the inspiration for their careers. In the grand tradition of cop-buddy shows of the 1950s and 1960s— *Car 54, Where Are You?*, *Adam 12*, and *Dragnet—Emergency!* followed two paramedic partners, John and Roy, as they raced around Los Angeles responding to one life-threatening emergency after another. With never a dull moment and medical emergencies occurring even while the two were on innocuous errands, there was certainly no time for the type of storytelling that paramedics engage in behind hospital emergency rooms, in the front seats of ambulances, or at coffee shops and bars.

The sometimes campy identification paramedics feel with *Emergency!* can reach amusing proportions, with the dividing line between them and their television counterparts blurring. Bill V., who had at one time worked in Southern California, recounts the story of buying the Land Rover driven by Roy on *Emergency!*:

Bill V.: I was flipping through the *L.A. Times* and I saw this Land Rover for sale up in Big Bear and so I called him up. And the guy who answers, he was like, "Oh, I played a paramedic on TV," and so I said, "Oh yeah, what show?" He said, "*Emergency!*" So I said, "Okay, yeah, so can I come up tomorrow and see the Rover?" So I did. It was Roy Desoto! Kevin Tighe, man. So the next day I drove it to work, and in the barracks there's the crews' quarters and if you're bored we used to watch TV. *Emergency!* was in syndication then, about ten o'clock in the morning and *Emergency!* came on and it just so happened that that first day I drove my Land Rover to work, it was one of those episodes where they had the Land Rover on, and I was down there showing my boss my Land Rover and the guys, they're like, "Hey, it's on TV right now, it's got the same license plate and everything!"

Because it does not pretend to be anything other than fiction, the television show paradoxically offers an acceptable representation of the profession. In the late 1980s, fictional occupational series such as *Emergency!* started being replaced by an ever-growing number of television programs referred to as "reality television."

Purporting to tell the "true stories" of a particular group—most often police, but in the case of *Rescue 911*, *Emergency Call,* and *On Scene,* those of emergency medical responders—these programs rely extensively on dramatic re-creations of medical emergencies. Among paramedics, *Rescue 911* is the most notorious. Hosted by William Shatner, best known for his role as Captain Kirk on *Star Trek,* the series re-creates ambulance responses to emergencies, followed by stylized post-incident interviews with the emergency responders and their patients. This portrayal of the profession has attained wide popularity with television audiences, but, among paramedics, the show is reviled:

George: I think *Rescue 911* is entertainment, I think that that's all it's meant to be. For the layperson who doesn't really know what it is we do, it might be kind of dramatic and kind of exciting, but for the people who are behind the scenes, who really know what goes on—that every call, every potentially bad call does not always turn out to be cake and ice cream with the patient afterwards—that's not realistic.

*Rescue 911* is also criticized by paramedics for showing events and actions which have little or no validity in the occupation, and, at times, would be downright dangerous:

Mark G.: For somebody who's in our business, it's a little too much to go home and flick on the TV and see 911 again, you know? It burns you out. We see it all day. So, pretty much, they suck. Pretty much everything they do on them is wrong. Most of the time.

Some feel that, instead of lending support to the profession, these representations detract from the paramedics' ability to perform their duties on scene in a proper and safe manner:

Lars: They always want to show the paramedics running. And then you get to the call and people on scene, they expect you to run. You're lugging seventy-five pounds of equipment and people want you to run up ten flights of stairs because they do it on TV. Then you're working some patient, and the crowd around you goes, "You've gotta save them! Do some of that *Rescue 911* shit!"

Popular expectations, derived from these media portrayals, clash with the paramedics' training and experience. As a result, people who call for an ambulance are not prepared when the paramedics do not run with reckless abandon to the patient's side, quickly load the ambulance, and leave the scene within a matter of seconds, but instead walk to the scene, ask questions, and at times initiate lengthy treatments before finally transporting the patient.

Another failing of the reality television programs, from the perspective of many paramedics, is the emphasis placed on responses to calls. Depictions of medics driving, arriving on scene, talking on the radio, starting intravenous lines, administering medications, and defibrillating cardiac arrest patients take up most of the time on these programs. No consideration whatsoever is given to the immense amount of down-time—the waiting at tedious post assignments, the cleaning and re-stocking of the ambulance between calls, and the filling out of paperwork—that constitutes the majority of the work day. During these long gaps, paramedics share their perspectives on the job with each other, and it is as much through these interactions as during emergency responses that they develop customs and beliefs specific to their occupation.

Most popular representations deny paramedics an opportunity to speak for themselves. Instead, a strong narrator assumes the position of authority, re-creating the call in a voice-over. When the medics are allowed to speak, it is within the framework of a highly structured studio interview. Even in dramatic television programs, such as the popular series *ER,* paramedics appear infrequently, and always in roles subordinate to the hospital staff. Medics deplore this lack of opportunity to present their profession in their own words. In this book, I want to show how medics talk among themselves about their profession, as opposed to how their jobs are presented on television. Unlike those TV stories, which contribute to a master narrative of the paramedic as a silent, unwavering hero, the paramedics' stories cover topics ranging from the problems facing urban America, the status of emergency medical services, and the problems with health care to the difficulties, frustrations, and rewards of their job.

Storytelling pervades our everyday lives and to a great degree structures how we view the world. We learn the beliefs, values, and norms of our culture through stories, respond to certain situations by telling stories, entertain each other with stories, and employ narration to voice our fears, hopes, frustrations, and joys. At times we use stories rhetorically to effect certain ends, to criticize individuals or groups, or to convince others that we are right.[1] Even at work, storytelling can play an important role in how we perceive our jobs and our relationships with coworkers and in how we carry out our tasks. In many cases, the stories employees and their managers tell play a major role in the functioning of the organization. Workers rely on stories of coworkers' experiences, coupled with their own narratives about work, as a guide to day-to-day life. Indeed, the manner in which workers "speak" the organization can be more important than how managers have codified the structure of that organization. The work of paramedics is informed more by the stories they tell each other about the company and their duties than by the thick personnel binder.

Even though it may be alluring to speak of the homogeneous culture of organizations and the concept of shared culture, the study of medic storytelling reveals a great deal of diversity both in behaviors and in attitudes. Medics do not all interpret similar events in a similar manner, nor do they all get along with one another. Far from being homogeneous, the medics' culture is marked by disjuncture and ambiguity.[2] Seen in this light, storytelling acts as a means for individuals both to interpret their experiences in the organization and to position themselves within that organization. Examining the role of storytelling among paramedics, in turn, affords an opportunity to develop a better understanding of how a medic views his or her occupation.

In the late 1970s and early 1980s, management literature touting the idea that work organizations function as minisocieties began appearing.[3] The majority of these studies, however, were unclear on their definitions of "society" and, more specifically, of the frequently used concept "culture."[4] Although it may be tempting to apply the work of sociocultural anthropologists to an understanding of the interaction of individuals with and within culture, such functionalist approaches necessarily require an emphasis on broad generalizations and thereby provide a deterministic model of culture, privileging the interpretive stance of the researcher.[5] Rather than attempting to portray something as slippery and dynamic as culture by using the broad brush of anthropology, a study focusing on specific symbolic behaviors — storytelling, for example — as part of culture will likely lead to a more nuanced understanding of life in an organization or in a society, with all its dynamism and contradictions.

Storytelling among paramedics occurs in numerous contexts, can be precipitated by various situations, has diverse purposes and consequences, affects different people in different ways, indicates numerous motives and intentions of narrators as well as of audiences, and offers varied interpretations of an event. The context of the telling (time, place, and audience) and the style (gestures, facial expressions, intonation, pitch, pacing, laughter, and silences) are equally important.[6]

Indeed, how, where, and to whom a story is told can have a profound influence on how one interprets what is told. Storytelling is always a situated event, and interpretation requires an appreciation of the performance's context. At the same time, it is imperative to recognize that a story produces multiple meanings for the narrator and the audience. The indeterminacy of meaning stems in large part from the importance of the individual, both narrator and audience member. Stories are not told by faceless members of a group; rather, individuals—each with his or her own unique personality, experiences, and narrating style—create what is generally referred to as "tradition."

Most of the stories medics tell center on their own experiences or on the experiences of medics they know. At times, they invent stories, or stretch the truth a bit, to make the conversation more engaging. These stories are known as "personal experience narratives."[7] In a study of personal experience storytelling, William Labov and Joshua Waletzky suggest that people tend to tell stories only about unusual, unexpected, or unique incidents.[8] While this conclusion generally holds true for medic storytelling, one must consider what types of events paramedics find to be unique, unusual, or unexpected. What may qualify as such an experience for a person not accustomed to responding to medical emergencies may be mundane and routine for a medic. As one medic puts it, "A lot of people find it hard to believe some of the stuff that we go through." Not surprisingly, paramedic storytelling tends towards the description of extremes—situations far removed from most people's experiences:

Bill V.: I've been to the nineteen-thousand-foot ridge on Mt. McKinley.

George: Is that right?

Bill: Yeah, I picked up seven Japanese climbers, frozen on the side of the mountain. The Japanese mountaineers, they don't turn back.

George: What do you mean? They get to the top, then what do they do? Jump?

Bill: No, no, you just keep going until you get the peak, if you don't die. If you die, you die. You don't retreat off the mountain. You make the summit or you die trying! And these guys, they [laughter] . . . I mean nineteen thousand foot on the side of Mt. McKinley, I mean it's deadly. These guys got caught in a storm, and all seven of these guys were frozen in the climb position. They were frozen, their ice axes in their hand, in the climbing position, man! They were locked in and just frozen like that! We had to break their arms and shit to get them in body bags, 'cause they were all frozen and shit. Snap!

Paramedics frequently play up this extreme aspect of the stories. As another medic notes, "I think the more you get into this business, the better you get at telling stories." In fact, some paramedics suggest that rookies, interns, and EMTs (emergency medical technicians) do not have the requisite experience to tell truly compelling stories:

Steve: If they've been an EMT for a long time they can tell some pretty compelling stories, it really depends on their experience. I think what happens with interns is that they're so excited about trying out their skills, and so their stories tend to be more like, "Yeah, and we started an IV and gave him this drug and it worked!"[9] and so we're like, "Oh, okay." Sometimes they'll have a good story, but sometimes it may just be the way we perceive it, you know, oh, it's an intern talking.

Hierarchies are a regular feature of the paramedics' work environment—both on the scene of emergencies and at the hospital—and so it is not surprising that hierarchies also exist among the storytellers. In this case, the more experienced medics are considered to be the best storytellers.

Paramedics tell their stories for other paramedics. Indeed, one of the most apparent characteristics of their stories is the ubiquity of technical terms, abbreviations, and radio brevity codes. This use of jargon makes the stories difficult for nonparamedics to understand, unless one happens to be familiar with the terminology of medicine and of emergency communication. In both of these realms, there is a deliberate tendency to obfuscate—medical personnel sometimes speak in shorthand so as not to alarm bystanders, while emergency dispatchers deliberately use code words to deter "ambulance chasers." The use of jargon among paramedics also helps them determine the boundaries of their group, since new recruits have to spend time with the other medics before they can understand what is being said.[10] Lars draws attention to the incomprehensibility of some of the jargon:

Lars: In New York, they had all kinds of great little terminology. People who lived in the housing projects were referred to as hamsters, and the projects were of course the Habitrail. So they'd be telling a story and say, "Oh yeah, we went over to the Habitrail to pick up a hamster," and they'd rattle off all these terms and I'd be like, "What the hell are you talking about? What do you mean you went to a Habitrail?" I had no idea what they were talking about for the first few months. Then I picked it up.

This use of jargon also contributes to the paramedics' self-presentation as authorities who have control over a specialized language.

A paramedic on scene, in public view of patients and bystanders, presents the persona of a highly trained professional carrying out a treatment-oriented performance. When only paramedics are around, they do not have to keep up this public presentation of themselves. Paramedic storytelling usually takes place between partners in the long periods of downtime between calls. For example, here Mary and Kathryn tell the story of a shooting they responded to:

Mary: This guy was delivering papers and he got caught up in an attempted carjacking. It was about four o'clock in the morning and he and his sister were out in his car. And he got out of the car to, I don't know, I guess toss a paper on a porch. [laughter] And somebody came up and wanted his car and he was trying to be a man about it and be tough or whatever. He got shot in his chest, right?

Kathryn: He got shot in the face and the chest!

Mary: Face and the chest?

Kathryn: Yeah.

Mary: And he was totally innocent, just you know out doing his job and they killed him. Just for nothing. Ended up not even taking his car. Just, you know, his life. And left like it was nothing, you know? And his poor sister was all wigged out and stuff. But you can't really blame her, she watched her brother get murdered. He was only like nineteen years old. Was it?

Kathryn: Something like that.

Mary: Yeah, that was fucked.

Kathryn: But the really hard part about it is that we thought the guy was going to live, so we pulled him out of his car and we started doing CPR on him, and he opened his mouth and he started breathing and he had a heart-beat, and that lasted for what? How long, Mary?

Mary: A minute.

Kathryn: About a minute or two. We thought maybe he was going to make it but he just bled out [hemorrhaged] completely.

In Mary and Kathryn's story, the distinction between teller and audience blurs. As Mark G. mentions, the stories emerge in the course of conversations and focus on similar experiences:

Mark G.: I just got a new partner, so I'm able to rehash all my cool old stories, tell them all over again, which is kind of cool. He'll give me one, and I'll give him one, then he'll give me one, similar situations. That's all I've been doing the last couple of days. It's been fun.

Some partners have heard each other's stories so many times that the narrative becomes a cooperative endeavor, as is treating a critical patient on scene. At other times, medics congregate near emergency room ambulance loading areas, since this is one of the few places where they have a chance to socialize.[11] In these situations, it is not uncommon for several paramedics to jump into the storytelling, which then takes on a competitive feel, with narrators trying to outdo each other. In these situations, the general rule of telling stories with firsthand authority does not apply, and, in the spirit of competition, medics may tell stories about calls that their partners have had or, in rarer instances, calls that they have "heard about."

   Understanding why an individual tells a particular story at a particular time is not a transparent task, and the best that the folklorist can hope for is to elucidate some of the meanings. In part, storytelling offers an entertaining diversion from the tedium of waiting at post assignments. It also gives the medics a chance to exert control over the narrated events. Through their stories, they can impose order on what are generally chaotic, unstructured scenes. Frequently in their stories, they position themselves as the calm in the center of a storm. As Jonathan A. Robinson writes, "We may grant that narrators will often endeavor to portray themselves as more clever, skillful, resourceful, or of higher moral character than their antagonists. This attitude is not to be disparaged, for it is not merely an attempt to exploit a social interaction to further one's self esteem. It is a semiritualized means of reaffirming both one's personal identity and socially sanctioned beliefs and values, particularly those that ascribe responsibility, hence blame or praise."[12] At the same time, the stories can be seen as a political act with the presentation of self taking on strategic importance. Through their storytelling, paramedics comment on the organization of their work environment, the relative competence of the personnel from other agencies, the abilities of other paramedics, and the merits or faults of other ambulance services.

Paramedics consider storytelling an opportunity to exchange information. For example, stories about combative patients, unexpected hazards, or surprising outcomes all provide medics with important experiential information. Thus, to some degree, the stories serve a didactic purpose. As one paramedic says, "There's nothing you can't learn on this job. Anybody who thinks they know it all doesn't know shit. There's nobody who can't teach you something about something. Once you stop listening then you're fucked. You'll never do any good in this job." The stories also build solidarity and, in the give and take of storytelling, the medics develop commonly held views, debate beliefs, and reinforce norms. As such, the storytelling contributes to their sense of shared community. However, not all paramedics are enthusiastic about their coworkers' storytelling. Cecil, for example, says, "Working in Oakland is a trip in itself. I'm not big on stories to tell you the truth. I hate listening to people tell stories and you just sit around Darryl for a while and all you hear is story, story, story. I don't know. This is the business of stories. Yeah, everybody's got stories, but don't bore me, that's kind of my attitude." Numerous studies of storytelling have revealed the differing degrees to which people participate.[13] Some people enjoy telling stories, while others prefer to listen. Some, like Cecil, readily acknowledge the existence of the tradition, but prefer not to engage in either the telling or the listening. At times, however, the storytelling is unavoidable and the person is forced into being an unwilling participant.

During the course of a shift, medics are stationed throughout the county according to a "flexible deployment system." One of the stipulations of their 911 contract is that they must reach the scene of a call within eight minutes of being dispatched. Rather than working out of station houses, they are assigned to "posts," strategically selected street corners that allow them quick access to various parts of the city. The concentration of paramedics in the city is determined by calculations based on call volume for specific sectors of the county at specific times of day. Because of this flexible deployment system, the medics work with a high degree of autonomy. In fact, the only time they spend at their central deployment center, "the barn," is at the beginning and end of their shift. During the next twelve hours, they are either at post, on the way to a new post, responding to a call, on scene, en route to the hospital or taking care of paperwork and other duties at the hospital. The standard work week at Regional Ambulance consists of four twelve-hour shifts. Two field supervisors patrol the streets, but they rarely manage to make contact with all of the paramedics on duty at any given time. Paramedics thus work with very little direct supervision, and many of them cite this relative freedom as one of the most attractive aspects of their jobs. The field supervisor, in turn, must walk a fine line between insuring that company policies are followed and respecting the experience and personal techniques of the individual paramedics.

Alameda County stretches along the eastern edge of the San Francisco Bay. While most parts of the county are densely populated, others are remote and isolated. The East Bay is known for its mild weather year round, with an average temperature of fifty-eight degrees and an average yearly rainfall of twenty-three inches, making it considerably warmer and drier than its better-known counterpart, San Francisco,

across the bay. A high ridge of hills runs along the entire coast, several miles inland. The coast itself is dominated by ports, naval bases,
and highways, and it is here that one finds the county's industrial concentration. From the coast, the land slopes gently upwards to the East
Bay hills; these areas, known as the flats, are part residential and part
commercial. A series of earthquake faults, most notably the Hayward
Fault, three to four miles inland, defines the eastern border of the
flats. Rising from the flats, the East Bay hills tower to heights of nineteen hundred feet and act as a natural barrier to eastward movement.
A developed network of parks—the East Bay Regional Park District—
dominates most of the hills, with huge stands of eucalyptus trees and
small redwood groves.

As one goes further north and east in Alameda County, one finds
the neighborhoods becoming more prosperous. While the hills are
dotted with luxurious homes, the areas surrounding the port are characterized by crumbling warehouses, burned-out and abandoned buildings, and large public housing projects. Highways crisscross the county,
with three major interstates and their tributaries carrying a huge volume of traffic on a daily basis. The BART (Bay Area Rapid Transit) system provides public rail transportation for the entire Bay Area, and
links much of the East Bay to the San Francisco area. The main city
in the county is Oakland, with a population of nearly 375,000, and
the majority of the emergency calls originate there, although the two
large communities of San Leandro and Hayward to the south and Livermore to the east contribute to the extraordinarily high call volume
that confronts the paramedics.

The population of Alameda County exhibits a remarkable ethnic and
racial diversity. According to 1990 census figures, 52 percent of the
population is white, 18 percent is black, 15 percent Asian, 14 percent
Hispanic, and the remaining 1 percent Native American. Many recent
immigrants from Mexico, South America, Eastern Europe, and East and
Southeast Asia contribute to the dynamic mix of people in the East
Bay. A variety of customs and languages makes up the county's rich
cultural fabric. Nowhere in the area is this cultural diversity more apparent than in Oakland. A large part of downtown Oakland is known

as Chinatown, and, although not as well known as San Francisco's Chinatown, the area is a magnet for the county's large Asian populations, not only Chinese but Vietnamese, Khmer, and Korean as well. Other parts of the city have concentrations of Mexican, Central American, and South American immigrants, and, in some areas, pockets of Eastern European immigrants are beginning to emerge. The signs that line the streets in different parts of the city attest to the numerous languages and cultures that contribute to Oakland's diversity.

As a city, Oakland suffers from the strong economic allure of San Francisco and the Silicon Valley, and unemployment and poverty are chronic problems.[14] Although unemployment in Alameda County hovers near the national average, in Oakland it pushes 11 percent. In recent years, Oakland has also vied for the dubious honor of being "murder capital of the United States."[15] Drug dealing, gang violence, random shootings, a paucity of meaningful employment opportunities, a faltering city government, overcrowded schools, and a strong-armed public housing police force all contribute to a pervasive sense of hopelessness in the poorer neighborhoods. It is in these disparate geographic, cultural, and economic environments that the paramedics work. In a single shift, the paramedics I rode with responded to a bicycle accident in one of the parks high above the bay, then plunged down the hill and responded to a medical call in a run-down housing project. After dropping the patient at the central county hospital, they went to the site of an industrial accident out by Oakland's busy docks. The next call came for a heart attack victim at a Vietnamese restaurant in Chinatown, followed quickly by one for a minor automobile accident on an interstate. After responding to a call for a confused patient suffering from an alcohol-induced seizure, the medics ended the shift by going to the home of a recent Russian immigrant whose limited English coupled with the medics' limited Russian contributed to the difficulty of treating the patient's acute stomach pains. In between each of these calls, the medics told stories as a way to fit these and other experiences into their general understanding of the job.

# TALKING TRAUMA

# CHAPTER

# 1

# DOES IT TAKE
# ANY TRAINING?

On a relatively slow summer day, paramedics Steve and Stephanie are eating lunch in a small deli in downtown Oakland. The conversation turns to difficult calls, ones that require medics to use all of their advanced life support skills, and the two start to swap stories. Steve sits back and, between bites of his sandwich, tells a story about a shooting:

Steve Y.: Let me tell you what happened. It was about a year ago, and I was working with a guy named Bob Wilson at the time. He's working for a fire department somewhere else now, but on that day, we heard a unit go out on a call for a shooting at Bosn's Locker. That's a bar up on Telegraph. It was just a standard call, and we heard them go out on the scanner. Then all of a sudden, we hear a frantic police officer call for five more ambulances. So we got there as the second unit in and it was just an amazing scene. Several people were shot—I think it ended up with ten or eleven people were shot, two were killed.

I remember when we were walking in, it was really weird. The thing that stands out in my mind is that apparently two guys with Uzis had come into the bar and just lit up the whole bar. And I remember we were walking in and we weren't really sure what was going on, and we opened the door and there was a crunching sound under your feet—like you were walking on potato chips. And I remember looking down at just thousands of spent shell casings, must have been at least five hundred spent shell casings on the ground! Then looking down on the ground, there was people just everywhere—one guy hanging over the bar, on his stool with a bullet in his head, and people down everywhere.

I was looking at the bar and there was this bullet path that had passed through the roof down the bar, like they had just swooped down the bar with machine guns. It was one of those calls where you just kind of stand there in awe, thinking, "I can't believe that somebody would callously walk in and do this."

It turned out they were just gunning for a fellow drug dealer, and just wasted twelve people in the process. You walk in and it was total devastation. That was probably one of the truly scariest calls I'd ever just walked in on. It was amazing. And then you've got to snap to it and get going, with all these people. When calls get that big, there's just a mess on top of everything else. You're in a tiny place with people who haven't been shot and people who have been shot, and it's just hard to get control. Plus, then the supervisor showed up. There were other people who'd been shot and actually fled the bar and then returned. I remember one guy got shot in the head and left and actually was able to come back into the bar!

Stephanie: It's really weird when people get shot, leave the scene and come back again! That's what happened the other night with the call for the six people that were shot. These people stopped back in on the way to the hospital, "Oh, can you look at me?" Yeah, you've been shot!

Steve: Walking in I'll never forget that feeling and looking down and seeing just a whole field of empty bullets and going "Oh, this is fucked."

Stephanie: They just stood at the door, hunh?

Steve: Yeah, two guys with Uzis. They said they reloaded three times.

Stephanie: I'm surprised more people didn't get killed.

Steve: Yeah, you know I'm surprised. But they killed an off-duty police officer and the owner, and then hit twelve other people.

Several days later, the supervisor who was called to the scene tells his story of the shooting and the difficult triage problems associated with this multiple casualty:

Tom B.: I became a field supervisor and I see a lot of multicasualty incidents and one of them in particular, which was pretty horrifying, was somebody stuck a machine gun in the door of a small bar, and killed two and critically wounded seven more. And when I got there, there was two paramedic units already there and police wouldn't let any of the patrons out of the bar. So, needless to say, the chaos was pretty intense. 'Cause people were screaming, "I need help over here, I need help over there!"

And to wade through all of these people with varying gunshots — nothing was below the waist — was tough. We had multiple GSWs [gunshot wounds] — in the chest, in the head, two fatalities. So I was looking at all of this and I was thinking, "You know, fuckin', I could be doing this all by myself!" You know, that rehearsal from the past in my mind really helped out. And we just had to say, "Okay, these two, they're dead." That's a pretty hard thing to do when you're trained to save everybody. You're geared to treat everybody you come across, and to have to say, "Okay, these two, they're dead, and we're not treating them," and then to have to wade through all the critical patients and decide who gets treated first, who's going to the hospital first and that kind of thing. So, that kind of wears on you. Sometimes I think about it and hope like hell I made the right decision, you know?

But I could have tied up all our resources on those two and transported them to the hospital, but what was it gonna do? There's seven other people who are still alive, probably stay alive if you get them to the hospital, rather than these two, they're dead and are pretty much gonna stay dead, you know?

In his story, Tom brings the question of training to the foreground. Although stunned by the brutality of the scene, he makes several difficult triage choices. Later, he wonders if he made the correct ones and, through the process of telling the story, arrives at the conclusion that he did. In his comments, he mentions the orientation towards saving lives that informs both the training and the actions of paramedics.

Paramedics at times confront situations that would overwhelm most people. Once on scene, they must assess the circumstances, identify the patients, and, in the case of multiple patients, perform triage. Then they have to develop a treatment plan, contact the base hospital and their dispatch, initiate treatments, and finally stabilize patients before transporting them. In life-threatening emergencies, time is of the essence, and all of these procedures must be accomplished quickly yet thoroughly. Despite all this, people approach paramedics and ask if the job requires any training. Darryl, an experienced medic, mentions that this question is one that thoroughly confounds him:

Darryl: The topper of them all is people who come up to me and ask, "Does it take any training to be a paramedic?" "Oh, none at all!" [laughter] "None at all!" You just get in the bus and you take off. Sort of like on-the-job training. I mean you'll figure this out—eventually. I can't believe it, people ask that though, all the time. All the time. "Does it take any training to be a paramedic?" "You just jump right on in, I had the uniform, it already fit from a Halloween costume!" Is that too much or what?

Darryl's sarcastic comments echo the sentiments of many medics who feel that the public has little appreciation of their skills. Most paramedics mentioned that the public often refer to them as "ambulance drivers," a term they find to be demeaning, since it ignores their significant training and suggests that the main responsibility in their work is driving the vehicle rather than caring for the patient.

The development of the field of paramedicine is closely linked to the history of Emergency Medical Services (EMS). Regrettably, this history is marked by fitful stops and starts, periods of unbridled optimism and energetic policy initiatives interspersed with long stretches of stagnation and backsliding.[1] Paramedicine first entered the American public consciousness in the mid-1960s with the frequent media footage of Med-Evac operations from Vietnam. It soon became clear that, while the expedient care and transport of the sick and injured was the focus of major efforts within the military, the same could not be said of civilian society. A survey of ambulance services in the United States conducted between 1966 and 1971 revealed that the majority of civilian ambulance care was provided by funeral homes as a community service.[2] In cases where the patient did not survive, this service also afforded funeral homes a degree of convenience and a potential source of revenue. It was an odd incentive structure, indeed, to have funeral homes providing for critically sick or injured patients. In most cases, the early ambulances were not designed for medical care during transport. The popular station wagons and hearses hardly had the room necessary for an attendant to assist the patient on the way to the hospital, and the equipment was inadequate for treating anything but the most minor injuries.[3] Instead, the general philosophy of most ambulance services at the time was "load and go" or, more colorfully expressed, "scoop and scoot."

The advent of the well-developed interstate highway system brought with it a concomitant rise in the number of highway traffic accidents, and, in 1966, the Department of Transportation (DOT) pushed for legislation that would provide better safety standards on the nations' roads. In 1971, DOT outlined the first training course for EMTs, followed soon thereafter by the Emergency Medical Services Act of 1972, legislation that effectively laid the foundation for a nationally consistent ambulance service and indirectly guaranteed the necessity of the paramedic profession.[4] But a lack of follow-through on the part of an embattled Nixon White House in the early 1970s threatened to derail fledgling state programs throughout the country. Two agencies, DOT and the newly formed Department of Emergency Medical Services, came to loggerheads over which one had a legitimate claim to policy development and implementation. The results of this aborted rush into the development of a national system of emergency medical care resonated throughout the late 1970s and into the 1980s. Even in the 1990s, some systems are woefully understaffed with insufficiently trained employees and still rely on the inadequate communications systems of the early 1970s. In many communities, volunteers, who, in the estimation of professional paramedics, are hardly qualified to handle the needs of a critically ill patient, are the only ambulance personnel available. By the early 1990s, EMS suffered from an abundance of legislative contradictions and a lack of coordination, with the result that some areas had excellent systems while adjacent communities had virtually none. Public and private providers found themselves locked in competitive turf battles, and hospitals that had once offered trauma care and emergency room services could no longer do so because of the astronomical rise in health care and insurance costs through the 1980s and 1990s.

The training to become a paramedic, the most advanced level for ambulance and rescue personnel, builds on the eighty-hour basic life support (BLS) EMT course established by DOT. There are now several levels of training, including the basic EMT, two intermediate levels, and the most advanced level, EMT-P, or paramedic. In Alameda County, basic EMTs provide backup assistance to paramedics, transfer patients between hospitals and their homes, and transport noncritical patients. As they discover the limits of their own training and the broader scope of the paramedics' practice, some EMTs return to school for the more rigorous paramedic training. The standard paramedic course consists of slightly more than one thousand hours of classroom and clinical instruction and a three-month field internship. Paramedics are trained in what is known as advanced life support (ALS) techniques, which focus on the care and transport of critical patients. During their training, paramedics learn the general principals of triage, how to conduct field assessments, how to read and interpret vital signs, how to look for indications of external and internal injuries, how to listen through a stethoscope to various organ sounds, and how to gather additional clues concerning a patient's condition. They also learn which drugs are used to treat which maladies and the contraindications and possible side effects of these drugs. Finally, they learn immobilization techniques, bandaging, the treatments for blunt and penetrating trauma, and the care of burns. Some of the more dramatic medical techniques that paramedics learn are those for restoring normal heart function and managing the patient's breathing. As paramedicine developed through the 1970s, more and more emphasis was placed on the expedient treatment of coronary events. In large part, this increased focus can be attributed to medical studies showing that, with early treatment, heart attack victims had an exponentially greater chance for survival.[5] Techniques such as defibrillation and intubation were incorporated into paramedic training along with the development of treatment protocols that included aggressive intervention for heart attack victims.

Paramedics also receive training in rescue techniques, including extrication of patients from badly damaged vehicles or collapsed structures. Sometimes medics have to crawl into confined spaces to stabilize their patients while the fire department works with heavy cutting and prying devices, such as "the jaws of life." Other rescue techniques, involving, for instance, the use of Stokes baskets [a wire mesh basket] and helicopters, can figure in their training. Unlike physicians and nurses, who are guaranteed a stable—albeit chaotic—environment, the medics must work in a variety of physical circumstances. A patient may be caught in a car that has fallen into a muddy ravine late one rainy night or be stuck in a bathroom on the fourth floor of an abandoned building used by crack addicts. The closest thing the medic has to a stable, controlled environment is the back of the ambulance, but even here it can be difficult to start intravenous lines, manage an airway, and provide continuous updates to the hospital, all in a cramped work space, while the vehicle is bouncing down a road.

Paramedics not only encounter difficult physical environments while on the job but also must contend with bystanders, other emergency responders, and traffic. On scene, they have to evaluate the information they receive from bystanders, defuse potentially explosive confrontations, coordinate their work with the police, and develop a cooperative relationship with the firefighters. Although one can learn most medical procedures, as well as theories of triage, crowd control, and cooperation, in the classroom, medics agree that such a setting bears little resemblance to the outside world. Accordingly, before medics can be certified, they must spend several months working with preceptors as part of their training. It is during this period, generally referred to as an internship, that the new paramedic develops an appreciation of how to balance the medical side of the job with the environmental one.

Paramedics generally choose the profession because of its medical aspects. One morning, Bill V., a medic for seventeen years and one of the most experienced at Regional, discussed his motivations for becoming a paramedic:

Bill V.: I was talking to my uncle, who was an ER doctor, and I was talking to him about maybe becoming a doctor and stuff. He goes, "Bill, being a doctor isn't what it used to be." He goes, "The malpractice and the specialization and as hard as it is to get into medical school, the effort doesn't equal the reward." He goes, "Bill, there's this new thing they have now, it's called paramedic and these guys are doing things that doctors weren't doing twenty years ago. This is a new thing, you ought to think about that." And ever since, I decided to be a medic.

My very first job, I was a lifeguard, and then when I was old enough, I was a beach lifeguard. When I graduated from high school, I went into the air force into para-rescue, because they were going to teach me how to be a paramedic, how to do all this other neat stuff. As soon as I could, I got to civilian paramedic school. It was something I've always believed in, you know? We are an honorable organization, an honorable profession, and we do a lot of neat things and do a lot of things in medicine that nobody else does, and the changes that I've seen the last seventeen years, it's phenomenal.

I tell these twenty-one-, twenty-two-year old guys I work with as a float — guys just out of paramedic school, just starting in this career field. They talk and they ask me all these questions and stuff like I'm the old man, and what I try to relate to these guys is that you've just been a paramedic for six months and you are still one of the first paramedics, you know? It's so new and so exciting, the changes.

You know, I remember not that long ago being in the ER and I brought in a pediatric full arrest and they're calling all these doctors in and all these other people from the floors in because Doctor So-and-So is going to do an intraosseous infusion on this child. Oooooh, he's gonna stick this needle in this kid's bone and give him fluids and give him drugs and revive this kid through a needle going into the bone, the medullar cavities. "Oh, this is wild. Oh, this is neat. Oh, wow!" Paramedics are doing it now.

I remember when they were doing external pacing. First time I saw that, they're talking that we're going to be doing it within a year, external pacing. And all the drugs we use and the skills we use.

George: All this stuff that nurses still can't do! We're doing pleural decompressions without even being told to. That's unheard of, where six years ago a paramedic had to make base contact to start an IV, now we're putting needles into people's chests.

Bill: Or their bones, or their necks!

In Bill's comments, the persuasive function of storytelling is clear. He draws attention to the relative novelty of the profession, as well as to the increasing medical skills that medics possess, and then uses stories to bolster these statements. In a comment typical of medics, George brings up a comparison between the skill level of medics and that of nurses, thus highlighting one of the most common topics in medic conversations.

On another day, Mark G. sits in the front seat of the ambulance and explains his reasons for being a medic:

Mark G.: It just gets you going, you catch yourself in the back with this patient and you stop and you go, "Wait a moment, this is just me and him here, I'm fighting for this person's life." And so I was in back and I was yelling, "Hey, don't give up. You better get your shit together. Come on, take a deep breath, come on fight with me!" It's hard for them to understand what's going wrong, they just know that they're screwed up and not feeling well. They don't know that they're on the edge of death, right, right on the edge. You gotta get them motivated, you have to get them and say, "Hey, I'm doing everything I can to save you, and you have to fight with me here!"

I remember when I was sixteen, the first real call that I did anything on was this guy who was like sixty-five. He got out of the car after dinner and had a heart attack and that was it, he was dead, you know? The family is standing around there, so I grab a defibrillator and start working the guy. Where I worked, it was such a small town, everybody knew everybody, so you get on scene, and it's like "Oh, that's so and so." And when you know them, it just throws you for a loop.

But up here is probably the first time that I've really been responsible, really on my own. When you're an EMT, or a firefighter, you always kind of have support around you. You're not the sole person responsible for this person. When you're out here as a paramedic, you're the first line of defense against dying.

I had one recently. A guy got in a motorcycle accident, it wasn't his fault, someone pulled in front of him, and it crushed his chest and his ribs and his lung, and he ended up having an airway problem and he ended up dying. I thought I was going to be able to save him — I did everything I could for him. I was talking to him, and he was talking to me, and I thought we were going to make it. But he ended up dying in the OR. It just throws you for a loop some-times, you know? It's like you know it happens, and you try everything you can to help this guy, and you feel so strongly about it, and then it just goes right down the tubes.

Then there's the people — we got on scene where this guy had shot him-self in the heart with a .357, and he was still alive when I got there, and the last thing he said to me was, "I can't breathe," and then that was it. I was like, "What's wrong with you?" "I can't breathe," and that was it. He was dead. That's it. That's the last thing he saw, that was me, and the last thing he said, "I can't breathe."

It's kind of weird, 'cause you're right there, and you feel like, "if I can just get a hold of him, if I can just get a piece of him, and just keep him until I can get him somewhere where they can do more, I can save this guy's life." It's not an issue of what color you are, or where you live or how old you are, or "Oh, they were gonna die anyway," you know? It's, it's like you and death and the patient, and you're on the side that needs to fight for the patient, and that's what you do.

Mark makes it clear that he does the work so that he can help people in need. Interestingly, this series of stories is free from the sardonic banter that characterizes much of his storytelling and that of his part-ner, Lars. Instead, it seems that some topics, such as interactions with dying patients, are treated solemnly. Although Mark mentions the re-wards of the job, he also notes the very real fact that many of the people whom he and other paramedics encounter die. Regardless of one's training or ability, there are limits to what can be done.

Possibly in response to their own limitations, or maybe as a means of countering the negative psychological impact of frequent encounters with death, paramedics tell stories of memorable "saves." While the definition of a save varies from paramedic to paramedic, most agree that it consists of reviving a patient who, without medical intervention, would have died, and of keeping him or her viable long enough for the paramedics to clear the hospital. One medic suggested that all saves were memorable because they occurred so infrequently, while others mentioned that the occasional save reminded them of why they do the job. Sometimes medics tell these stories to reaffirm their life-saving abilities in light of the critique proffered by others in the medical profession. In any event, the stories allow the medics to present themselves as trained individuals able to save lives under challenging conditions. Bill L. recounts the story of one such memorable save:

Bill L.: I remember we had the same type of call as that last one. He was Code Blue — dead as a door nail. Upper-middle-class family up in the Oakland hills, and the whole family was gathered. Probably about a dozen family members there. And the guy wasn't initially responding to any of our advanced life support efforts, so the family is saying, "What can we do? What can we do?" And I say, "This guy needs you more than he's ever needed you in his entire life. You guys really need to be supportive for him."

So the whole family gathers in this big ring, all holding hands, all holding each other and they're going, "Come on, Dad! Come on, Dad!" You know, he's got these twenty-, thirty-year-old children. "Yeah, you can make it, Dad! You can make it!" And the guy, it was incredible. We gave him another medication, he goes into a rhythm that we can shock, so we shock him. We got a rhythm back with pulses! And the guy walked out of the hospital like four or five days later. And we had been working on him for like twenty minutes!

Bill R.: Wow.

Bill L.: Very interesting. So, sometimes I just feel that there's no life left in the room, for that person. If you're into that spiritual thinking and I believe it. Sometimes you go in, you can feel like there's definitely a lot of life still there.

Although Bill refers to his medical skills in the story of the save, the main focus is on the emotional help provided by the family. The switch in verb tenses in the story offers an intriguing glimpse into how Bill charges his narrative with the energy of the event. As he progresses from the introductory description of the patient and the scene to the critical moment when the family gathers in support of their dying father, he switches from the past to the present tense, and includes direct speech, a change that not only heightens the narrative tension but also increases the immediacy of the action. Once the family has gathered around the father, Bill lapses back into the past tense briefly, but switches once again to report on the dramatic defibrillation and the patient's miraculous survival. In the resolution of the story, Bill once again returns to the past tense, restoring the patient to the realm of experience. After Bill R.'s evaluative comment, Bill L. turns the focus of the story back to the spiritual aspects of the work — while medical skills save the patient, the family's support emerges as an equally important element of the save. Through stories like this, Bill L. also contributes to his reputation as a "spiritual" medic with a "Zen" approach to patient care.

Paramedics feel that their skills and abilities are unappreciated not only by the general public but also by the medical personnel and other emergency responders with whom they work. One early morning, Tom B. sits on the back of his ambulance with his rookie partner, Jim. They have just had an encounter with a mobile intensive care nurse (MICN) who had questioned their treatment of a gunshot victim. Tom was finally vindicated by the head of the trauma team, who commended him in front of the MICN and the nursing staff. Half an hour after the confrontation, Tom, still somewhat angry at the nurse, commented on the common misperceptions of paramedics' abilities:

Tom B.: One of the things about prehospital care that I don't think is recognized in the medical industry, from the AMA [American Medical Association] all the way down to your average citizen, is that we do a job that a lot of people admit they wouldn't want to do, number one. And that a lot of people can't do. That's evident by some of the mistakes that are blatantly broadcast in the field.

You read these articles in the newspaper about paramedics who don't realize somebody is alive, they said, "Oh yeah, this guy's dead," and they were alive, you know?[6] So it's obvious that not everybody can do this job and do it right.

The thing about this job is that it's a specialized field and I think, until we get our little requirement—you've gotta have an AA degree or some kind of BS degree in order to be a paramedic—we're not gonna get the total respect for the technical ability that we have. I mean, we do life-saving steps that a physician would do if he was in the emergency room, for life-threatening injuries, right? You have somebody who has a punctured lung from a car accident. Well, we have the technology to decompress their chest. Let the air out of their chest through a needle. We can inflate their lungs, we can use an advanced airway.

And nurses, you know, they say, "Oh, you're just paramedics and you don't know anything." Well, that's not true. Yes, we have a limited scope of what we know about in the general field of emergency medicine, but we do prehospital care. We take care of life and death emergencies and we go to chaotic scenes and try to establish a little bit of order in order to get the job done that needs to be done.

You take a physician, throw him in the back of a bouncing ambulance, and they have a difficult time starting an IV, you know? Take a nurse or a doctor and throw them in the middle of a tenement hotel on the third floor with a status seizure and it's you and your partner because somebody thought it was a Code 2 call. And it's just two of you, and you've got to manage an airway, and you've got to manage the whole scene, because you've got tenants that are standing there going, "Gee, why don't you do something, do something, do something?!" So you have to do security for you and your patient, you have to treat the patient, and you have to get them out of the scene that you're in, you know? And a lot of people don't respect us for what we do out here.

I mean, there are people who understand, that've been out here and have had to find out for themselves that, "Oooh, that's crazy. I don't want your job," you know? But there's a lot of people in the medical community who really, truly do not understand what we have to go through to do our job. And I know it sounds like, "Oh, poor me," but it's a specialized field, just like respiratory therapist is a specialized field, just like being an EKG technician is a specialized field.

Fire and police, they understand what we go through, because they're right there side by side with us, you know? But a lot of physicians who are not emergency room physicians or aren't trauma physicians don't understand what we're doing. And the times that they're out there, faced with the crisis, a lot of them, they may not admit it, but they know deep down inside, "Thank God somebody who does this stuff every day is here to take over." Or, there's the fool-headed ones who ain't giving it up and they're making bad mistakes. They don't know their ACLS protocols, they don't keep current, you know? They're not up on the latest technology of emergency care, and they're physicians who do general practice. And it's just a lack of education. It's not what they do every day, so you can't expect someone who runs a medical office to know all the latest of everything.

Medicine is such a specialized field, your general physician doesn't know how to do everything. When he has a patient who has a kidney problem, he sends them to a kidney specialist. When they have a patient that has a brain tumor, they send him to a neurosurgeon. The general physician, the general practitioner, usually doesn't take the patient with the brain tumor into the OR and treat it. And that's the same thing with doing prehospital care. In-the-field care is a specialized field that if you're not in it and doing it, then you really should stand back and let the people who do it every day do it.

But it's a specialized field and I wish that we could get more recognition, naturally, in the medical community as a whole. Yeah, we make mistakes, but so does everybody else, you know? Physicians make mistakes, paramedics make mistakes, nurses make mistakes. And all you can do is hope that you'll learn from your mistake. Unfortunately, somebody's gonna pay a price for that, but it happens on internships. Physicians make mistakes when they're in their training, you know? And they chalk it up as a mistake. A paramedic makes a mistake in the field and it ain't necessarily treated as just a learning mistake, you know? We're held to a really high standard, and that's good, it keeps us in line. But there's a lot of people out there that think we're just a bunch of renegades and that ain't it.

Although Tom's comments are directed both at Jim, a rookie, and me, an outside observer, they act as an elaborate response to the condescending MICN and, by extension, to the entire medical establishment.

As Tom points out, medics view themselves as specialists in prehospital care, a notion found in many of their stories. Because of this specialized training, they resent the encroachment of nurses into their territory. The more experienced the medic, the more intense the resentment. Tom also voices the common complaint that hospital personnel have little appreciation of the demands of a paramedic's job. He dwells on the fact that, rather than offering support and encouragement, nurses and physicians frequently challenge their medical skills.[7]

Perhaps in retaliation for such affronts, paramedics tell stories which comment directly on the abilities of the medical personnel with whom they interact. The tension between paramedics and nurses has been noted by other researchers,[8] and this tension at times extends to conflicts between paramedics and physicians. Medics on scene are treated (and expect to be treated) as the medical authorities. Once at the hospital, however, they find themselves at the bottom of the ladder, a position reinforced by television programs such as *ER*. Frequently, the hospital personnel adopt the stance "Okay, now let us take over," which angers the medics. Steve, for example, tells a story of a memorable save he and his partner had—in the emergency room of a hospital:

Steve Y.: Oh, I've got a great one for you. Me and Lars, we were up at this one hospital. See, Highland's real good at handling acute things and stuff, but this hospital, if something happens to their patients, like say the patient comes walking in and develops something very acute while they're sitting here, the hospital staff just freaks, they have no idea what to do.

We had one, when we were sitting in here. It was like Lars and I were the messengers of death that day, everybody we came near, fucking died. We couldn't believe it! And so we're sitting inside and Lars is talking to a nurse in there, and I go in to use the restroom. I come out a few seconds later and here comes this nurse flying out of one of the rooms going, "It's a code! It's a code!" her hands flailing above her head, just freaked out.

Apparently one of the patients had come in with mild chest pain, gotten on the bed and just died. A fairly young man too, so we're all "Okay, no big deal." But everyone in the emergency room, you look around and it's an ant farm, everybody's banging into each other and running all over the place. Then this nurse turns to us and says, "Oh! Get these people out of here." And Lars looks at her says, "We're not security!" [laughter]

So I go in there, they've got a nurse in there doing chest compressions like she's giving this guy a rubdown or something. It was just ridiculous. The guy's in a rhythm that should have been shocked right away, and they've got a doctor in there trying to tube him instead of just shocking him and restarting his heart.

So we go in there, where the nurse is doing shitty CPR, and we just push her out of the way, and I'm all, "Lars, they won't do anything, go get a crash cart." So Lars grabs a crash cart and goes in and defibrillates their fucking patient and starts his heart again! In their ER! While a doctor is trying to tube the patient! It was just unbelievable, I just couldn't believe it! The guy most certainly would have died if Lars had not defibrillated him. And the guy did fine.

In Steve's story, the competence of the nurses and the physicians is called seriously into question. Furthermore, the initial disparagement of the paramedics by a nurse who equates them with security is countermanded by the medics' decisive action. Here, the only people with the skills and abilities to save the man, while managing an unruly crowd—of medical personnel!—are the paramedics.

Firefighters are renowned among paramedics for offering less than adequate care. Most medics believe that firefighters would rather fight fires than respond to medical emergencies, and therefore resent the attempts of fire departments to assume the responsibility of providing emergency medical care:

Bob: Let me tell you about fire. I will not name the fire department that this happened, or the city that happened, it shall be nameless. But two weeks ago I walked into a mental housing facility and saw this lady, probably in her mid-fifties, and she was pulseless, apneic [not breathing] and she was sitting up in her chair with her face down on her chin. And the firefighters had a naso-canulla going with this patient, right? And they're just kind of standing there looking at her. I'm like, "Um, guys, I think she stopped breathing!" Well, after that we pulled her to the ground and started working her up. But, oh, the atrocities!

In this case, the firefighters not only have initiated improper treatment for a critical patient, but have shown themselves inept at diagnosing as clear a problem as stopped breathing. Bob delivers his final evaluation with a giant grin, and the ironic tone of his narration emphasizes his appraisal of the firefighters as incompetent bunglers when it comes to medical matters. Possibly because of an occupational bond between emergency responders, the stories about firefighters' medical incompetence are usually tempered with evaluative comments such as, "But what can you expect? They're just a bunch of firefighters."[9]

Medics expect far greater medical competence from the emergency room nursing staff. One point of contention between nurses and medics revolves around "field orders," since medics must ask permission over the radio to initiate certain treatments. While an attending physician is the final authority in these cases, the medics generally receive their orders from the MICN on the radio at the base hospital. Usually these interactions are fairly routine. But in cases of critical patients or patients with unusual conditions, medics feel that, since they are with the patient, they are able to make better judgments than a nurse sitting in a radio booth several miles away. On the same night of his confrontation with the MICN, Tom tells a series of stories about paramedic-nurse interactions which highlight a poor working relationship between the groups:

Tom B.: We had this patient with a phenothiazide reaction, a dystonic reaction, and they're in real severe distress. So I was telling this MICN everything she needed to know to give us a drug order, and then she's refusing to give it to us. Now we'd been having problems with her a lot. So, we had the radio on voice — you can have the thing on voice so you don't have to pick up the handset to talk to them — and we didn't know it. And my partner was all pissed off, "God dammit! I hate this fucking bitch! She always makes me repeat every fucking thing two and three times! Why can't she get it right the first time?" And I go, "Yeah." I was sitting in the back with the patient and I had already told him I was gonna give him some medicine to square him away. And, you know, I told him, "Man, I can't believe that she won't give us the medicine to make you feel good!" So I go, "Yeahhh, she's a fucking bitch!" Well, all that was on tape, you know? So, yeah, she was fuming. That was pretty funny.

So we get there and she gives us this lecture about, "We're the ones who decide how a patient is treated," and all this shit. And I'm like, "You're on drugs, lady!" I said, "When we call you for drug orders, that means we need something. Other than that, we don't bother with you." And she's just sitting there on her little power trip. So finally I said, "We just won't talk to you. From now on, we're disrupted!"

So, we pick up the microphone like I just did, "Alco, Paramedic 47, we need a medcom channel to Highland base." And we never turned the thing on, you know? We'd just sit there and wait, "La la la la la." And Alco would go, "Uh, 47, Highland's standing by on channel 6." "Yeah, we can't get through! Can we get another channel?" And they'd be, "Yeah, try channel 4." So then we'd be waiting, "la la la la la la la la," you know?

Or if we really wanted to hassle them, we'd just pick up the microphone. "Highland, this is 47, with stat medical traffic." "This is Highland, MICN So-and-So, go ahead." "Highland, 47, stat medical traffic." 'Cause you know, it gets their blood all pumping and stuff to get all ready, to keep expecting to do something. It's like, we never talked to them. "Can't copy, too bad." Click.

It used to be we had good relationships with MICNs, you know? We'd call them up, and you'd already given the medicine and they'd just give you the orders for it. But not anymore, man. You can't guarantee you're gonna get an MICN who's gonna cooperate. So, it's like, now, you've gotta wait. And when you're on the third or fourth floor of a building you ain't got time to get ahold of everybody. I mean, everybody knows that you just treat 'em and you call and talk about it later. But, nahh, they don't like that no more. Patients don't get the medicine they need, they don't get treated anymore, not like they used to. 'Cause you never can tell whether or not you're going to get your drug orders.

There is a delicate negotiation that goes on over the radio between medics and base hospital nurses. Medics describe the patient and suggest a treatment, which inevitably is modified and augmented by the nurse. The medic evaluates the treatment and at times suggests other possible ones. In this case, Tom and his partner override the MICN's medical authority by turning off the radio. This subversive gesture allows Tom to assume authority for the patient's treatment, which he feels he is more qualified to do than the distant and uncooperative MICN.

Although in many cases paramedics and nurses have a good working relationship, medics react negatively to instances when nurses treat them as anything less than equals, as is apparent in Steve's story of the emergency room code and Tom's story of interactions with the stubborn MICN. Paramedics feel that both groups have their own specializations and that the nurses should accord them respect, given their experience with treating patients in the field. As a continuation of his commentary on this subject, Tom relates another experience with a nurse who acts improperly:

Tom B.: Tricyclics, these are drugs they give to depressed people. Well, tricyclic overdoses kill a lot of folks. 'Cause they give them just enough to keep them from having to be there every day, but they give them enough that if they took all of them, it'd kill them. And the sad part about those overdoses are, those are hard to counteract in the field, because they go through all kinds of heart rhythms—constantly changing, you know? You can do a lot of resuscitative efforts and then it turns out to be for nothing. They end up dying anyway.

But I was on one—that was at Providence Hospital—and this guy had been in the ER for twenty or thirty minutes maybe. And this nurse, she hadn't really done anything for this guy, you know? And then they decide, "Well, we're gonna put a nasogastric tube in him." Well, just about the time she shoves that n-g tube in, snap, Code Blue. And my partner and I were there. This nurse, she was a little overwhelmed. So, we ended up initiating the code—getting IV's in him. He didn't even have an IV in, you know? He'd been walking around the ER. So, we put an IV in, started CPR, started ventilating him, getting him ready for intubation.

The doctor walks in, we tell him what's going on and he starts in working this code. We worked on this guy for forty-five minutes. Forty-five minutes, we gave him probably everything they had in their crash cart. I mean, second- and third-line drugs. Ended up getting a good rhythm back. And he ended up getting discharged with no deficits—no brain damage or anything—a few days later. You know, that's pretty incredible.

In this story, Tom, his partner and the emergency room physician are the ones who save the patient. The nurse's care is less than adequate; she is unable to handle the pressure of the patient suffering from cardiac arrest, and she eventually fades from the story. By the time the physician enters the treatment room, nurses are conspicuously absent and the save becomes a cooperative effort between the medics and the physician.

In contrast to their attitudes towards nurses, medics hold most emergency room physicians in high regard. In the field, paramedics are essentially borrowing the attending physician's medical license, and therefore feel a substantial responsibility to those doctors. At times, however, they tell stories of the incompetence of some of these same physicians:

Melinda: This was during my internship. We had this patient in there in the ER, okay? And we had him on a mask. But when we brought him into the treatment room, he was just lying there and the mask wasn't plugged in. And so my preceptor pointed that out to the nurse, who said to the doctor, "What do you want it on?" and he said, "Two." And my preceptor said, "I don't think that's gonna work, with the mask unplugged." [laughter] And so the doctor said, "Okay, crank it up to six." The guy was clueless. He did have the good sense to call for an anesthesiologist to come tube the guy since he wasn't competent to do it himself. But anyway, our patient wasn't in good hands, I wouldn't have wanted to be that patient. There were several people who were referring to that one doctor as "Dr. Death."

Yeah, there are usually a few clueless doctors. They're not all clueless, not at all. But, in fact, it's always about tubing. We brought somebody in to this Dr. Death and the patient was having a lot of trouble breathing and she was a little swollen around her neck. And I was gonna tube her on scene, but she was screaming for a couple of minutes and I couldn't see her cords, so I didn't.

And we got to the hospital and the doctor tried and he bloodied her mouth. By the time the nurse anesthetist had gotten there, the poor woman was beginning to come to, we had given her some epi or something, and she was coming around. And the nurse anesthetist was just sort of holding her cheeks and saying, "It's okay," and asking the doctor, "Are you sure this woman needs to be tubed?" They couldn't see her cords either.

Medics expect physicians to be able to diagnose the patients brought in to the hospital. In the ER, these diagnoses occur in a semipublic space with other well-trained medical personnel present. Since these personnel — including the attending physicians, the residents, the interns, the nurses, the X-ray technicians, and the medics — have competitive relationships with each other, and turf wars are legion, the physician's performance of diagnosis and treatment occurs under great scrutiny.

While cleaning the ambulance after a response to a minor shooting, Mark tells the story of a victim brought to one of the county's designated trauma centers:

Mark G.: I was at Eden one time when they brought in this person who'd been shot with a shotgun in the back, and the doc took the X-rays on the back and he goes, "There's two pellets lodged next to the spine." Now this guy didn't get shot anywhere near the spine, so I was kind of hesitant. So I looked at the X-ray and I noticed that they had little Phillips heads on the spots where he thought there were pellets next to the spine. Turns out they were screws from the backboard. He was all flipped out, that it was pellets near the spine! [laughter]

Perhaps stories about "Dr. Death" or other dangerously incapable physicians allow medics to place themselves on an equal footing with physicians, which would put them in a higher position than nurses. The subversive intent of these stories is to undermine the medical hierarchies, which consistently leave medics stranded on the bottom rung of the medical ladder.

In their stories, paramedics do not present themselves exclusively as well-trained heroes who always respond appropriately to medical emergencies. At times they acknowledge the limitations of their training as well as the mistakes they make in the field. Tony tells a story of failing to treat accident victims with the proper care:

Tony: I don't know, it was one of these things. I shouldn't be telling stories about my mistakes [laughter], but we fucked up big time on that call. At this accident, one guy had a broken neck and the other one had a concussion. And we transported them, but we didn't "C-spine" them, we didn't do anything. That was during my internship. And we found out later that one had a broken neck and the other one had a basal skull fracture, some shit. Yeah, the two of them were fucked up and we didn't take care of them right.

Although Tony expresses some reluctance to talk about failures, he may tell this one as a training story and to remind himself to learn from his mistakes. Not surprisingly, the story is situated during his internship—a time for learning. Bill L. tells an amusing story of diagnostic mistakes:

Bill L.: We got on scene of this one call, and this guy had atypical vital signs. Got an EMT crew that responded along with us, back when we had a tiered response. And I'm checking the guy out, he's got left-sided deficits and I'm in one of those self-pontificating moods, I was a new paramedic and I'm saying, "Yeah, boys, this guy's got classic stroke symptomology." I can show them several examples along with the vital signs that all suggest a cerebral event. I said, "But, just in case, I'll give this guy sugar. But, you know, that's not gonna do any good. Some people think maybe it could cause some harm." I give the guy some sugar and he wakes up. Says, "Thank you very much," you know, and has no complaint. It's like another episode of eating serious shit.

In his story, Bill constructs an interactive setting reminiscent of the hospital, except that here he positions himself as a teacher at the top of the medical hierarchy. As in the stories of hospital staff who arrogantly dismiss medics only to be proven wrong later, Bill discovers that his authoritative proclamations are incorrect. Yet here it is the patient's recovery, and not intervention by the EMTs, that highlights Bill's mistake. Thus, unlike the stories situated in the hospital where the physician's authority is diminished by a medic's diagnostic acuity, Bill retains a semblance of medical authority. Despite his misdiagnosis, he initiates the proper treatment and restores the diabetic patient to normalcy. Even when a paramedic makes a diagnostic error, he still manages to provide correct treatment; he can then step back and laugh at his own unsuccessful attempt to show off.

Bill V. tells of a far more dangerous situation—giving a patient the wrong drug. The first story, culled from his early air force experience, resonates with the second story, which is based on his experiences working in Los Angeles. In part, these stories highlight the dangers of fatigue that every medic experiences on the job:

Bill V.: Had another jump mission, that's where I learned for drugs, when you give drugs, "right drug, right patient, right site." That one got sent home! It was on a Japanese merchant vessel, this was fifteen hundred miles northwest of Hawaii, and these two Japanese cooks got in a meat cleaver fight! [laughter] And these fuckers—

George: Well, I've been to Benihana, I've seen how they wield knives!

Bill: Well, these guys fucked each other up! It was like ha! ha! ha! ha! Two of us jumped in on these guys. It was like two in the morning when we finally got out to them. From March Air Force Base, this is like a sixteen-hour flight!

George: Another sixteen-hour flight.

Bill: It was long ass, maybe ten hours. No, it was a long time, it was like sixteen hours. Have you ever flown over the Pacific Ocean at night? Ever been to Hawaii or something? I mean it's dark. You're at forty thousand feet and, as far as you can see, blackness, just blackness.

We got fifty miles out from this boat and the radar officer went through RCC—which is the Rescue Coordination Center in Indiana. That's like the world international rescue coordination center, all international rescue goes through there for the communications and coordination. So the radio operator, through a satellite linkage, calls RCC and through an interpreter says, "Hey, tell them to flip on their lights on this ship." And it lit up like a frigging city, man! It's like "whoosh!" You see this glow off on the horizon, right? They put a dinghy out in the water, we jump into the water. Parachuting into the middle of the ocean in the middle of the night, it's like fucking, "Ahh! Ahh! Ahh!" You have a diving mask but you don't want to look under water 'cause you know whatever is under water you're food to!

So we get on the boat. Anyway we're working on these guys, there's three medics, doctoring up, we did retaining sutures, giving them plasma—we carried plasmanate and Ringer's and saline, after their blood loss. And it was like the second day out and they were doing a lot better, they were coming around to where they could feel pain and they were conscious and oriented and stuff.

They hadn't bled to death and I was doing my watch and I went to give this guy fifty milligrams of meperidine, Demerol, and I was tired and I pull out the tubex and put it together, and I look at it, "meperidine." I prepared the site, and I look at it again, "meperidine." Right patient, right drug, right site. I look at it again, "meperidine!" Put it in the hub of the IV tubing and squiiiiirt, 100 milligrams of "meperidine." Pull it out, recap it, the guy says, "Ahh ahh ahh ahh ahh ahh ahh AHH!" Starts breathing fast, he starts getting all weird in his bed, and I go, "What's wrong? Ask him what's wrong!" He says something and I go to the interpreter, "What did he say? What did he say?" "He said he feels like his heart is going to explode!" I go, "What?!" "He says his heart's going to explode!" I look at it again—epinephrine! [laughter] I gave this guy a milligram of 1:1000 epi IV push! Woops! Threw it out the porthole, "Tell him he'll be okay in a few minutes." [laughter] Man, that was terrible.

Fatigue, man, I wonder how many people fatigue has killed in this business? I remember when I was doing the strike thing about six months, eight months ago, I was all beat to death tired after commuting between here and Southern California. I was in the ambulance, right? This guy, pulmonary edema patient, give him Lasix right? Lasix. Lasix [mimics getting ready to push drug]. Lasix. Plugged it in. Lasix. Just getting ready to push it and I look down again before I pushed the drug—lidocaine! [laughter] Ooooooo. Fuck. The mind plays tricks on your ass.

The humorous retelling of what were at the time sobering experiences contributes to Bill's presentation of himself as an in-control authority able to laugh both at the scenes he encounters and at himself. This ironic and self-deprecatory stance is found in many of the other medics' stories as well, and is one of the most common stylistic aspects of paramedic storytelling.

Each county develops its own treatment protocols, all with varying degrees of "aggressiveness." The protocols help the paramedics decide on treatments and determine destination hospitals. "Standing drug orders" further allow them to exercise judgment in the field without having to make hospital contact.[10] But the protocols can also hinder the medics in their attempts to treat certain patients. One area in which they feel that the protocols are not aggressive enough is in the treatment of pediatric emergencies. Moments after detailing his motivations for becoming a paramedic, Bill V. recalls a pediatric case that led him to question the adequacy of treatment protocols and the odd priorities of a system that allows far more aggressive treatments for geriatric patients than for pediatric ones:

Bill V.: We had this call, a pediatric full arrest again, and it was a twenty-five-minute ride to the hospital. At the time we couldn't intubate peds, we couldn't do intraosseous infusions. I'm sitting there doing CPR and ventilating this baby and I'm seeing my own kid's face and this kid's face.

George: Knowing that you could do more if they'd just let us!

Bill: I had the tools right there, but I didn't want to go to jail for practicing medicine without a license. And we got to the hospital and the doctors and nurses in the emergency room take over my patient care from me and they start doing the ACLS treatment that I could have done, started twenty-five minutes earlier. And as I had tears rolling down my face I said, I said, I told them right there to the doctors, and they knew me pretty well, 'cause you know I'm me.

George: So old?

Bill: No, in Southern California I was not old. I did not consider myself an old-time paramedic until I came up here. But I'd been around and they knew me and I said, "You know this is fucking criminal that, with the training that's out there and with the equipment that's out there, that resuscitation could not start on this child until I got to the hospital." We fucking do everything to save the ninety-year-old person that's been sitting in a convalescent hospital for the last four years rotting and God finally lets their heart stop so they can get on with the great adventure. And we do everything, all these heroics to re-suscitate an old man dying of cancer, but we can't take those same skills and the same technology and apply it to an infant or a child or a young person!

I just told them, I said, "This is fucking criminal and it's all your fault! 'Cause you ER docs can do something about it!" I walk out, they just sat there and went, "You're right." I just turned around and walked out.

Bill is not alone in these concerns; other medics also mention the constraints placed on the scope of their practice by protocols which are drawn up without their input. The criticism of protocols occurs frequently in medic storytelling and constitutes another attack on the medical establishment.

These stories tend to focus on the results of the inflexibility of the protocols, although medics express a certain ambivalence toward this subject. On the one hand, medics admit that protocols cannot reflect all possible scenarios. On the other hand, they acknowledge that the protocols protect them from having to make decisions concerning the viability of certain patients. For years, paramedics in Alameda County were not allowed to pronounce a patient dead, usually referred to as "calling" a patient, in the case of blunt traumatic injury resulting in cardiac arrest. These and similar protocols required the medics to treat patients whom they felt had no chance at survival. Jason, for example, recounts a story of one particularly horrific episode with earlier protocols:

Jason: I don't know, there was a lady about eighty years old one time, and she had apparently been depressed and she jumped from the eighth floor of a retirement building. She was instantly killed. But in those days, we couldn't call the patient that had a blunt traumatic arrest, we had to transport to the closest hospital so that they could pronounce the patient. So we actually had to transport this lady that had fractures everywhere and she probably had all sorts of internal injuries, and we had to transport her to the hospital. It was pretty shocking. That's one of the worst calls that I've had in the past, she was pretty dead, and we had to transport her. That's what was really bad, nobody was going to save this lady and we had to transport her. Nowadays, we can, if you're blunt traumatic arrest and you're asystole on the monitor, we can pronounce you dead, and the coroner's gotta go out and pick you up, that's about it. That's probably the worst call.

The protocols prevented Jason from using his judgment — developed through training and experience — to exercise medical restraint.

Paramedics struggle with fatigue, a demanding work schedule, difficult calls, frequent challenges to their abilities, and an abundance of uncertainty; all of these environmental factors contribute to their job stress. When discussing these aspects of the job, they occasionally tell stories about the medic who turned to amphetamines to keep up with the relentless pace, or the one who became addicted to painkillers to escape the psychological overload associated with responding to one traumatic call after another. Mark G., when asked about such stories of drug abuse, responds, "You don't hear about it so much now. But this one partner I had, he told me stories about how back then they'd have some of their supervisors on heroin on some of their calls." Stories about drug abuse were generally situated in other EMS systems or in different companies. Regional Ambulance had a policy of drug testing for their employees, but they were also willing to help employees who had substance abuse problems receive proper counseling and help. I suspect that medics were unwilling to tell me stories of recent drug use because I was not an insider. Of the paramedics I talked to, Bill V. was the only one who openly discussed his own drug abuse:

Bill V.: I quit cocaine on the job, almost died. It's pretty crazy down south. You're working ninety-six-hour work weeks, four twenty-four-hour shifts straight, running twenty-five, twenty-six calls a day. You're twisted, not that it's an excuse or anything.

Well, drugs are pretty crazy, everyone is doing cocaine, smoking weed and shit, selling it, on duty you know, to firemen and cops and everybody else. It was about my fourth day on straight, I was twisted, and I started having chest pain. About three o'clock in the morning, I'm having chest pain and shit, having a hard time breathing, I go out in the ambulance, hook myself up to the monitor. We're talking about ten multifocal PVCs a minute! I'm fucking freaking out, I'm thinking, I've got my baby boy, he'd been home from the hospital like two weeks, and I'm thinking to myself, "You fucking asshole, who in the hell do you think you are?" Thinking if I died, my son would never know me. People would ask my little boy, "So, Bill, what do you know about your father?" "Oh, he was an asshole who died of cocaine." I just said, "Fuck it, that's it, last time." Common sense.

I was like the first of all my friends who stopped. You know, misery loves company. Living the lie. I was lucky. Hey, every profession, every group, like the ER doc. One of our best ER docs, I mean this guy was on top of it, all of a sudden, it's like, "Hey, where's Doc Smith?" you know? "Oh, he's not around anymore." Found out he'd been fucking slamming morphine on the job, and he was giving his patients placebo. It's everywhere.

I think it's helped me a become a better paramedic going through the circle and living through it. It's helped me become a little more compassionate and a little more understanding and able to reach these people who are in the same condition that I was when you're sitting there holding their hand while they're freaking on whatever substance they're on and telling your patient, "Hey, I've been there too, I'm no virgin too, I know what you're going through and you can't stop it." I've been able to touch people that way, if anything for that moment, you know? I look at it this way, the bottom line, you have to quit. You can either go to jail and quit, you get education and quit, or you can die and quit. Fortunately I got educated and scared and quit.

Bill notes that he is considered "the wise old medic" at the company, and as such it is particularly fitting for him to tell this series of cautionary tales. In a narrative move typical of his storytelling, he links the paramedic drug abuse to the larger issue of drug abuse among emergency medical personnel, including here the story of an emergency room doctor succumbing to the same type of pressure; thus, the story serves the function of incorporating the medics into the community of medical personnel, one from which the physicians and nurses try to exclude them.

The medical training paramedics receive does not prepare them for situations on the street. Their own experiences and those of other medics, communicated through stories, contribute to their ongoing development. The medics also tell their stories as a means for commenting on the perceptions that the public and medical professionals have of their skills and abilities. Many of these stories position the paramedics as equal to or better than nurses and physicians at handling medical emergencies. The nurses' claims that medics should be kept on a short leash are countermanded by stories of medics stepping in where nurses have failed. The politics of the work environment are brought to the forefront in these stories; mistakes are scrutinized, and generally the medics emerge as the most able group. When they do make mistakes, these are often depicted as humorous and easily corrected. The stories also reveal the high degree of self-deprecatory humor that pervades medic work culture. This ironic stance emerges as one of the medics' greatest strategies, not only for keeping critics at bay but also for putting distance between themselves and the scenes of medical emergencies.

# PLACES YOU WOULDN'T GO FOR A THOUSAND DOLLARS!

On the way to the hospital with a young patient, Steve begins telling stories about unpredictable scenes. The sunny afternoon and the sedate atmosphere of the patient's neighborhood—one of Oakland's numerous housing projects—contrast markedly with the story Steve tells of volatile bystanders and explosive violence in the same project:

Steve Y.: We've had people get assaulted. Me personally, I've had people swing at me and stuff. Nobody's ever pulled a knife on me, but one of the funniest things ever—I thought this was just ridiculous—we got a call to the projects for abdominal pain. And it's a girl we'd run on countless times. We get there and she's fine, she's just got PID [pelvic inflammatory disease]. It's just an infection. And so we're talking with her and stuff and she gets up and she's walking around the house. There's nothing wrong with her.

Anyway this next-door neighbor, Fred, he's a drunk, he's about fifty-five, sixty years old, he's a pain in the ass, every time we go over there we have a hard time with him. But this time was just particularly bad. He starts goin', goin' off, "You white motherfucker this, you don't care and dadadadah!" You know, take better care of her. And there's nothing wrong with her, except she needs some penicillin. So finally this guy is being so obnoxious that I turn around and I go, "Fred, get the fuck out of here!" And then he just goes ballistic. Now the rest of the family — the two sons — get a hold of him and they're all, "Yeah, Fred, get out of here!" So they grab him by the shoulders and shove him out the front door.

Anyway, I'm thinking, "Okay, great, Fred's gone." So I'm going out to the unit to throw the patient in the back and I'm just about to get in the front seat, and here comes Fred out the front door with a 9 mm! And he's hot, you know? But at the projects, there's two steps right at the front where you step down onto the walkway. So he's shitfaced, he comes out with his gun waving, takes a step, misses the front step, and goes just face down on the pavement! Knocks himself silly. I mean he wasn't moving after that! And his gun spins down the sidewalk.

Well, two teenagers about four doors down see the gun spinning down the sidewalk, run up, steal his gun, and run off down the street. And so just as I'm stepping in thinking, "Oh, this guy's gonna shoot me if he's sober enough to shoot straight," this whole thing unfolds in like ten seconds, you know? Boom, bang, gun goes away, kids steal it. I just looked at him and shook my head, got in the ambulance and drove away. Didn't call the police or anything. He was starting to move around after we left. But it was just the funniest fucking thing I'd ever seen.

The police know about the danger out here. The police know and the fire department knows it, but we don't know it. And there's been a couple of instances where if the guy laying on the ground had been armed or had felt like shooting us, then we would have been at his mercy. That really stinks 'cause all the company's gotta do is get a better line of communication with the police department or fire department, but because of their lack of problem-solving abilities, somebody's gonna get killed. It's just a matter of time. I mean I've been out here two and a half years and I've never seen anybody get killed — and it just surprises the hell out of me that nobody ever has.

Paramedics are often called to unfamiliar areas, sometimes late at night and to neighborhoods rife with crime and violence; the danger associated with these places can cause anxiety.

Sitting on the hood of the ambulance outside of a 7-11 store in the early morning hours, Kathryn and Mary talk about the dangers of the neighborhoods where they work:

Mary: You go into places you wouldn't even think to go for a thousand dollars!

Kathryn: Even if you were Superman!

Mary: Somebody could pay you to walk down a block of MLK [Martin Luther King, Jr., Boulevard, a major street in Oakland and Berkeley] and you wouldn't do it.

Kathryn: Yep.

Kathryn and Mary: But you would with your uniform on.

Mary: Yeah, you'd go down for no big reason.

Kathryn: Yeah, and tell the biggest meanest ugliest people out here in this city—

Mary: To shut the fuck up!

Kathryn: Yeah, just to shut up. Stop being stupid. Sit down or I'm gonna take you down! And we do actually, too. [laughter] We'd never, ever try to do anything like that in our street clothes. [laughter] I wouldn't even drive my car in those areas. [laughter] Really, with bulletproof windows. But there's something about the uniform. Pretty stupid, hunh?

Mary: I thought you'd never say it. One day somebody is gonna get shot out here. They really are. It'll probably be me!

While the tone of the discussion is flippant, Mary and Kathryn voice genuine concern about their safety, and, in part, the swagger of their storytelling belies the anxiety produced by entering a darkened hallway in a rundown tenement at two A.M. Such banter allows Mary and Kathryn an opportunity to voice their fears in a manner consistent with their presentation of themselves as in-control authorities unperturbed by danger.[1]

Mary's and Kathryn's conversation also reveals a common belief that their status as paramedics affords them a high degree of mobility in areas where they would not normally be welcome. Tom R., operations manager of Alameda County, concurs in this assessment:

Tom R.: If there's one person angry against the establishment and uniforms, there'll be three or four others that recognize, "Wait a minute — paramedic — they're sacred, don't touch them." And so it's real reassuring, I guess.

Where I get fearful is walking in someplace that I shouldn't be. It's kind of a fluke, you know? If I walk up in the middle of a drug deal, and they don't know anything, they just see blue, and think, "uniform." That's really the scenario that one of us could get hurt in. Not that they recognize you're a paramedic, and think, "I'm gonna shoot a paramedic." I just don't feel that would ever occur. I don't think the people are against the paramedics.

Oakland is an example. Those people. I don't know how to describe it other than they watch out for us. They treat us differently. That city can be pretty dangerous, and I'm sure you've noticed that. You've got to watch yourself. In uniform, in a company vehicle or an ambulance, I feel very safe going into that city. I don't know if that's maybe stupidity on my part, but I feel somewhat safe. I wouldn't go into some of those same areas in my own car. I don't know how to describe it, but as a civilian up there, I would be very shaky. But as a paramedic going in there, we're afforded a certain amount of courtesy that is hard to describe unless you've been there. But they very much watch out for us.

Tom has an optimistic view of the paramedics' ability to move unimpeded in areas where they might otherwise be singled out as targets. He goes so far as to suggest that medics are "sacred," and therefore immune from the ill will of potential assailants. Perhaps such an attitude allows him not only to enter these areas himself but also, as the person responsible for all of the paramedics in the county, to send them into situations which may in fact put them in harm's way. Other medics are less optimistic about the public perception of them and instead tell stories which underscore Mary's closing remark: "Somebody is gonna get shot out here, they really are." Stories of medics being assaulted or attacked are, in fact, common. In all of these stories, however, the medics escape unharmed either by chance, as in Steve's story, or by their own quick action.

These narratives point to another fascinating aspect of the paramedics' interactions with the environment. Kathryn draws attention to her feelings about the city when she is not in uniform, contrasting it with her experience of the same place while she is on duty. Parts of the city she and other medics consider off limits because of potential danger become accessible when they are working. Medics who are on duty no longer hesitate to travel along certain streets or into certain neighborhoods but enter these places as a matter of course.

Location becomes attached to experience—a particular place has certain occupational associations, and a posting to that spot frequently triggers those memories. For example, to introduce a story about a cardiac arrest, Ken mentions that "I had a real good story right across the street from that building right there." Ken no longer refers to the call as such, but remembers it entirely as a narrative. In other cases, a post—one near a freeway overpass, for example—has topographical or environmental features resembling those at the site of a memorable call, and the similarity leads to storytelling. Thus Kathryn says, "Oh, that bridge is a lot like the one that the car went off. Remember that one, Mary?" The subsequent narration provides a means for reinterpreting the place. Mary and Kathryn mention this close relationship between place and memory:

Mary: You know, different places, different corners, different buildings, they all have stories for you. You know, you'll be at work and you'll drive by a place and think, "Oh, that's where we worked up the code," or "Oh, that's the building where we had the overdose." I did a call for a shooting in the park over there. Isn't that right, Kathryn?

Kathryn: What's that?

Mary: Just how places become associated with calls in your mind? You don't really think about it off work. But when you're driving around.

Mary suggests that these associations between place and occupational experiences apply only while she is at work. At the very least, the process of being at work foregrounds the work-related interpretation of her environment. Presumably, other nonwork experiences then inform her interactions with the same places when she is not at work. Lars concurs with this conclusion:

Lars: Usually I don't look at the city the same way as when I'm at work. I don't think, "Oh, we did a shooting right near here," if I'm going past a restaurant or something. I'd be more likely to think, "Hey, me and Melanie went on our first date here." But the next day, I might be in the same place at work and then I'd think, "Hey, I did a shooting right near here!" first, and then I'd think about the date." [laughter]

Of course, it is impossible to separate completely these two conflicting views of the city. But, while many medics admit that calls color their impressions of neighborhoods, streets, parks, or highways, they also suggest that work impressions of those places which occur to them while they are off duty are secondary to their nonwork impressions.

The city emerges in the paramedics' stories as the setting for their occupational adventures, and, in this narrative guise, it is frequently compared to a foreign land. Traveling into the city offers a window onto foreign cultures:

Bill V.: When you're dealing with some of the Asian cultures, they've got tiger balm and they're burning crazy incense. I remember the first time I came on one of these scenes, this person had these round burn marks all over their forehead and their chest and their arms. This guy's got a stomach pain! I'm going, what are all these burns on this guy? Well, they heat up coins and put them on you.[2] Culture! The culture, especially in Oakland, it's like going around the world in an afternoon! Like go to some of these Asian homes and play guess the carcass hanging from the ceiling! [laughter]

George: Name that carcass!

Bill: Uhhh, mammal!

George: Okay, good.

Bill: Really screws you up when they cut the paws off of it so you can't tell if it's a dog or cat.

George: Sick!

Bill: It's true. Or squirrel. "Uh, I think that one is squirrel!" Birds are easy 'cause they leave the heads on.

In many paramedics' eyes, going to work is equivalent to visiting a foreign country. As Mark G. quips, "It's a little like *Around the World in Eighty Days,* but here it only takes twelve hours!" The neighbor-hoods are described as foreign, dangerous lands, where the patients speak a different language and their food practices are surprising, all characterizations that help heighten the excitement and exotic nature of the job. Bill's stories are told not as a malicious, xenophobic con-demnation of his patients' practices but as the awestruck musings of a tourist confronted with something utterly foreign. What heightens the narrative amusement is that these examples of culture shock take place in the familiar setting of the city.

Most of the stories about the work environment allude, directly or indirectly, to race. Street names and the reputations associated with those areas provide a signal regarding race to the initiated listener. While generally unwilling to talk about it openly, paramedics are keenly aware of the racial tensions pervading Oakland. In Alameda County, many of the patients whom they transport are African Americans, while the majority of the paramedics are white. This phenomenon, added to the alliance between the medics and other emergency services, par-ticularly the police, means that, in the view of many patients, para-medics are associated with members of the "white establishment."[3] Their blue, quasi-military jumpsuits, along with the large, baton-like flashlights (carried as much for self-defense as for illumination) and black jump boots, contribute to the image of a close alliance with law enforcement.

As a result, white medics responding to calls in predominantly black neighborhoods occasionally find themselves the target of built-up frus-trations among an economically and politically disenfranchised popu-lation. It is not uncommon for medics telling stories to report, in di-rect speech, racial epithets used by patients and bystanders, such as Steve's mention of Fred's tirade against "You white motherfucker this." Another medic jokingly said that, after a few shifts on the job, he be-gan to think that his name was "white-ass honky." Conversely, few medics include overtly racial derogatory characterizations of patients in their stories.[4] It would, of course, be misleading to suggest that there are no medics who exhibit racial bias. The stories, however, tend to show racism being directed toward the medics, who, in turn, present themselves as performing a noble task despite the environmental difficulties. In this chapter's opening story, for example, Steve is presented as the victim of racism, even though he is trying to assist a black patient.

Nearly all paramedics tell of instances in which crowds on scene felt that they were not receiving care equal to what would be provided if the patients were not from a minority group.[5] A popular rap song, "911 (is a joke)," and the accompanying video depicting overweight, uninterested white medics casually eating lunch while an African American patient lies in distress, fueled this sentiment in many of the neighborhoods where the medics respond.[6] Bill L. and Bill R. mention the difficulties this particular song posed for them:

Bill R.: Basically, there was a time when there was a rap song, "911 (is a joke)." And that got a little scary sometimes, because the people who are going to give you a hassle are usually the young hell raisers. But usually you don't have any problems. We're pretty much neutral. I mean, we don't like to give people a hard time, so they don't give us a hard time. It happens, though.

Bill L.: There's only been a couple of times when I've actually had to drop things and run.

Bill R.: Well, most of the bad times we get are people who are angry because we've taken a few minutes and it seems to them that it's been a long time. Or, sometimes when we go and we have to stage, waiting for scene safety. That's when people hassle us.

People's preconceived notions of what constitutes proper care can conflict markedly with the medics' responses. When the paramedics are predominantly white, and their actions lead to delays in service, it is not surprising that they would be accused of providing unequal or inadequate care. Storytelling provides medics with an excellent forum for exploring these racial tensions and affords them an opportunity to evaluate different strategies for dealing with racially motivated anger. Nevertheless, as both Tom R. and the general paramedic story tradition suggest, most instances of violence directed toward the paramedics do not stem from racial tensions but rather from individual aberrant behavior.

Many people are misinformed about the paramedics' mission, a situation which inevitably leads to misunderstandings. Sometimes, people deliberately abuse the 911 system, a source of great frustration for many paramedics.[7] Medics cite the poor education of many of their patients as a major contributing factor both to abuses of the system and to difficulties in providing expedient patient care. After responding to the fourth call that morning for complaints that did not require emergency care, Darryl voices his frustrations:

Darryl: I don't know, people are fools. You deal with some real fools. This is the biggest babysitting job you'll ever do in your life. It is, you know what I mean? You're babysitting. And the funny thing is, you're babysitting adults. You're babysitting adults. With their silly-ass problems and everything. And some problems are so minuscule, you would not believe! People call you up to ask you what to do about their kid with a fever! Okay, Parent of the Year. You know what I mean? "Give them Tylenol." God! But, yeah, you deal with some real peaches.

Calls that are not true emergencies become especially annoying when they come at the end of a twelve-hour shift, forcing the medics into overtime. While waiting to get off one early morning, Tony tells such a story:

Tony: We responded out of Hayward, really late, like about 1:45. And I was about ready to get off shift at 1:45, but the system was in depletion. So, we had to stay up in service and couldn't go off duty. And units are starting to clear, but it was still depleted in Oakland. And we were like at the borderline of Oakland and San Leandro. We were pretty sure we were gonna get off and we were like, "Score!" Probably another three minutes and we would be cleared for the barn, cleared to go off.

Well, a call came down in Oakland. And it was Code 3 for a hand injury. We hauled ass to get there, really pissed off. We get there, and there's a lady in a third-floor window waving us down from her apartment, "I called! It's me, I called!" And we see her hand, she's got a towel wrapped around one hand. We're like, "Dang! This is nothing." And it was not far from a hospital, like maybe ten blocks from the hospital.

So we get up there, and I'm like, "What's the problem?" and she says, "Well..." She unwraps her hand, and she shows me her hand. There's no blood on it. I'm like, "What's the problem?" I'm ready to walk out already. And she says, "I was sleeping, and a jagged edge of my nail caught on my blanket. And when I pulled back, it tore my nail halfway back. And it's really painful." And I said, "And you called 911 for that?!" I was just really pissed off, so I started walking out. And she says, "Where are you going?" And I said, "We're going home."

But then I turned around and I said to myself, "All right, I've got to relax here." And I went back to her and I said, "Let me see your finger." I looked at her finger, and I said, "There's this stuff they coat blankets with now, it's a fire retardant chemical. If it gets into your bloodstream, I've seen it kill the tissue around the nail and they end up having to amputate the finger. And if it gets bad enough, they have to amputate the hand." I said, "We need to take you to the hospital."

So, I took her to the furthest hospital she would allow me to take her to. [laughter] Took her in, told the nurse exactly what had happened here and asked her to please keep this woman in triage for as long as possible.

Patrick: So you made the fire retardant story stick?

Tony: Yeah, I made the story stick. And she went to the hospital with this. And I was happy. That was my gratification. [laughter] That was my gratification. It's like, this lady, she's an idiot. So I didn't feel so bad after all.

Tony's actions were no doubt prompted by the fast-approaching end of his shift and the worry that he would be sent on one more call. He enjoys telling this story because it stands as one of the few cases in which he successfully punishes an abuser of the system while appearing to perform his task admirably. Whether or not the narrated event occurred as it does in his story is immaterial.[8] What is important is that Tony is able to exact narrative revenge. In this sense, Tony's story allows him to explore the possible range of action at the scene of a nuisance call. In his conduct toward an undeserving patient, Tony plays out a fantasy that many paramedics entertain; in addition, his stature among the others probably increases as a result of his telling the story. As part of the brinksmanship associated with their storytelling, medics sometimes play a game of "narrative chicken," daring each other to see how far they can push the bounds of acceptable behavior without getting caught. Here, Tony goes quite far, yet the patient remains unaware of his manipulation.

Many medics mention that abuse of the 911 system arises from a pervasive lack of education, with people not knowing what constitutes an emergency or being unaware of the availability of noncritical care programs and less expensive transportation options. Bill V. mentions communication difficulties arising from poor education coupled with arcane medical terminology. His comments, along with the other discussions of 911 abuse, contribute to the sense that the profession involves "babysitting adults," as Darryl put it:

Bill V.:It's like dealing with a bunch of children out there. They really are, they're a bunch of naive scared children. Best way to describe it.

Tim: Do you have any examples?

Bill: Without sounding like a racist? 'Cause I'm not. It's like when you're talking to these people, you're doing a history on them, and they refer to their bodily functions like, "I had a wee-wee" or "I had a poop." You know, a forty-five-year old man! Or referring to genital pain, "My wee-wee hurts."

George: C'mon man!

Bill: It's true! It's true, isn't it?

George: Yep.

Bill: I heard "done fell out" on the scene in the backyard.

George: Fell out of where?

Bill: No kidding. We're in the middle of this backyard, there's no trees in the backyard, guy's laying on the lawn, and I'm like, "So what happened?" "Ah, he done fell out [lost consciousness]!" "Where did he fall out of?" You know, there's no ladder around, he's not a skydiver. It's a one-story house, he's fifty feet away from a window. "What did he fall out of?" "He done fell out!" Then, I caught on to what she meant. Or "chicken breather"? Have you heard that one?

George: Chicken breath.

Bill: "Hey, help her, man, chicken breathe, man! Chicken breathe!" [She can't breathe.] I go, "Chicken breathe?" Then there's another one, "So, what kind of medical history does your child have?" "Well, about a year ago she had smilin' baby Jesus."

George: Smilin' mighty Jesus.

Bill: I go, "Smiling baby Jesus?" "Yeah, smilin' baby Jesus!" Spinal meningitis! "What other kind of medical history do you have?" "I've got the sugars, I had the seizures." "What kind of medications do you take?" "Peanut butterball." Phenobarbital, or dial-a-tan, dilantin. Ha! Public school system at its finest! That's when you move into your veterinary medicine mode.

Tim: Which is?

Bill: Feely touchy. You know, poke at it, if it don't hurt, it ain't broke type of deal.

Although told with a great deal of humor, Bill's short stylized depictions of interactions with patients highlight both his frustrations with what he feels are inexcusable communication problems and the uneasy suspicion that a critique of these problems may characterize him as a racist. Bill ends by referring to "veterinary mode," thus making a startling comparison between his patients and animals.

Tony, a Latino medic, and his partner, Patrick, engage in nearly identical banter one afternoon while discussing the abuses of the 911 system:

Tony: "Done fell out." It's like, "What do you mean, done fell out?"

Patrick: Yeah, fell out of what? [laughter] Fell out of the car? What do you mean?

Tony: What's that? "Yeah, he done fell out! He was right there, and he just done fell out!" Oh—done fell out. Gotcha. "Done fell out." That, and "peanut basketball."

Patrick: What's peanut basketball?

Tony: It's like, "What's he taken?" "Peanut basketball and dial-a-tan." Oh, phenobarbital and dilantin. Gotcha! Seizures! Little red pill.

Patrick: Yeah, that's what these old grandmas tell you.

Tony: "Yeah, I know what I'm taking. I'm taking this blue pill, a little red pill, and a pill with a big red line in it." "All right, thanks." [laughter] "Yeah, take two of those a day with these." But, what Hispanics say, "Che can breathe! Chicken breathe!" for "She can't breathe!"

Tony and Patrick vent many of the same frustrations felt by Bill and George in dealing with a poorly educated population. They imply, however, that as a paramedic gains experience in these situations, he or she acquires an understanding of the language of the inner city, and develops skills for dealing with inarticulate patients. These situations then cease to be problematic and instead become a subject for amusement.[9]

With short narratives such as these, medics present themselves as being experienced by recalling a time when they were dumbfounded by the responses they received from patients. The humor is generally directed at their own naïveté, particularly in the "done fell out" stories, in which the medic tries to discover the place from which the patient fell. These highly stylized stories of typical patient interactions reveal two conflicting levels of language: the patients' language, which the paramedics must learn to interpret, and the language of pharmacology and physiology, which paramedics feel that they have mastered. The mispronunciations, malapropisms, and popular characterizations of medications and illnesses become the object of scorn in these stories. Thus, in one respect, it is the patient's abilities, and not the patient, being derided; the patient is still treated.

While medics express their annoyance at being called to the scene of nonemergencies and voice displeasure with the communications problems that confront them on scene, they are aware that an unwillingness to respond sincerely to people's complaints can be construed by patients and bystanders as either elitist or racist:[10]

Jason: Don't give them attitude. You can't say, "Hey, you don't need an ambulance, you gotta take a taxi." Don't say that. Instead say, "Hey, what happened?" Check it out, put an ice pack on, they're gonna think you're the greatest guy. I mean just treat people nice. Don't give them facial expressions. Sometimes paramedics go, "Oh, man, you called an ambulance for that?" People gonna get irritated, they're gonna get mad.

Matt: That's the way my partner gets.

Jason: Just be nice. Be nice and people gonna be nice to you, and at the end of the day you're gonna be mellow. If you give people attitude, they'll give you attitude and by the end of the day you'll be stressed out. Just be nice.

Matt: Notice that those are also the people who get punched!

Jason: Yeah, just be nice. Especially Latinos and black people, they like a lot of attention. They do. I don't know why, but they do. Give them attention, they'll be happy with you.

Emergency scenes are generally unpredictable, and approaching the scene with a proper attitude can spell the difference between a safe environment and an explosive one. As Matt notes, a paramedic whose attitude is perceived as hostile can become the victim of assault. Even with precautions, however, paramedics occasionally find themselves in situations that threaten their physical well-being.

Paramedic story tradition is replete with accounts of crews responding to mundane calls only to be confronted with enraged patients and bystanders, crews unwittingly arriving onto unsecured scenes, or the intrusion of street violence into the ambulance itself. Despite numerous precautions, medics are sometimes the victims of assault:

Darryl: Yeah, we're shot at, we're assaulted and everything. It's funny how we're there to help people, and how a lot of times when we go there, we feel like beating the people. I mean that's really bad, because we're there to help people, and we now feel like beating you. So, you probably deserved being beat up in the first place!

Unlike Tom R., the operations manager who adopts the passive stance of suggesting that paramedics are "sacred," Darryl proposes a position more in line with the one taken by Kathryn and Mary. Darryl's view is tempered by the threat of frequent interactions with violent patients. Certainly, his braggadocio contributes to his self-confident approach to scenes; some medics even mention that bluffing can be the best protection. As Matt puts it, "Never let them know you're afraid!"

Sitting in the front seat of his ambulance at a post renowned for being dangerous, Tony smiles at his partner, Patrick, puts down his burrito,[11] and tells the story of an assault:

Tony: I got a knife pulled on me, one time. We went to this apartment house, and we were like, "What's going on?" And the woman there tells me that her children were sexually assaulted about three weeks ago. And I was like, "All right, well, we'll request the police department for you, 'cause there's nothing at this point that we can do for you. We'll be glad to take your children, if you want." And I look over at the children, and they're just playing. And she was like, "Oh, well, I don't want that, just give me the police department." So I said, "Okay."

But she was really diaphoretic [sweating] and was really anxious. She did not look well. So I said, "Are you okay?" and she said, "Well, no, I'm feeling really bad right now." So I said, "Do you want me to check you out?" And I checked her blood pressure and her pulse and all that was really high and really rapid. Then I started asking her questions and I saw a crack pipe next to her and a little plastic bag. And I said, "Have you been doing any drugs today?" And she looked at me really angry and said, "Why?! Just 'cause there's a pipe there?!" And I was like, "Well, no, that's a question I need to ask you to figure out what's going on here." And she said, "You think I'm a druggie!" And I was like, "No, I'm not saying that at all!"

And then she pulled out a big old knife from underneath her pillow—we were sitting on her bed—she pulled a big old knife from under her pillow and took a swing! [laughter] I said, "Listen, forget it, we're out of here!" And I started backing out. Then she came chasing at us. And so my partner grabbed the airway bag and smacked her on the side! [laughter] And then we both took off. And waited for the police to show up.

She and her two kids, in the meantime, got up and left the apartment complex. We followed them for a little while, but they took an alley and so I don't know whatever came of it. But that was my knife experience. Never been shot at. And I wanna keep it that way, too. Other medics have been shot at.

In part, the story stands as a cautionary tale. Tony and his partner have no reason to expect anything out of the ordinary, and the attack catches both of them by surprise. Many of the calls paramedics receive come over the radio as "unknown medical," and these can be particularly dangerous since the medics respond without any assistance from either the fire department or the police department.[12] In such cases, they have little information to work with other than an address, which, although it can give certain clues about the environment, rarely provides a clear picture and, when alcohol or drug abuse is factored into the equation, an otherwise normal scene can become unpredictable. Thus, a tale such as Tony's helps reinforce the belief among many medics that what are innocuous-sounding calls can quickly become threatening. The tale also reinforces the sentiment expressed by Darryl that medics will strike back.

Tony relates the story with a great deal of humor, perhaps using it as a means of defusing the threat; rather than being a story of terror, it becomes an amusing story of medics cleverly retreating from a dangerous situation. At the end, Tony also comments on the threat posed by handguns. Thus, the story resonates well with Steve's story of the fumbled assault, with one amusing reversal; whereas Steve mentions that he has never been stabbed, Tony remarks that he has never been shot. As in Steve's story, the threat—in this case the patient—eludes capture and remains on the street. Even though Tony and his partner win the battle by beating a hasty retreat, they quite possibly have lost the war, as the potential exists for the patient to strike again. Thus, rather than decreasing anxiety, the stories generate more, and precipitate a mood of watchful readiness.[13]

While medics are not shy about restraining unruly patients, they emphasize the close working relationship they have with the police:

Darryl: People quickly find out that we're not going to play around. You strike one of us and it's just like striking the police! We'll be all over you. It's a felony, first off, to assault us and we'll be all over you before the police get there. And then the police will be all over you afterwards, too, and everything. But people get shocked when we turn it around and tie people up and beat on them or something or other. Because they think that we're Nurse Florence Nightingale there to help people and everything. That's not what it's about. I'm not going home with a black eye. There's no way. There's no way!

Darryl expresses clearly the extent to which he is willing to assume the role of the police in their absence, a position not as much endorsed by other medics. At times, Darryl even likens himself to a medical version of the police:

Darryl: "Medical arrest." I think I thought that one up. Sometimes you have patients that are legally within their rights to refuse treatment, because they're still lucid enough to answer the appropriate questions to be a consenting adult and everything. But you know they're having a medical problem that's life-threatening. I'm not talking bullshit, I'm talking about a life-threatening illness and everything and they don't want to go to the hospital. Typically, it's like elderly emphysema patients, they're just tired of going to the hospital. They don't want to go to the hospital, they don't care if they die, and they're just going to stay in there until they do, you know? Well, in reality, what would probably happen is they'd go unconscious and the family would call us back, but why? I'm basically a lazy person and you've got us there right now, let's deal with the program, let's take you to the hospital.

So I just bullshit people. "Look, you're under medical arrest. You have no rights here. You're under medical arrest and you're in violation of the paramedic penal code if you resist medical arrest." And I quote some bullshit like section 4, paragraph 3, subtitle fucking 3.2, which gives us the right to put you under medical arrest. Usually, you can bullshit people into going to the hospital, they'll go with you and everything. You don't have a choice, you're under medical arrest. "Uh, you're not going to put me under arrest, are you?"

This cop asked me, he goes, "Does anybody ever fight you? " I said, "Yeah, the same assholes that fight you when you arrest them fight us!" [laughter] It's no big deal. Most citizens you can bullshit, they don't know any better. You can tell them they are under medical arrest, be done with it, and drag them off to the hospital. It's in their best interest. No judge or any jury would ever convict you. I guess technically that could be kidnapping. But if you really think they have a medical problem and they have a life-threatening illness, what jury or judge would convict you? It ain't gonna happen. Morally, I find it easier to lie to people than it is to leave them to die. I don't think that's very moral either. But yeah, we lie to people all the time. "You're under medical arrest, that's what you are." [laughter]

In this case, of course, the patients pose no threat to the medics, but rather are threats to themselves. Darryl pretends to have the authority of the police—making use of their vocabulary and their right to detain criminal suspects—as a means for expediting his own work. Within the story, Darryl suggests a close relationship with police, relating a conversation with a "cop" as an integral, and amusing, part of the narrative.

The general belief about the close relationship between medics and police and the specific belief that the police will respond quickly to paramedic calls for help find reinforcement in the storytelling. One evening Lars tells an involved story of being assaulted:

Lars: We're sitting there at the little AM/PM at West Grand and Market, and I went in, heated up my dinner, came out all hungry, psyched to eat. So I get in the unit, and I was sitting there, taking off the cover of my spaghetti and I've got my drink, and suddenly the door opens, and this woman reaches inside. "Hey, hey, you gotta take me out of here! Drive me down the street!" I'm like, "What is this, Yellow Cab?!" And she's all, "Oh, you gotta drive me down the street, drive me down the street!" I'm looking at her and I'm like, "Why, what's wrong?"

And this guy comes around the ambulance. Now we're parked right next to this minimarket, so the wall is right next to the ambulance and she kind of moves in between the wall and the door. And this guy comes right up and starts yelling at her, "You fucking bitch, you fucking whore! You motherfucking bitch!" And he grabs onto her. So she grabs onto my arm and my leg. And he's yelling and screaming at her, and I'm like, "Oh! Sir, you should calm down." "Fuck you, motherfucker!" And I said, "Well, listen, if you don't let go of her, she's not gonna let go of me."

So, he lets go of her and he's standing there and he goes, "Okay, let go of him, bitch!" She's like, "No!" I'm like, "Well, why don't you just step back?" And he goes, "Fuck you! I can do whatever I want, this bitch is my wife!" And he grabs her and starts punching her in the face. I'm like, "Fuck this!" So I put my feet up on him and I push him away—I should have kicked him hard, but I pushed him away.

Now this crowd of people has gathered in front of the unit. And this guy turns on me, "You motherfucker! You white mother! You punk-ass white motherfucker! You kicked me! You just fucking kicked me for no reason!" He's saying, "You fucker, you just kicked me!" So all this crowd is hearing is that this white paramedic just kicked this black guy in the chest. So now we have an angry crowd in front of us. And he gets up in my face, "You motherfucker! I'll fuck you up! Let's go right now!" And he pulls off his jacket.

Meanwhile, I'm sitting here hitting the little 11-99 button, which means "Help!" And my partner's on the radio, like, "Could we have Code 3 PD here now!" And he tells them West Grand and Market, but somehow they get it as 10th and Market. So they're sending all the cops to 10th and Market.

And this guy's up in my face, the woman's holding on to me, the guy's right in my face screaming, she's holding my arm and my leg, like I'm the human shield here. And then he just cracks me, right in the mouth. And I'm like, "You motherfucker!" I want to get out and fight him, but there's this big crowd of people. And it's like, "Fuck, these people are going to kill us." You can hear people are kind of grumbling, "White motherfucker, kick his ass." So now he's also insisting, "Yeah, go ahead, call the cops, motherfucker! You're going to jail!" He's telling me, "You kicked me, you're going to jail!" I'm thinking, "Oh, yeah, OPD is really gonna come out and want to hear what this guy has to say."

So, the dispatch asks us, "Are you guys Code 4? Are you guys Code 4?" So my partner just takes the mike and keys it up and leans it over, and all you hear is this, "I'm gonna kill you, you motherfucker!" You hear it all over the county! They're like, "I don't think they're Code 4." Then you hear on the scanner—we had our scanner on—you hear the police going, "It's not at 10th and Market, it's at West Grand and Market!" And so two seconds later, you just hear sirens from all over. And these cop cars just pour into the parking lot.

It's great—as soon as you hear the sirens, this big crowd of people just— whoosh!—disappears. They're all gone. So the cops come in and I'm like, "Yeah, he hit her in the face, he punched me in the face." And that was all it took, they all just grabbed the guy. So he starts trying to fight with the cops and you just hear "Wham!"—they throw him up against the side of the unit, he's still trying to fight them. Throw him down on the ground and they hand-cuff the guy and throw him in the back of a police car. Then they turn to me, "What happened?" I give them the whole story—turns out the guy's out on parole. The woman, she's been punched in the face a bunch of times but she doesn't want to press charges. I'm like, "I want to press charges! Bring the form on, let's press charges!" So, we press charges on the guy, turns out that he doesn't go to a normal hearing, he goes to a special parole hearing. So, I don't know what happened to this guy, whether they threw his ass back in jail or not, but I'm hoping they did. They're like, "You haven't heard from him, have you?" I go, "No, why? Should I be worried? Might I hear from this guy?" And they're like, "Oh, well, he's out on the streets." "Oh, good." So somewhere there's some guy out on parole, he walks around Oakland, looking for me. After that, I went out and bought a bulletproof vest, which I obviously have on today. [laughter] Today, I'll run into him. [laughter] But yeah, that's my story.

Here, Lars openly praises the police for their rapid response while simultaneously criticizing the dispatchers for their failure to respond and communicate properly. Another compelling aspect of Lars's story is the violation of the seemingly safe area of the ambulance. Many medics refer to the front seat of the ambulance as their "living room," and see the vehicle itself as a safe haven from the dangers lurking outside. Unwisely, Lars leaves the door open, and thereby invites the threatening outside into the sanctity of the ambulance.

The racial tensions associated with work in Oakland also inform the story; yet here, race is used by the assailant as a secondary weapon in an attempt to galvanize the crowd to turn against the medics. Lars provides a further comment on the judicial process in which a felon is not confined but rather is allowed to remain free. The story underscores the concern among medics that particularly violent patients or bystanders might come "gunning" for them to right past wrongs. Whereas other medics have described occupying a position of seeming invincibility, Lars tells of a situation in which he is nearly powerless and must rely on the police to save him. At the end of the story, he mentions his purchase of a bulletproof vest and then laughingly points out that he is not wearing it. On another day, Lars provides a different ending to his story:

Lars: So they throw this guy in the back of a police car, and then the cop asks me, "Why didn't you smack him with your flashlight? Where's your Mag-lite?" And so I pull out this little minimag [penlight] that I carry, and these cops are just cracking up. They're like, "You call that a flashlight? *This* is a flashlight!" And he pulls out this giant thing with like five batteries in it. I mean, it looks like a friggin' battering ram. [laughter] I finally went out and got one.

Lars's substitution in an otherwise stable narrative reveals a fascinating aspect of medic storytelling, namely the continuous quest for some kind of ending, despite the evidence that there are no clear endings, since there are always more patients. Telling stories allows medics to provide endings—and thus both structure and closure—to what are often unstructured and open-ended experiences.

In other stories, medics express more suspicion of the police. These stories, however, generally refer to police harassment—for example, pulling an ambulance over for "failure to signal"—as unusual behavior. The improper actions are attributed to CHP (California Highway Patrol) officers, referred to by many medics as "AAA with guns," or officers from smaller, suburban police departments, unaware of how critically important medics can be to their survival on the streets (or at least how critically important medics believe they can be to the police). At the end of the story, the medic usually calls out "Hope you don't get shot!" to the departing police officer. This ambiguous attitude toward the police is not an anomaly; in fact, ambiguity is a major aspect of paramedic work culture. Information at scenes is ambiguous, relationships with other first responders and medical personnel are ambiguous, relationships between medic crews are ambiguous, and the information that comes over the radio is ambiguous.[14] It is not surprising, then, that such attitudes are explored, negotiated, and reassessed time and again in storytelling. For example, an ambiguous evaluation of the fire department can be found, even within a single paramedic's storytelling. Late one night, while waiting to get off, Stephanie tells a story about an assault and the admirable performance of a firefighter:

Stephanie: This poor woman was walking home from school, it's about nine o'clock in the evening and some thugs came up and hit her over the head with a two-by-four that had nails sticking out of it. And so we got there and she'd walked about half a block down the street and it was a pretty dark street. Of course she's got this huge gash in her head and she's crying and stuff and one of her front teeth is missing, it's just gone, right?

So the fire department gets on scene and we're trying to C-spine her and all this stuff and one of these rookie firewomen comes up and says, "Well, do you want me to go look for the tooth?" And I'm thinking that it's a nice dark street and it happened a block away and I'm like, "I don't think you're going to find it and we sort of need to go, 'cause we're gonna make her a trauma activation."

So we're getting her all loaded, we get her packaged and put her in the ambulance and we're just about to take off—I mean the driver's in the driver's seat—and just as we're about to take off we hear this knock on the back door of the ambulance! And it's the firefighter! And we open the door— of course you can't save teeth unless it has a root—and here she is and sure enough, she had her tooth and her root and everything! The whole thing intact! She'd gone all the way down the street and found it. It was just the most amazing thing you'd ever seen. Her whole tooth.

So we rush her to the trauma center and the doc says, "Oh, the tooth!" and puts it right back in and gives her a couple of 4 by 4s [four-inch-square sterile gauze dressings] to bite down on and, with all the rich blood supply, they thought it would just take like that. But I thought it was so impressive this firefighter, I kept saying, "No, no, you're never gonna find it, you're never gonna find it!" And here's this beautiful woman—you know she would have had a false tooth the rest of her life—she was probably twenty or something. And it was just amazing.

Steve Y.: That's an amazing story.

Stephanie: Yeah, it's an amazing story. I just opened the back door and there was the tooth. It was unbelievable. I think it was Lars I was working with. And so we wrote a letter of commendation for the perseverance of this firefighter who just took it upon herself to find the tooth. I just kept brushing her off. She scanned the whole place and ta-dahh!

Steve: Fuck, what are the chances of finding it?

Stephanie: I don't know.

Steve: Put some money down on the lottery before that!

In the story, the focus moves notably from the brutality of the assault to the firefighter's perseverance and the victim's recovery. Stephanie and Lars, frequent critics of the fire crews in their stories, even go to the length of writing a letter commending the firefighter. Significantly, the firefighter is a new recruit and a woman. As such, she is not representative of firefighters in general. Stephanie's story is somewhat rare because she endorses not only the fire crew but also the hospital medical staff. At the same time, she reveals the deeply ambiguous attitudes integral to paramedic culture.

A far more common type of assault story focuses on the extreme brutality with which people are attacked. His memory jogged by a posting in a warehouse district in East Oakland, Lars tells the most memorable of these stories:

Lars: This last weekend I was riding around as a third person on units, 'cause I'm supposed to be testing new heart monitors. And they're like, "Oh, you don't have to do patient care." Which was crazy. We had so many traumas and stat calls, I ended up doing tons of patient care, you know? I mean, what the hell, you've got a third paramedic there, you know?

So we get a call in deep East Oakland, real bad part of town. O-K Corral type stuff. We get a call for an assault and we get there right behind the police. And there's this guy laid out in the street. And, yeah, he's been assaulted. They assaulted him with a Buick! And then they assaulted him with a pickup truck! They had beaten this guy up—I guess there was some drug deal thing going—but they had beaten him up, thrown him down in the street, and then they ran him over with this car. And then they ran him over with this pickup truck.

So, he's all sprawled out in the street, and we come up. We don't know where the fire department is, they didn't show up 'til the very end of the call. But, luckily, we've got the three of us to work on this guy, 'cause he's in cardiac arrest. And his legs are just sort of ripped open, bones sticking out all over the place and there's blood everywhere! So I'm cutting off his clothing, we're doing CPR and one of the guys goes to intubate him. So, he puts his hand on the back of his head and, as he's putting in the laryngoscope, he's like, "Yuck! My fingers just went inside his skull!" We're suctioning, but we pull up the suction 'cause it's not sucking up much stuff. "Oh, there's a big chunk of brain on it!" [laughter] It's like when you've got a milkshake and you're sucking, and you get a piece of ice through your straw? It's like, "Oh, brain."

So we get the brain off and we get the guy intubated and we're working on him and we get him on the backboard. I go to put him on the backboard and one leg sort of flops off this way and one flops off the other way. So I get him on, I'm trying to arrange the legs so they look almost anatomical but they're just all over the place! We strap the guy down and we're giving him CPR, we get him in the back of the ambulance and then the fire department shows up. "You guys need a hand?" "Uh, we got it."

So we start out Code 3 to the closest hospital, 'cause on traumatic arrest you just go to the closest emergency room so they can go, "Hmm. Dead." So it's me and this one other medic in back trying to start some lines and some CPR and I'm bagging this guy. I'm supposed to be testing these new heart monitors and what I've been doing with other people is having them wave their arms and stuff, move their legs to see if I can get the monitor to screw up. Well, I'm sitting here bagging this guy, there's blood shooting out every-where and running all over the place, and I'm like, "Sir! Can you lift your arms? Thank you." The machine seems to be working fine. [laughter]

So, we get to the emergency room and we're wheeling him in, riding on the gurney, doing CPR and we go right by the waiting room. And there're all these people in the waiting room and it had to have been the most disgusting thing any of them had ever seen 'cause this was really up there. It even ranks up there for gross things I've seen. And they're all like, "Uhhhh." We go scooting by and we go into this room and we're like, "Here he is!"

Now we thought they're just gonna go "Oh, dead." But they start working on the guy! They're giving epinephrine and atropine to stimulate the heart and we're going, "I don't know if you want to stimulate that heart—there's no brain!" I mean, we left half of them on the scene. I'm like, "You want me to go get the rest of it, it's out in the unit." So one nurse was like, "Oh, how's his pelvis," I'm like, "Oh, that's out in the unit, too." But at one point they thought they got the heart beating again. I'm like, "Oh, good, yeah. He'll be asparagus." But finally they said, "Aw, he's dead." No kidding! Oh! What a shocker! I thought we had snatched his life from the gaping jaws of death! So, he died.

In this case, Lars's sarcastic tone puts distance between himself and the event. He further distances himself from the environment, labeling the area the Wild West. Just as in many other stories of accident victims, Lars describes the violent uncovering of otherwise hidden organs, and, as in many of those stories, he likens the discovery to something far more innocuous—here, a frothy milkshake.[15] The startling analogy (brain matter stuck on a suction unit and ice caught in a straw) is, in fact, a common feature of medic stories—extraordinary sights are compared to mundane ones. Lars, of course, is a master at making these surprising comparisons. Finally, he offers amusing criticism of the medical workers who attempt to save a patient he has already determined to be dead. In particular, he singles out the nurse who asks a moot question—if the man is in cardiac arrest and has suffered severe brain damage, the condition of his pelvis is inconsequential. For Lars, the medical treatment approaches the grotesque, since the patient is so clearly dead. But in Lars's capable narrative hands, the story does not devolve into a depressing rumination on the horrors of the assault and the ghoulish attempts to revive the patient; instead, he turns it into a burlesque.

Possibly the most dangerous calls that paramedics respond to are shootings. Usually, medics arrive after the scene has been secured, but sometimes they arrive with, or even before, the police. Darryl and Tom tell the best-known story at Regional Ambulance about a shooting. As in many of the stories concerning the dangers of the job, they are able to persevere and successfully save their patient, despite daunting odds. At the same time, they openly admit to overwhelming fear which colors their judgment, leading them to interpret innocuous events as dangerous threats. Early one evening, as *Cops* plays on the station house television, Darryl tells his version of the story. Despite the "drama" on the screen, everyone in the station listens to Darryl's tale:

Darryl: Me and Tom, we were cruising around at three or four. No, it was probably later than that, actually, 'cause we were really close to getting off. So it's probably around five o'clock in the morning, four-thirty in the morning, around in there. And we were listening on the police scanner and stuff and we heard a call for multiple shots fired and a person screaming. And whatever way you look at it, in Oakland, that's a shooting.

It was at Hale and Cary, which is right off of 98th Avenue and stuff. And I didn't hear Hale, but I heard Cary and I thought they said "Cherry." Cherry's another street sort of about five miles away or so. So we start heading that way and I'm looking it up on the mapbook, and it just didn't make any sense. Well, then they put it back up as, "Police are arriving at Hale and Cary." And I said, "Oh, it's Cary! Okay, this makes more sense." So Tom turns it back around, we shoot down San Leandro Boulevard and start coming up 98th Avenue. So we're driving and stuff and we're going to take a right on Edes.

Before we get to Edes, we come over the railroad tracks to the street called Railroad right there and I look over to my side—I was the passenger—and I look over to my side, and there's this car, T-boned into a tow truck. The back wheel is spinning, right, and there's a lot of smoke in the air and the wheel's spinning, but all the rubber's off of it and it's just the metal grinding into the pavement. And it's digging into the pavement going, "Grrrrrrrrr." And I'm thinking, "Huh, that's a real trip."

So I say, "Hey, Tom, flip it back around, this doesn't look right, let's check that out." So, he flips it back around, comes up to the car, we flip the lights on and stuff, and we put ourselves out on the radio, "We're investigating" what we believed was an auto accident at the time. And I walked up to the car and there's a white male adult slumped sideways in the car with his head on the window sill of the car. And his foot's just mashed down on the gas pedal! And that's what's causing the back wheel to spin and stuff.

So I give him this radical trapezius pinch, which usually stimulates somebody, and he doesn't even move! And he's got this pale, ashen, I-don't-have-any-blood-pressure-because-all-of-the-blood-bled-out-of-my-body look to his face. I go, "Hmm..." I'm watching him, and I reach over into the car to turn the engine off. I turn the engine off. At the same time, I sort of step back and look what we got and stuff. 'Cause I'm looking, I'm thinking, "Why is he unconscious, blah blah blah." I'm looking at the damage to the car—you're thinking all your paramedicine weirdness, why somebody could be unconscious.

What does a car do, when it's at full tilt and you turn the gas off? It backfires like nobody's business, right? And right as I turn it off and it's starting to go "Buuhhhh" down like that, I step back and it's got about fifteen bullet holes in the door. And I look over at Tom and I say, "Tom, we've got the shooting right here," 'cause it was right around the corner from Hale and Cary. I go,

"Tom" — right as I'm saying, "Tom, we've got the shooting right here" — "bam! bam bam bam bam bam bam bam!" It starts to backfire, man! We were like all over the ground.

We're laying down and stuff and I'm looking at him and he's looking at me and I'm trying to figure out where it was coming from. Well, it was backfiring, it only took like seconds to transpire, to figure that out. But at the time, you know, we were scared. There's nothing but what could be a gunman on the other side, we don't know, and on the other side of us is this fence, 'cause it's a wrecking yard. And there's these gnarly pitbulls, "Arr arr arr arr," you know? So it's either jump the fence and get chewed by the pitbulls, step out here and get shot by this homicidal maniac coming back to finish this idiot off. And Tom looks up at me and goes thump thump thump right on his chest. 'Cause he had his vest on, but I had left my vest in the ambulance. And he looked at me with this "Ha ha! Got my vest on! You don't!" And I looked right at him and said, "I hope they shoot you in the fucking head, motherfucker!" Just like that! Then we figured out, "Oh, it's backfiring!" So once it backfires and everything, we're like, "Ha ha! It's backfiring!"

Well, the back seat's now on fire from the wheel spinning around and now the back seat just erupts. "Whoosh!" It just flashes over! So Tom runs back to get the fire extinguisher 'cause I'm trying to pull this idiot out of the car, and he's not coming. The door mechanism is jammed, 'cause there's a bunch of bullet holes in it and I reached in — the flames are now licking out — and I reached in and I found the seat belt, snapped the seat belt and I just grabbed him and I'm pulling him out. Well, Tom runs up with the fire extinguisher, gonna buy us some time. And he goes squirt. Nothing! "Ooooh! It's not even charged!" And he throws it on the ground! He goes, "Damn Allied!" 'cause they always had equipment that didn't work and stuff like that.

And so we drag him out of the car, and by now the whole car is fully involved. I drag him out, sit him on the ground, Tom runs up with a backboard, flip him on the backboard, and so we're gonna get him to the ambulance to do our business and strip him and stuff. And these two dudes come walking up. Two black guys. Now it was five in the morning, but you're not really thinking that, right? And I think it was a weekend, but what does that matter? And these two guys come walking up and one of them is holding a newspaper — maybe I've watched too many gangster movies, but you know how you see how the hit man always has the pistol underneath the paper. You know what I'm talking about? Well, he's carrying a paper like that. I'm thinking, "Ohmigod, ohmigod, ohmigod! Here it comes. He's gonna kill this guy, he's gonna kill us all, oh no! Mr. Wizard, I don't wanna be a paramedic anymore!" And they walk up and he all looks mean and nasty, and what does he say? He goes, "You guys need any help?" Turns out they were two ordinary Joes with a cup of coffee and a paper on their way to work. It was incredible. I couldn't believe it. Scared me shitless. Haaa!

So, we get him in the back of the ambulance, and we put ourselves back on the radio, "We've got a fully involved car fire." It takes longer to tell the story than the time it transpired and stuff, 'cause it was only seconds to minutes, and here it is I've been telling the story the last twenty minutes! But we get him in the back of the ambulance and put out on the radio that we've got a fully involved car fire and we've got this shooting victim there and we need the police there and stuff, 'cause God knows who's gonna to show up next to our party here! We're by ourselves in the ghetto, you know.

So we're stripping him in the back and we pull off one of his cowboy boots. And we pull his cowboy boot off and there was a slug, in the cowboy boot. And the slug fell out of the boot and I put it in my hand. It's a bloody slug, sitting there on my hand and the cops pull up and they go, "What do you guys got? What's going on here? There's a car fire?" And I go, "There's a shooting right here," and the cop goes, "Well, how do you know?" "What do you mean, how do I know? Hold your hand out!" He holds his hand out and I dropped the bloody slug in his hand. He goes, "Oh, God!" And I go, "Is that shooting enough there for you, dude?" That's a shooting, isn't it? Incredible. That's my story about Tom B.'s and me car-fire-crash-rescue-shooting-radical-ness. There it is. [laughter] That was it, boy, right there.

So just to conclude this whole story. This idiot had this big old gold chain and these nuggets on the end of his chain and evidently it fell off or got lost. Well, we went and saw this guy two days later in the ICU, and he goes, he says, "Did you see my chain? I lost it. Did you guys find it?" No "thank you." No nothing. Can you believe that?

Alone, with malfunctioning equipment, at the scene of a bizarre accident, Darryl and Tom emerge in the story as part road warriors, part

Keystone cops. While they eventually manage to control the scene and save the patient, the process is so filled with adrenaline-fueled bungling and the undermining of preconceived notions that the story becomes a slapstick comedy. The final evaluation of the victim as an "idiot" is in line with attitudes other medics express towards many of their patients. The final twist comes in the recovery room, which does not resemble the idyllic scene of medic and patient, life saver and grateful victim so common in media portrayals of the profession; instead, the patient asks them for his gold chain.

On a different day, Tom has a new rookie partner, Jim. With a great flourish, Tom puts on his bulletproof vest, referring to it as a "prop," grins at Jim, and launches into his version of the same story. Tom's version closely mirrors Darryl's, with the expected shift in perspective. Tom offers greater detail on the street names and the route—perhaps because he was the driver—and an elaborate description of problems with the radio system entirely missing from Darryl's story. Not surprisingly, Tom describes Darryl's actions as being frenetic and his own as being calmer. Despite the differences in emphasis, Tom's story is quite similar to Darryl's. The stability of the narrative across versions is indeed one of the most notable aspects of these two tellings.

Stories abound about the dangers of paramedic work. To some extent, medics use these stories as an opportunity to explore various situations and examine potential outcomes. They also tell stories as a means of elevating their job status, while critiquing the performance of other emergency providers. Stories of danger and derring-do are always engaging, and the unique work environment offers abundant opportunity for surprising experiences. The stories at times help alert other paramedics to potentially dangerous situations and, in this sense, they contribute to the enculturation of new medics and the ongoing education of current ones. Many medics also comment in their stories on the social ills afflicting large American cities, particularly the pervasive racial tensions which accompany working in the inner city. But few paramedics feel that the danger associated with the job would lead them to abandon the profession. Rather, most enjoy the adrenaline rush that comes with responding to crime scenes or going into dangerous neighborhoods, and many relish telling stories about such responses.

# 3

# THERE WAS BRAIN FOR
# HALF A BLOCK

Bill V. adjusts his seat further back so the shade of the overpass covers his face, laughs, and begins yet another story:

Bill V.: I had a buddy, he and his partner, these guys worked for Goodhew L.A. This is before they had the paramedic debriefing and shit. You know, the stress debriefings? His buddy committed suicide. Ross Zentner knew these guys and he was involved with this, too.

The Cerritos air crash where that fucking airplane—it was like Labor Day—and that airplane went into that neighborhood?[1] Well these guys were cruising down the 605 freeway in L.A.—I think it was the 605—they're cruising along and they see this airplane go down right next to them in this neighborhood. It's like, get off the off ramp and they're there. And they were the first guys on scene, before fire got there, before anybody got there.[2] And they're driving through this neighborhoood. You know, driving over body parts, and there's guts and shit hanging in the trees, and there's houses burning, there's cars out front on fire. You know, everybody was in their houses at this time, everybody's in there eating, you know? Whole complete families were wiped out and these guys were driving through just like going, "What do we do?"

George: Yeah, where the fuck do you start?

Bill: Well, anyway the whole thing went down and for some reason these guys slipped through the cracks as far as afterwards. The people who responded officially, before they were allowed to go home, they were all taken and they went through the whole debriefing thing, you know? Mandatory stuff. Well, these two guys slipped through the cracks and went on their merry way. Well, five days later, the partner of this guy blew his brains out.

George: Oh, man!

Bill: Just freaked him out. Can you imagine that one? Ugh. You see some terrible things.

The most visible emergencies to which medics respond are accidents. Indeed, the earliest history of paramedicine and the development of the field in this country are intimately tied to transportation safety. While accidents involving automobiles constitute the majority of these calls, Alameda County paramedics also respond to those involving trains and, occasionally, boats. Most paramedics have seen countless minor fender benders, which rarely become the subjects of stories, but they also at times encounter remarkably gruesome wrecks, and these inevitably end up being described in narratives. Far less common than automobile accidents are those involving airplanes and helicopters, and the very novelty of these disasters makes them perfect material for storytelling.

For an automobile accident to be memorable enough to become part of a medic's long-term story repertoire, it must include an event that makes it significantly different from other such accidents. Usually, the notable element is the exceptionally horrific death or the miraculous survival of the victims. While routine accidents must enter the medic's narrative repertoire at least until the patient report is given at the receiving hospital, they do not endure as subjects for stories, since the experiences that would be recounted are universal among paramedics and therefore uninteresting. But these countless small accidents and minor complaints do form an experiential base for the medics and provide them with a guideline against which to measure other incidents.[3]

After dropping off a patient who suffered minor injuries in a fender bender, Mark F. tells a story of a far more gruesome accident:

Mark F.: I think the one I remember the most was about six years ago when I worked in Santa Monica as an EMT. We had these two guys in an MG going down the California incline, they rolled over and they had the top down — they were Recaro seats[4] — and they skid for about a hundred feet to where they stopped. And their seats didn't collapse backwards like they normally would and from their heads to their knees was just totally ground round. Their skin got completely torn off.

And you know that was kind of gruesome seeing that, but you know the worst, the funniest — funny — but the weirdest part was that, all the way to the back of the car, you'd see two little red marks like you would if you dragged a pencil eraser across a desk. And you know, once you flipped 'em over, there were these two guys sitting there with no faces! It took us about five minutes to figure out if they were male or female, 'cause they were nothing but a mass of blood from the front down. And it was just two guys just out for a good time, beer bottles in the car and stuff like that.

In his narrating, Mark catches himself on the word "funny," and his slip is revealing. Paramedics, when telling stories such as these, usually laugh and characterize the events as "funny." Here, though, the "funny" element is not the event itself but the mental image Mark conjures to help himself organize the events and categorize the accident scene. The victims become further removed from the realm of normal human interaction because their defining features — their faces — are erased. In this story, the victims actually appear as representations of the countless, anonymous — faceless, as it were — victims of automobile accidents that medics encounter in their work. Trauma to the face and head is a common feature in paramedic stories, perhaps because such injuries place identity and thought in jeopardy. The construction of identity — and, by extension, the person — has, in Western tradition, long been linked to the face, the brain, and the heart.[5] Medics frequently respond to accidents in which life is lost — a person has ceased to be — and it is interesting to note the emphasis in the stories on the violent destruction of the physical aspects of self. By focusing on the erasure of the face, for instance, Mark has the opportunity to treat a body, and not be concerned with the person.

Mark identifies himself as an EMT at the time of the accident, and the story thus is situated in his training period. In general, paramedics tend to remember and recount stories of grisly accidents encountered early on in their training. Lack of experience undoubtedly contributes to the psychological force of the scene, and subsequent experiences rarely supplant the shock of these initial accidents. As medics gain experience, stories from their training period take on a secondary significance as well. The stories serve not only as emotional guideposts but also as experiential ones. By telling these stories, medics can gauge their own development and their increasing ability to handle emergency scenes. The psychological burden of dealing with traumatic death can further be alleviated with the dark humor that pervades many medic stories.

In the story of the Cerritos air crash that Bill V. tells at the beginning of this chapter, the medic receives no counseling, no "debriefing," and, as a result of not being able to tell his story, he commits suicide. Storytelling can act as a continuous debriefing. Indeed, one of the main elements of Critical Incident Stress Debriefing (CISD), as the counseling process has come to be known, is narrating a troublesome call in the presence of cohorts.[6] Other medics express their empathy with the responding medic and help defuse the stress associated with the call. In an informal setting, when the memory of a scene seems overwhelming, another medic inevitably has a story of an equally gruesome one; the retelling of the story, often accompanied by laughter, can be reassuring.[7]

Stories told as a kind of informal debriefing actually have little interest for nonparamedics. Over breakfast one morning before a shift, Lars tells a story of a traffic fatality:

Lars: Sarah and I were working together and we were headed down from Oakland to Hayward, we were driving down Mission Boulevard, and the road's all blocked off. And we asked a cop, "Oh, what's wrong?" He says, "Oh, some car wreck, I think it's a fatal." We're like, "Okay, can we go by?" "Oh, yeah, sure."

We're driving down and the crew that was on the scene was like, "Hey! Stop!" We stopped and they're like, "You gotta see this. This is really gross." So, we go walking over there and this guy was flying down Mission Boulevard, something happened to his car, it spun around—he was doing in excess of a hundred miles an hour! It spun around, hit a curb, went flying up in the air and, biff!, impacted a telephone pole—backwards—at over a hundred mph.

And the car was just obliterated. Completely. The trunk was under the front seats, the front seats were both pushed up and out. And the guy went up and his head hit the top of the car and the door and everything. He was dangling out of the car on the pavement. His legs were all broken and mangled up inside the car, his head's there on the pavement, and the entire top part of his skull had been ripped off. And there was just brain for half a block. Brain bits. I mean his skull was empty, like a bowl. You could look up through his nostrils and see, you know, the sky! His face was all contorted and there was just brain everywhere. We needed a truck company to come with the jaws of life just to get the body out of there, it was so messed up.

And you know we're hanging out, talking with the crew, looking at it and going, "You're right, that is disgusting." And one of them's doing the paperwork for a dead body and he's like, "You ever done one of these?" and I'm like, "Oh, yeah." He's like, "Uh, what should I write for the chest?" I'm like, "I don't think it matters what you write for the chest. He's got no brain!" So we just hung out while they did the paperwork and waited for the fire department to come and cut the corpse out of the car.

Here, Lars's joy in telling the story seems oddly misplaced—the focus rests entirely on the condition of the accident victim and, in particular, the loss of his brain.[8] Lars dwells on the violent uncovering of body parts and organs generally hidden inside the body and, indeed, the other medics on scene seem to be excited about the situation, urging Lars and his partner to stop and see "something gross." As Mark did in his story, Lars makes a striking analogy, here between the victim's empty skull and a bowl.

In the stories, medics who cannot talk, even laugh, about such star-tling scenes either "wash out" or are described as inexperienced rook-ies who eventually develop the experience to deal with these scenes. Undoubtedly, repeated exposure to traumatic injuries and fatal acci-dents inures medics to the initial shock of such scenes. Nonetheless, many medics tell stories about becoming physically ill at the scene of gruesome accidents, although, as in Mark's story below, these episodes nearly always occur during their training period:

Mark F.: My biggest pet peeve is people who don't put kids in child seats. One of the first calls I remember in East L.A. was this young Mexican couple. They didn't speak any English and they were driving a '68 Chevy Impala steel dash and they had gotten into an accident and the lady was holding onto her baby — it was about two months old — and she didn't have a seat belt on. Well, she went forward with the baby against her chest, and the baby hit its head against the steel dashboard and was just squashed like a grape.

She was fine, the baby saved her, but her baby's head was split open like a grape. Just split open like a melon. I think I'd been in this business like two months at the time, and I calmly looked at her and turned around and vom-ited. [laughter] It was one of the most disgusting things I've seen! But you know she's sitting there in just a state of shock and here I am throwing up and the firefighters and the paramedics are looking around and they're all go-ing crazy. No one was hurt, except this kid's head was split open.

The focus on the brain in Lars's story and the erased heads in Mark's MG story may be a metaphoric allusion to the stupidity of the victims. It perhaps seems fitting to the paramedics that people's foolish actions would result in accidents causing grave injury to their heads. The same analysis could apply in the case of the dead infant, with the child's head acting as a horrible replacement for the mother's.

Stories of accidents also place the medics in a position of authority, offering them a vantage point from which to criticize the habits of many of their patients. Driving drunk is considered by most medics to be among the most stupid things one can do; the accidents caused by drunk drivers are a routine element of the work environment. Surprisingly, medic stories do not focus exclusively on the narrative punishment of such scofflaws. Darryl comments on the vicissitudes of responding to accidents involving drunk drivers:

Darryl: Yeah, you see all kinds of stuff. As I was saying earlier, you're really surprised by the little amount of trauma that a body can take and the massive amount of trauma it can take! And the little amount, people die, and the massive amount, somebody will live and stuff.

Man, I've seen, believe it or not, a head-on accident in the parking lot of a Macy's sale. What do they have, those white sales, is that what they have? The parking lot was completely barren except these two cars that hit each other head on. This little old lady and some other idiot. How do you do that?! A barren parking lot! Completely empty, morning, nobody there, and somehow they managed to hit each other head on.

Well, it was just enough trauma to kill her, you know? Barely any damage but, you know, a little old lady driving a big car, a big old gnarly steering wheel and that's enough to kill an elderly person and stuff. And then you get these drunks who just mangle their car and they wrap it around a telephone pole and split it in half and it's upside down and it's like, you can't even identify what kind of car it was, let alone what color it was! And you walk up and ask, "Where's the patient?" And it's the guy standing next to you going, "Yesh shir, I was driving." And there's nothing wrong with them! At all! It's incredible, you know? What is the moral of that? When you drive, drink! No [laughter], God, man, that's really weird! Human life is really weird like that, I guess, I don't know. But I've heard some stories.

Although Darryl generally punishes stupidity in his stories, here he is confronted with a contradiction. His response is to beat a narrative retreat into a philosophically existentialist position. In his story he ultimately recognizes that life—and death—are unpredictable and that all one can do, when confronted with these contradictions, is laugh. Undoubtedly, this gallows humor, the treatment of death with irony, and the swagger associated with confronting death as an oddly amusing event allow medics a much-needed emotional outlet for coming to terms with the horror of many accident scenes.[9]

Other common stories about car crashes tell of medics who risk their lives while attempting to save accident victims. Interestingly, many of the victims do not survive, despite the medics' efforts. One afternoon, in the ambulance loading area of Highland Hospital, Doug tells a story of an automobile accident emblazoned in his memory:

Doug: About three weeks ago, I was just getting off work, so I was still in my jumpsuit. Well, I'm going home, getting on 680, getting ready to get off my exit, by my house, and out of the corner of my eye I see this thing moving— it was a car. And all of a sudden, I see a body fly out, and I saw the car land on its top, but it had no top because it was a convertible. So I get out and I'm looking for the fire engines and the ambulances, but there are none because I'm the only one there. And I'm in my jumpsuit.

So I get out of the car, and everyone is running to me asking me what to do. I'm going around and I haven't even seen the patients yet. And as I look over at this convertible car, I see a man pinned down, the car's on his legs, and he's flailing around trying to get out of this car. But I see his buddy who got ejected up walking around, trying to pull him out. And then the car caught on fire from bumper to bumper.

So I run over to get the guy who's not pinned, to try to get him out of the car, or out of helping his friend, and I couldn't get him out and he caught on fire. So I'm pulling this guy out who was on fire, trying to get his jacket off, his clothes off, and at the same time I'm trying to keep him away from his friend who was on fire and moving around in the car. And I couldn't. This guy was on fire from head to toe, he was moving around, he was like three feet from me and I couldn't grab him, couldn't touch him.

That was the nightmare of the call. I was there by myself and didn't even have gloves, didn't have fire equipment to help put out the flames, didn't have a radio, didn't have anything. And it was so frustrating trying to keep the guy from helping his buddy, it was like my decision to say, "Okay, he's dead." He wasn't dead, he was just on fire, fully involved, but there was nothing I could do for him. It just drug on in my mind for about two or three weeks, and I went to counseling and everything. It was just a nightmare call, something that I never ever want to do again.

In this case, it is the frustration of being on scene without any assistance that makes the accident memorable. Doug emphasizes that, while his dress identifies him as a paramedic, he is completely unprepared for the situation. Except for the jumpsuit, he has none of his normal accoutrements; in fact, he is missing the most basic equipment, gloves. As such, the wreck represents a fundamental breakdown in his ability to work as a medical authority at the accident scene.

Doug's story also highlights an important aspect of medics' experiences on scene, which is that, in most cases, paramedics do not witness the events that lead to their being summoned. Usually, when they arrive, the events have already transpired, and they react to the situation. Thus it is rare for a story to include a detailed blow-by-blow description of an accident. Instead, in the course of their stories, the medics hypothesize on the cause of the accident (this speculation ultimately enters their official storytelling in the patient report for the hospital). Because of their physical and temporal remove from the accident itself, the scene is less chaotic by the time they arrive, with traffic having already been diverted. The wreck is a past event; for all intents and purposes, the patient has always been in the state in which they find him or her.

Doug's story also reveals the various narrative levels that are incorporated into medic storytelling. First, there is the story of the accident itself, which has usually ended by the time the medics arrive, so that their job, in part, is to reconstruct this story. The second story begins with their arrival, and concerns their actions on scene. Internal to this one is yet another series of stories, namely those they hear from the police, bystanders, and the patients themselves. These stories, in turn, are included in the story the medics tell about the accident as part of their official patient report. Finally, they incorporate all of these stories, to a greater or lesser extent, in the one they tell to other medics during narrative sessions. When the first story has not ended before the medics arrive — or when the story plays itself out in front of them — they are forced into a narrative crisis. Doug, for example, is no longer dealing solely with aftermath. His story resonates well with Bill V.'s story of the Cerritos aircrash. In both cases, the medics witness a devastating accident and are unable to respond with their usual competence. In Bill's story, the medics do not know where to begin, while in Doug's story, he does not even have the most rudimentary equipment. The inability to "cope with the situation" ends with a medic's suicide in Bill's story, while, in Doug's, he falls into a crisis of confidence and seeks counseling.

Not all paramedic stories about automobile accidents concern gruesome death. In fact, medics take delight in telling stories about miraculous survivors of car accidents, possibly both because such cases are rare and because the victim's survival offers the medic an unexpected "out" from the stress of treating a critical patient. Telling these stories of exceptional patients can result in one-upmanship, as a brief exchange between Jason and Matt attests:

Jason: I had a car accident one time. This car went under a trailer and it took us about an hour to get them out. And they walked out without no scratches at all. It was an old lady and her daughter. They were fine. It took us about an hour to take them out, but if you looked at their car, you'd go, "Wow, somebody died in here!" But it was a miracle they were alive, nothing happened to them.

Matt: That's like something we got at 880 and A Street two weeks ago. We get there and there's this trailer parked over this car. I guess this guy tried to change lanes and he just wedged his car under it. I get out and I turn to my partner and I say, "There's probably a dead body in that car." And then we walk over, and there's this guy sitting in there, and there's only one space in the entire car where anybody could have possibly survived and the guy's sitting there! He was bleeding, but he was fine!

Here, the medics are caught off guard by what they deem to be unsurvivable accidents. While experience tells them that a scene probably involves a fatality, and the expectation of encountering a dead or seriously injured patient forces them into an emotionally defensive mode, the discovery of the survivor offers a welcome release. Retelling the event allows them to reexperience that release.

Accidents involving trains are far less common than ones involving automobiles.[10] Accordingly, medics who have stories to tell about such accidents are likely to tell them. The most common of these accidents involve pedestrians and, as Stephanie laughingly suggests, "usually the train wins!" She herself tells a story of responding to one such incident:

Stephanie: But here's a good one. We had a call for a train versus pedestrian and so we get there and practically canceled on scene because the coroner had already arrived. But, of course, it's my first call and my preceptor wants me to see this. We're walking up there, it's kind of a steep bank up to the railroad tracks, so we're walking up the gravel bank and as I'm looking down I see some pink stuff on the ground. I think, "Oh, it's like bubble gum or something."

And then I see some more of it as we're going up towards the track and it turned out to be this woman's brain. So I looked at the bottom of my shoes and made sure I hadn't stepped in any. [laughter] It was kind of gross but I was prepared for anything. This woman had thrown herself on the tracks in front of this train. And she was totally atraumatic from the bottom of her neck down. At the bottom of the neck, she had a really dark bruise, and her head, it was just like an ax or something had hit it. I don't know how the train did it. She still had her little tennis shoes on and her little summer outfit and she had her purse in her hand. So that was my very first call as an intern. Of course, we didn't transport her. It was pretty gross. [laughter]

The story, told over lunch, is punctuated by laughter. But Stephanie draws a hauntingly stark image of the victim, with her "little tennis shoes" and her "little summer outfit." Here, the everyday aspects of the victim's dress contrast sharply with the bleakness of the scene. As in other accident stories, Stephanie turns her narrative gaze toward the victim's uncovered brain, and, like other medics, makes an analogy between the brain's appearance and a more innocuous item. Interestingly, these comparisons generally involve food items—fruit, bubble gum, and ground meat, for example. Indeed, medics often make comments that reflect this culinary focus, and, while these comments are intended to be humorously ironic references to the nauseating elements of the call, the comparisons also diminish the humanity of the victim. After all, now the medics are dealing with mundane, inanimate items rather than people.

Other stories of train accidents concern amputation.[11] The most common of these stories entail the transport of an amputated limb. As a response to a medic's comment that EMTs never run interesting calls, Larry, an EMT, tells a series of stories about body parts:

Larry: There's one EMT unit went in on a call Code 3. Turned out this guy amputated his leg from a train accident and the medics were taking him Code 3 to the hospital. And the EMTs were following Code 3 with the leg, doing the ring down. "Yeah, we're coming in code 3, we've got the leg on ice and we'll be there in one or two." Yeah, it's kinda fun. Something different.

We get the calls where you take people into Ralph K. Davies with their finger in a cup. This one guy we had, he was making a bird house and there was a saw there and this blue jay attacked him and he was shooing the bird away and boom his hand went right into the Skilsaw. Cut his finger off. So he went to look for his finger, but decided he was getting really dizzy— "I think I'll sit down and call for help." And we ended up transporting him and his finger to San Francisco to Ralph K. Davies for his reimplantation. He's doing fine. Those are some interesting stories.

The first story derives its interest from the separation of the patient and his leg not only at the accident scene but also on the way to the hospital. The humorous implications of transporting the limb alone, including the difficulty of describing the "patient" over the radio to the receiving hospital, are apparent to medics who hear the story. However, despite Larry's intention to refute the paramedic's challenge, the hierarchy between EMTs and paramedics is still obvious, with the medics transporting the patient and the EMTs transporting his limb.

Darryl also tells a story of amputation and transport, but emphasizes the paramedics' mistakes on scene:

Darryl: At downtown BART, this guy hurls himself into this BART train and whoosh, it runs him over and amputates his leg below the knee. Well, this didn't happen to us, but I was sitting at Highland when I observed this ambulance come in, it was two management people who were working overtime that day. One of them's a supervisor here, and the other one's a paramedic here, too. Both of them are really cool and good paramedics, but they had left this brown bag with this extremity in the bag, right?

And they got to Highland, and they both dumped the patient off and they come out, "Yeah, we got a cool call, it was—" you know, whatever, "blah blah blah, run over by a BART train," and this other craziness. And I'm sitting there writing paperwork and everything, going, "Yeah, whatever, girls." All of a sudden one of them comes out and goes, "Did you see the brown bag? Where's the brown bag?" And they're looking all over the back of the ambulance— "You got the brown bag?" "I didn't bring the brown bag, did you get it?" "No, I didn't get the brown bag, where's the brown bag at?" "It's at the BART Station!" With this guy's foot still in the bag!

They fuckin' close up the ambulance and they take off for the downtown BART station, you know, woo woo woo! They get there and they found it, on the platform, not disturbed at all, a leg in this bag! And they left it there—all these people going back and forth. Can you imagine someone looking? Ahhhh! Fuckin' loop! Can you believe that? They left it there! That's a funny story, hunh? Can you believe that? It's true. It's almost like I'm making it up, but it's true.

The two medics emerge from the hospital after a particularly memorable call and immediately launch into a story of their exploits. The story is, of course, intended to bolster their status among other medics but, during the course of the telling, it becomes apparent that they have bungled their call. Interestingly, the women are able to recover from their gaffe, although the call no longer serves to build up their status. Their mistake (and the victim's foot), initially hidden from public view, are both brought out into the open in Darryl's narrative.

Darryl's story is fascinating for numerous reasons. He readily acknowledges the developed tradition of paramedic storytelling within the narration itself, and provides an analysis of the main motivation for telling such stories, namely to impress other medics with "a cool call." Paramedics openly admit that they get excited about the opportunity to respond to a unique scene. Tom, for example, in his story of the shooting, says, "I was kind of bummed, 'cause I wanted to go to the shooting!" In the hierarchy of calls, a shooting is almost always "cooler" than a car accident. "Cool calls" not only offer medics an opportunity to exercise their skills but can also be transformed into a story. A "cool call" narrative lets the medics position themselves vis-à-vis other first responders and medical professionals as competent, in-control authorities able to handle even the most demanding crisis calmly and efficiently. During the telling, the attention of other medics is focused on the teller—the responder to the "cool call." Darryl himself frequently uses storytelling in this manner. But in this story, he clearly undermines the position of the medics, thereby strategically reversing the effect of their "cool call."

While Darryl always triumphs in his "cool call" narratives, here other medics who attempt both to run the call and then narrate it fail in a situation that he implicitly suggests he could control. The call, in fact, sounds rather mundane to him, and his dismissive comment, "Yeah, whatever, girls," when they begin their story suggests that he has little interest. But his dismissive attitude towards these women is not solely motivated by a desire to present himself as a seasoned veteran. The two medics who botch the call are identified as "management," and the story points to a substantial tension between field medics and their supervisors. In the story, then, Darryl is able to jibe at the abilities of field managers to run a call. In fact, leaving the foot on scene almost constitutes "patient abandonment," among the most serious offenses of which a medic can be guilty.

Darryl appears to make a negative assessment of women paramedics, dismissively referring to them as "girls." This attitude, however, is tempered with his evaluative comment, "both of them are . . . good paramedics," and expresses a certain ambivalence. While the majority of the male paramedics I interviewed did not express negative attitudes toward women medics, some of the women I interviewed felt that there was bias against them.[12] Interestingly, they attribute the majority of this prejudice to the fire department crews:

Melinda: You get that attitude of "that's a man's job, you shouldn't be doing it" mostly from firefighters. I was working with Mark one time and we had a patient who fell and she was a small girl and for some reason I was carrying equipment and, I don't know, didn't happen to be right there when they picked her up to take her to the ambulance. And so Mark got one of the firefighters to help him lift and the firefighter got real huffy about it and said, "Well, if she can't lift, she shouldn't be doing this job." And he just kept going on and on all the way down four flights of stairs. All the way to the ambulance, that's all I heard. It's like, "Well, look, if you don't want to lift her, set her down and I'll lift her, I don't need to hear your comments all the way down to the ambulance and neither does the patient." He just kept rambling.

The number of female paramedics is high, and, as male paramedics attest, their performance quickly dispels any lingering chauvinistic attitudes. Darryl's story may express a residual distrust of women medics, given his own aggressive style of paramedicine. However, his great delight in telling the story may be attributed more to the bungling ineptness of the supervisors' attempt to work as field medics than to a dismissive attitude toward women. The narrative victory Darryl scores with the story undoubtedly contributes to his zeal. While the "girls" seemed to have a "cool call" story to add to their repertoires, the telling of the story is interrupted by the discovery of their gaffe, which immediately allows Darryl to seize the narrative as his own. Rather than being able to use the story to increase their status, the women now become the object of Darryl's derision, in a story he uses both to build himself up and to knock the other medics—and, by extension, management—down.

Airplane accidents are possibly the least common of all vehicular accident calls in Alameda County, and few paramedics have experience with them. Accordingly, given the overwhelming propensity of medics to tell personal experience narratives, few airplane crash stories are told.[13] In fact, at Regional Ambulance, only Bill V. and Darryl had stories of airplane crashes to tell; these were considered by other medics to be thoroughly amusing, and were well known in the company. Darryl starts his narration with another story, one detailing a mass casualty automobile accident:

Darryl: We got a call, it was a carload of people from San Jose, some Mexican guys and stuff. And there's probably seven or eight of them in the car, I guess, including girls, right? Six, seven, eight patients, something like that? Was it a rollover or did it crash into the center divider or something like that? I forget really what it was, but they'd screwed their car up royally and they're all there, and we had eight patients. We're trying to deal with them and stuff. It was a busy night, so obviously you can't fit eight patients in an ambulance, so we're having to call more ambulances. And I got on scene with the supervisor, and he started coordinating everything, started calling ambulances, and he assigned me to call ambulances. So I called more ambulances than we needed, shoved all the patients in, and they were all gone. And we're standing at the side of the freeway, going, "Ha ha, no paperwork, no nothing!" And then, right after that we get a call for a plane crash at Oakland airport.

Derek: Oh, yes! Those two guys!

Darryl: So, we go straight from over there, and we zip over there and these two guys are both—one was an Australian air force pilot and one was an American air force pilot—one was an F16 pilot and the other was an F18 pilot. And they had crashed a twin engine Beechnut. Beechnut? Beachcraft. And it crashed, big fireball, and they were both burned. About 30 percent burned, second or third degree, which is bad, but they were dealing with the program rather well and stuff. The thing I remember the most out of it, was how much of a stud that the American—the American was our patient, right?

Derek: Yeah.

Darryl: The American F16 pilot, said, goes, fucking, didn't want any morphine because it made him feel out of control, and he's never been out of control in his life. I thought to myself, "This is a man with raging burns, fucking, over 30 percent of his body, and he doesn't want any fucking morphine because it makes him feel out of control. He's never done drugs before and he doesn't want to start. I'm thinking, "That's a man!" Incredible. End of story. You know what I mean? It almost was, like, "Oh, God, all these people running around selling their bodies, selling everything they owned to get dope," and this dude needs it but he doesn't want it because it makes him feel out of control. What a stud! Total stud.

Derek: That's a real man!

Darryl: They were real men, real men. That's right.

In his stories, Darryl often mentions the alliance he feels with the police, and projects an image of himself as a rough-and-ready medic, eager to swoop in on even the most dangerous situations. In conversation, he makes frequent allusion to riding professionally on the rodeo circuit, and he styles himself as an urban cowboy riding his ambulance through the Wild West of Oakland. This presentation of self meshes well with the image of the fighter jockeys who become the victims of an airplane crash. Considering the undertones of patriotism that infuse his participation in the rodeos, it is not surprising that Darryl goes to special lengths to emphasize that it was the "American pilot" whom he treated. The pilot's remarkable stoicism in the face of extraordinary pain constitutes the main focus of Darryl's story. Darryl tells numerous other stories that emphasize the stupidity or cowardliness of many of his patients, even including in this story mention of the great lengths to which people go to obtain drugs. Here, the air force fighter pilot emerges as a competent hero, one who is so in control that he can shrug off excruciating pain to avoid succumbing to the temptations of narcotics.[14]

Numerous medics suggested that Bill V. could tell airplane stories, and, during an early afternoon lull, he began to tell them. Apart from providing another level of medic stories describing unusual accident scenes, these stories offer an interesting glimpse into Bill's personal storytelling style. They also provide an opportunity to explore the links a storyteller makes between stories. While it is rare to have the time and audience to tell three or four involved narratives, on this day the radio was surprisingly quiet, a symptom of what many medics call "ride-along syndrome." The majority of Bill's stories about crashes are culled from his experiences as a member of an elite air force pararescue squadron:

Bill V.: Oh, airplane crashes, you want 'em we got 'em. Up in Alaska I did probably thirty of them just off the top of my head. The thing about airplane crashes—it's funny, especially small airplanes—it's like everybody's all strapped in and when you get on scene, there's this airplane stuck in the side of the mountain. And do you know what the injury is on all the patients? 'Cause they're all strapped in and that sudden high speed impact? You get to the crash, the windshield's blown out. [laughter] You'll have two dudes in the front seat of this helicopter and their heads are up in the bushes! Their heads pop off! It's the only thing that's not strapped in. It's like, errr slam! [laughter] It's fucking sick shit, man! [laughter] That's some sick shit, man.

I was on one plane crash. Four guys. Pop pop pop pop! Four heads up there in the fucking bushes above them, man. It's like, if they had their heads — it's like you look at them, and you'd swear that if their heads were strapped back they might have lived! I had this one plane crash, have you heard of Red Flag? It's the big North American military exercise in the Mojave desert every year. It goes on probably three months at a time. It's a big, big exercise. Well, these two guys in an F-4 — you know that's all that's in an F-4 — they were doing this bombing run, and what they were doing is, is they were bombing on the other side of the hill. The technique was, apparently, they're skimming along in the bushes, and you come up over your hill, and as you come up over the top of the hill, you turn upside down and as you're coming up copping a negative G — you're upside down — you let loose the bombs. The bombs get along a trajectory and they're able to come away and flip. Well, I don't know what happened, but these guys were upside down and something went wrong and they — fucking — these guys ejected while they were upside down! Doing about 450 mph!

George: Oops, pulled the wrong lever!

Bill: About a hundred feet off the ground. It took five days to find these guys, to find the wreckage! All it was was this black spot in the desert, this charred spot. Biggest piece of the airplane was about the size of my fist and the only body part we found was a foot in a boot. Teeth, hair, and eyeballs all over the desert, man. That was pretty crazy.

George: Well, there's an airplane accident for you.

At the beginning of his tales, Bill alludes to responding to numerous air crashes, which immediately sets him apart from other medics. In fact, in his storytelling, a crash that would be a unique experience for other medics is routine for him. This opening to his air crash stories reflects his own image as an "old medic," one whom "the younger guys look to" both for guidance and for interesting stories.

Bill also revels in telling stories that border on the outrageous, punctuated by gruesome discoveries and horrific injuries. Even though some of the episodes he recounts seem patently absurd, such as the one in which the heads of the air crash victims popped off, he tells the story with such good-natured conviction, and backs his story with the authority of so many years of experience, that few medics care to challenge him.[15] Those who do are generally countered by a shocked and forceful "It's true!" Also, the stories are so entertaining that most medics do not want to challenge them, since the danger, the daring, and the surprise of Bill's stories indirectly reflect on them as well.

Bill's three stories of air crashes build on each other, and a clear associative line can be followed in his progression through the tales. The first story is a generalization, and probably stems from his desire to present the most outrageous aspect of plane crashes that he can think of, namely the instantaneous decapitation of the victims caused by the aircraft's sudden deceleration. George's encouraging laughter prods Bill into providing a specific example of such an accident, and, after his own evaluation of these scenes as "some sick shit," he tells the story of a particular crash. Interestingly, whereas specificity of location characterizes many medic stories, Bill's takes place in an undesignated setting. This uncharacteristic lack of precision could be due to his temporal remove from the narrated events (he is, after all, telling a story about a call that happened many years ago); it may also be attributable to the nature of the response. Paramedics who drive to their calls are intensely aware of location, since they must plot a route to the scene and consider the environmental dangers associated with it. In this story, however, Bill is ferried to the scene of the accident aboard a helicopter, and is not expected to assist in navigation.

Time also tends to play an important role in medic narratives. Medics are required to note the time of the call and the time of their arrival and departure; accordingly, they tend to include these referents in their stories. The implications of time are used as a narrative cue and can inform story audiences about other environmental considerations — darkness, fatigue, and end of shift are all linked to time and appear as salient aspects in various stories. However, in the case of Bill's stories, time of day plays no role whatsoever since it does not influence the response. Bill's third story in this sequence of airplane stories picks up on the theme of surprising amputations while continuing to focus on rare accidents, in this case the inexplicable crash of a jet fighter. He expresses awe at the amount of time it takes to locate the crash scene and at the complete obliteration of the victims. Generally, medics do not have to search long or hard to locate their patients; in this case, however, they have been reduced to their component parts— "teeth, hair, and eyeballs all over the desert."

After George's understated evaluative comment, Bill continues talking about air accidents, but switches from personal experience to a secondhand story. At the same time, he moves the locus of the stories from the remoteness of Alaska to terrain that is much closer to the experiences of other California paramedics. The story that opens this chapter includes a reference to the horrors of amputated body parts and to the strange juxtapositions of these parts with vegetation: "I mean, there's guts and shit hanging in the trees." Although told with humor, the story ends abruptly with a paramedic's suicide and an expression of disgust—"Ugh." Bill and George are relatively silent and contemplative after this last story. The feeling of distance from the episodes in the Alaska stories has been decreased with the story of a Southern California air disaster, and the notion of horror such a site might entail is present in the front seat of the ambulance. The paramedic's suicide then becomes a cause for serious reflection, despite the dark humor that has informed the three lead-in stories.

Along with vehicular accidents, paramedics at times respond to mass casualty incidents like the Cerritos air crash and to major natural disasters. Many medics currently working in Alameda County responded to the Loma-Prieta earthquake that rolled through the Bay Area in October 1989, causing the collapse of the Cypress Street freeway structure,[16] as well as to the Oakland/Berkeley Hills firestorm which destroyed thousands of homes in October 1991.[17] While most jokingly tell stories of "being off" that day or of being assigned to a "boring" part of the county, others tell of calls directly related to the disasters.

Major disasters, or other events which generate substantial media attention, provide medics an opportunity to present themselves and their profession to a large audience. These public presentations are choreographed by the press and dovetail nicely with other media portrayals of medics. Any performances that do not mesh with the media image of the medics can easily be excised in the editing process. The 1995 bombing in Oklahoma City was one such event; paramedics and, more notably, firefighters, were cast in the predictable role of quiet heroes, "just doin' our job."[18]

The "Baby Jessica" incident in 1987 also focused a great deal of public attention both on the toddler stuck in the bottom of a well and on the paramedic, Robert O'Donnell, who saved her by sliding through a lateral tunnel drilled from a parallel evacuation shaft.[19] The soft-spoken medic instantly became the center of a media feeding frenzy, and told his story on numerous television talk shows. Seven years after the event, however, O'Donnell committed suicide. Family members and former coworkers all speculated that the attention generated by his one spectacular "save" left him emotionally stranded.[20] Once the spotlights faded and he had told his story for the thousandth time, he was no longer able to find an audience willing to listen to his narrative. Coworkers apparently quickly soured on his repeated tellings of the "save" and on the meteoric media success he enjoyed, and he was eventually forced out of his job.[21]

"Hero stories" such as O'Donnell's generally do not go over well among medics. While the media love to play up these stories, and non-medics like to hear them, medics themselves tend to ridicule those who attempt to tell such accounts. Unless a story is told with ironic humor and a degree of self-denigration (both elements of Darryl's and Bill V.'s stories), other medics are bound to challenge and ultimately mock the narrator. George, for example, begins to tell a story of the 1991 firestorm, after Bill expresses reservations about responding to disasters:

Bill V.: Now let these youngsters do that disaster stuff. Get chased by all those sparks and that kind of stuff. Too scary, man. "Yeah, that's me right there, see that's me right there! Yeah, that's me." It's funny, that's the story he told his wife. "Yeah, I was there, baby."

George: Me and my girlfriend, we were supposed to go see Michael Bolton the day of the fire. I was driving down Tunnel Road, you know, half an hour into it and driving through these walls of fucking flame.

Bill: Here comes a hero story! Driving through fucking walls of flames, man!

George: We're in a gasoline-powered van, thought I was going to explode at any second.

Bill: Burned the tires right off the car, right?

George: Absolutely, I was driving around on rims.

George sees an opportunity to position himself as a medic willing to engage the risks associated with disaster response, but Bill immediately challenges his story. By the end, George is left with no choice but to mock his own performance.

In the exchange, Bill further mocks paramedics who deliberately seek out such scenes so that they can point themselves out to friends and relatives on the evening news. While many medics admit to "getting a kick out of being on TV," and some keep scrapbooks of newspaper clippings about calls they were on, these stories are generally excluded from cohort storytelling. One evening, Ben tells an amusing story of being on the evening news but missing the coverage:

Ben: The worst part about it is, I get home, my girlfriend's mom calls me. "Hey, we saw you on TV." "Which channel?" "Two!" "All right!" I'm sitting there from six o'clock on with my videotape and my remote control just waiting for it, the ten o'clock news comes on, not a word about it.

Jake: Aww, shit!

Ben: I never saw it, my partner never saw it, nobody ever saw it except my girlfriend's mom. That's my interesting call story.

Here, Ben's attempt to capture his media debut, presumably to show friends and thereby bolster his stature, fails. Instead, he ironically comments on waiting at home with his remote control. Lisa mentions a similar episode:

Lisa: We did this one call that was on the news. Missed it, though. It was supposedly on channel two. I watched like all the channels trying to catch it. It was in the paper somewhere, too, but I missed that, too.

The medics have turned these attempts to catch glimpses of themselves on television into self-derisive stories. While admitting that they wanted to see the media performance, they are also laughing at their own preoccupation with that performance, thereby subverting any attempt to buy into the "hero" portrayal foisted upon them by the media.

The stories that the paramedics tell about the two major Alameda County disasters, like many other medic narratives, tend to focus on surprising or unexpected events. Some continue in the vein of many other stories, with frequent critiques of the separate groups involved in the emergency response. Some stories echo the medics' fascination with remarkable patients, while others rely on dark humor and odd juxtapositions. For example, Darryl tells of shaking a dead person's hand while searching for survivors on the Cypress structure after the Loma Prieta earthquake:

Darryl: And right near us there was a hand hanging out of the fucking car that's totally smashed and everything. I looked at it, and I shook it. This, this dead hand, and I said, "Glad to meet you!" and everything. And this guy that I was there with went, "Oh, God! I gotta be stuck underneath here with this maniac!" You know? It was too much!

Rather than focusing on the gruesome results of the disaster, other stories revolve around issues of access. People want access to scenes and to information during disasters, and paramedics are often able to acquire both; stories reflecting this situation allow the storytellers to support their self-presentations as authorities. Tom R.'s story of his experiences with the collapsed freeway stresses the paramedics' access to scenes and the resulting emotional impact:

Tom R.: The earthquake hit at 5:04. I got in here at about 5:30, and by 6:30, I was up at the Cypress structure. And it was something that you can't describe. You can't. You can look at all the video footage you want to, you can see it on TV a hundred times over again, but unless you were physically there and saw it, it just has no impact. You can't understand it. Boulders. I mean,

I'm talking, boulders as big as this room. Just thrown, just like a pebble, up the street, off this structure. And just thinking about that thing going and anything in its path was going with it, you know?

And if you happened to be walking down the street, you went with it. Vehicles, people in vehicles, thrown off the top. I mean, these people were driving down the road, and all of a sudden, they were just thrown off the top of it. Not a crash, not a swerve, nothing — thrown over.

Some of the ironic things I learned up there was, we're always taught in an earthquake — what's the lesson? I mean, everybody knows it. What's the lesson in an earthquake? Stand under something heavy, right? In an overcrossing, underneath these big bridges, what they have is concrete supports. They stick down, maybe four feet lower than the bridge, right? So, all of these people driving along this bridge. We couldn't figure it out, when we're pulling bodies out of these cars, we couldn't figure out why the cars were in park. Why would the cars be in park if they're doing sixty-five miles down the freeway? Why would the cars be in park? But they went underneath these big beams, thinking that was gonna save them. And the ironic part — luckily the freeway was sparsely populated because of the World Series going on across the bay — I remember looking at all these cars, and these cars would be right in the middle under these beams. The beams are probably two feet wide or so and four feet high. And if that car would have been a second sooner or a second later, they'd have missed this whole beam and the car would have survived. Because there was big gaps of space where that car could have survived. But all these cars were lined up under these things, underneath these things.

And I remember thinking, "Man, that's real ironic. Just a split second," and each of these columns are all lined up like that. And then we realized that the reason is that these people pulled underneath them, thinking that was gonna save them. And that's actually what killed them. So it's just one of those weird paradoxes that everything you've been taught killed them in this scenario.

Like Darryl in his earlier comments on automobile accidents, Tom focuses on the vicissitudes of fate; here, education has killed the motorists.

Tom B. also tells a story about the earthquake, but, rather than focusing on responses to the victims, he points out how the disaster gave him an excellent excuse to avoid transporting "bullshit" calls:

Tom B.: Yeah, I did system calls, you know? On the day after the earthquake. It was pretty cool. 'Cause we were in red alert, we just pulled up, man, and if it wasn't a real medical emergency, we said, "Too bad! See ya!" and left. No paper, no nothing, no explanation. It's like, "We're in the middle of a national disaster! You want me to take you to the hospital for what? Pfft, bye!" [laughter] That's right. "No, you don't understand, man, this ain't normal operating mode. Your stubbed toe will have to wait. Good-bye." Get back in the ambu. "See ya!" Next! You know, we were having none of that silliness.

Rather than telling stories about the emergency scenes precipitated by the disaster—these were adequately covered by the news media—Tom instead discusses how the earthquake affected his own work, remembering with delight how he was able temporarily to sidestep patients who were not truly critical.

The Oakland/Berkeley Hills firestorm was the other major disaster experienced by Regional paramedics. Not surprisingly, few, if any, of the fire stories center on heroic saves, instead emphasizing the breakdown in communications among emergency services, the paramedics' inability to respond to calls, or the horrible condition of the fire victims. Mark tells several stories about the day the fire started:

Mark G.: This weather, it's just like the day of the fire. I hope that doesn't happen again, the fire. That was a big fire. I remember it started out the day before, it was just a little area, and we were listening to it, and then Sunday night it started back up and then it just went. We were staged up at 24th and Broadway, and we got reassigned. I don't think we ever got there, but we were driving down the 13 when the fire was coming over the freeway. There was fire on both sides, and we're driving through this, and the windows, you touch them and you burn your hands 'cause they're so hot, it was intense. A scary fire.

I was at Highland when all those people got caught in the Caldecott tunnel. And there was this guy who got out of his car, and he had this shirt on, and all off his skin had just fluffed off his body, it was just hanging down beneath his arms. The guy got out of the car, and I was like, "Hunh, that's a weird jacket, I've never seen anything like that before," and then I realized it was his skin. It was sick.

Then we got called up for the fire chief and the cop that got killed up there. They lost a fire chief and a cop up there, and they found like a dead baby underneath him, he was laying on top supposedly trying to save the baby. They told us to go up there and pick them up, and they went to investigate. And that was it, we just hung out for the rest of the day. It was crazy. The next day, too.

Mark recounts how his initial curiosity about the burn victim turns to horror when he realizes that the man's jacket is actually burned skin. Like many medics, he does not relish these disasters, but rather "hope[s] that doesn't happen again." His obvious discomfort in talking about the fire chief and the police officer killed while attempting a rescue underscore how unnerved he was by the event. Unlike many of his other stories, which are generally quite humorous, this one is informed by serious introspection.

Most people think of accidents when they think of paramedics. Indeed, the news media contribute to this portrayal of paramedics as heroes on the scene of car accidents, train derailments, plane wrecks, and natural disasters. But paramedics' stories about these events have a notably different focus. For the medics, one grisly accident is much like the next. An accident, in fact, only becomes worthy of narration when something happens to set it apart from all other accidents—some aspect that makes it a "cool call." Consequently, paramedic stories about accidents generally involve one-upmanship. A good call can be parlayed into a good story, and a good story allows the medic to take center stage during the telling. Since much narrating among paramedics has a strong undercurrent of competition, a story such as Darryl's airplane tale can be played as a trump card. Among themselves, medics are highly suspect of "hero" stories and deride those who tell them; accident stories as a rule are replete with ironic statements and black humor. The medics tend to express a ghoulish fascination with violent death and dismemberment and their interaction with the corpses. Perhaps stories like these offer the medics a chance to "debrief" themselves: by discussing the scenes and making light of traumatic injuries, they distance themselves narratively from their patients, and release the stress that results from encountering such scenes. Cautionary tales, such as those of a paramedic's suicide, alert other medics to the need for this kind of debriefing, thereby offering yet another incentive for the storytelling tradition to continue.

# 4

# YOU SEE THE WEIRDEST
# THINGS OUT HERE

Bill R. and Bill L. have spent the better part of the afternoon swapping stories and debating health care policy. They are not ordinarily partners, but have both worked for Regional for several years. Bill L. has a reputation for being calm and deliberate. Bill R. is known to be fun-loving; while experienced and competent, he also enjoys some of the odder calls that medics occasionally receive. Many of his stories on this day have featured sarcastic humor and grotesque remarks. For example, after Bill L. tells a story of a patient who lost his leg in a train accident, Bill R. rummages about in his knapsack and produces a rubber arm. "Body parts, extra," he says with a grin, as if the arm were standard ambulance equipment.

Standing in the parking lot of a convenience store, chewing on a microwave burrito, Bill R. once again regales Bill L. and me with a story:

Bill R.: This happened in San Francisco probably somewhere in the eighties—eighty-two, eighty-three, somewhere in there. I wasn't working for the department of public health, I was with King American.[1] Carol Dodo was the first topless dancer in the Northbeach area—a part of town that sprung up for

topless entertainment and such in San Francisco. Well, in her stage was a piano that would rise out of the bottom of the floor. And it would rise when
you'd have a stage show.

Well, she was gone, she was no longer at the Condor club, but one of the
managers and one of their dancers were staying late after closing one night.
So they were entertaining themselves on this rising piano, and they thought
it'd be a kick to make it go up. So, they got carried away, and the piano went
up and up and up and up. And eventually, it pinned the guy into the ceiling.
See, the ceiling opened, you could go up, unless you were caught right on
the edge where it would just crush you.

Well, it crushed this guy when he was on top of this girl. And this happened somewhere around two-thirty, three o'clock after the club closed. And
they were stuck up there until six-fifteen when the janitor came in. And, it
crushed him, broke his back and crushed him. But this girl had to lay under
him for three hours, until the janitor came in. We didn't get the call, we weren't
initial response, but we were so close, and it sounded so good, that I had to
run over there and witness this one for myself. Very entertaining call there.
Very unique. Very unique.

"Jumping calls"—responding to calls that have been given to other
units—usually occurs when a "cool call" comes over the radio. In
this case, the call is so intriguing that Bill cannot pass up seeing it,
and thus he has the first-person authority to narrate it. The odd and
unexpected nature of emergencies surfaces repeatedly in paramedic
storytelling. At times, story sessions can be marked by an implicit competition over who has responded to the strangest call. Medics mention that these unusual calls contribute to their enjoyment of the job.
While responding to traumatic accidents or entering dangerous neighborhoods gives the medics an "adrenaline rush" and contributes to
their images of themselves as urban warriors, the "weird" calls provide them with "a good laugh."

Among the strangest calls are emergencies that do not involve human patients at all. A surprising number of stories feature medics providing emergency medical care to animals, usually saving them from
burning buildings. Lars tells the most well-developed of these "puppy-

save" narratives. In a typically ironic refiguration of the well-known representation of a firefighter carrying a child from a burning building, he conjures an image of one carrying a puppy:

Lars: We got a call for a house fire and we had to go standby in case someone was in the house that was burning. Now, we get there and we checked, there was one woman in the house and she was like, "Oh, I'm fine, I'm fine." There's no one else in the house and she's worried about "my dogs. My dogs are inside!"

And so, we're sitting there and this fireman comes out and he's got these little smoldering balls of fur. And he puts them down next to us, and it's these three dogs. And one was dead, this dog's out of it. The other two dogs were sitting there gasping for air, you know? And their fur is all wet and smoldering and stuff. I listened to their lungs and you could hear the fluid in their lungs. And they're just suffering from major smoke inhalation. It was me and Bill D., and his girlfriend was riding third, she's an EMT.

So I turned to her and I said, "Get the airway bag!" And she's like, "What?" I'm like, "Get the airway bag, we're working up these dogs!" So we get out the airway bag, and I put them on oxygen and stuff. Bill comes over and he's like, "Are we working these dogs?" I'm like, "Oh, yeah, you bet." So, I go, "Oh, let's put them in the ambulance!" We put them in the back of the ambulance and get them both on high-flow oxygen. And there's this emergency pet clinic right down the hill here. We were down in San Leandro. I'm like, "All right, well, let's bring them there!"

He gets on the radio, "5-2-5. There's nobody hurt in this fire, the people are all okay, but we've got these two dogs that are critical. Can we bring them to the emergency pet clinic?" And there's dead silence on the radio. So finally one of the supes said, "Yeah, Okay, go ahead, just go Code 2." So we went Code 2. "Woo woo woo woo!" Lights, sirens, you know? Code 3! And we called the dispatch and had them call this pet clinic, so they're all waiting for us. And they're by the door, and here comes this ambulance in, lights and sirens! Pull it in, get out, we've got the dogs on oxygen and we come running in. Give them a full medical report on the puppies. I was thinking about intubating one of them, 'cause it was looking pretty rough, but he started to pull through and by the time we got to the pet clinic, they were sitting up and breathing a lot better. And we got them inside, and by the time we left, they had one of them in a warmer, 'cause he was all cold and shivering. And their lungs had cleared up and they'd started lines on 'em, and the dogs did great! They survived. So, we saved two out of three dogs. That was pretty cool. We were happy.

Others told variants of this same call, and its frequent repetition as a secondhand narrative suggests its ability to create meaning for the medics. Puppies are the purest form of innocent victim—helpless and completely dependent on the medics. Also, unlike many other patients, the puppies cannot talk back. Finally, the dogs can be seen as extensions of family. Indeed, many people consider their pets to be part of the family, so that the death of an animal can be as traumatic as the death of a family member. Lars's story also reveals the lengths to which medics will go to preserve a life—any life—as is emphasized by his willingness to break the rules and transport the animal Code 3. Thus, the story illustrates the life-affirming mission of the medics. On the other hand, the treatment of the puppies indicates a direct relationship between patients and animals in the medics' minds.

In a twist on the "medic saves dog" story, Brian offers the somewhat surprising story of an "auto versus canine" accident:

Brian: Here's a nasty story. Anyway, Terry goes out there, this is in Morgan Hill, this is years ago, like eighty-four, eighty-five, right? This dog is in front of the station, biff, gets nailed by a car, everybody's like "Ohmigod!" So about ten people are standing around the dog and he walks out there with the life pack 5 and says, "Oh!" And they're all saying, "The paramedic's gonna save the doggy!" And he whips out the life pack 5, paddle check, and poof! Smoke comes up, flames the dog, he goes, "Oh, well," turns around and walks away. And everybody's going "Ahhh!" Funny as hell.

The crowd's expectation that the valiant medic will strive to save the dog is skewed when the dog is electrocuted with a portable defibrillator. The equipment is certainly designed to save lives, and the bystanders have in mind a picture of paramedics, defibrillator paddles in hand, saving a heart attack or accident victim. But in this case, the victim is not a human—an inversion of the normal scene—and the defibrillator takes on inverted status as well, becoming an instrument of death. Although it was probably the most humane treatment for the dog, the paramedic's callous "Oh, well" stands in marked contrast to the expectation that he would try to save the injured animal.

While at times appearing in medic stories as patients, animals can also be the cause of emergencies. Dog bites and cat scratches are mundane calls, and do not offer much in the way of novelty; accordingly, they are rarely mentioned in medic stories. However, attacks by more ferocious animals, while as rare as airplane crashes, do make good subjects for narration.[2] Not surprisingly, it is Bill V. who offers a series of stories about responses to emergencies caused by bears:

Bill V.: When you were on alert you know, as soon as you activated, you had to be on the airplane in like ten minutes, ready to fly, from anyplace on base, you know? So anyway you get in the airplane and after they do the preflight checklist, you know, the pilot starts briefing you on what the mission is. And these three guys from L.A. got mauled by this bear, this grizzly bear.

Well, I got the story from the guy who lived. What happened, these guys were hunting moose and this is towards the end of their trip and they hadn't any luck with catching any moose, shooting a moose. But they saw this grizzly bear walking along the tree line, so these guys sniped this grizzly bear. And they wound it and it goes running into the woods. Well, these fools go after it, looking for it. Well, this grizzly bear is hiding behind some trees, and as they go in, this bear jumps out and grabs the first guy by the head and starts shaking him by the head and shoulders. Grrrrrr! And the other two guys are going, pop pop pop. The bear spits one guy out, grabs the second guy, starts doing the same thing, shaking him by the head. I mean this last guy is still shooting at this bear. The bear spits the second guy out, jumps the third guy—and dies. He was all torn up.

After we loaded him up in the helicopter, put his two buddies in body bags, we tied up this bear underneath the helicopter and took him back to base. This bear weighed eight hundred pounds and his front paws were the size of a plate, with like six-inch claws. That's when I started reading up.

George: That's scary shit!

Bill: Oh, I started reading up on grizzly bears. A grizzly bear at a dead run, his heartbeat is only like ten beats a minute. You can take his frigging heart out and he can still eat you up. They shot this thing seventeen times in its chest before it died. After that they started giving us .44 magnums to carry with us on missions, because of bears.

George: Is that right?

Bill: Yeah.

George: Where the hell was this?

Bill: Up in Alaska. We started putting M60 machine guns in the helicopters, too. M60 will tear up a grizzly.

George: That's one of the big ones with the two legs on it?

Bill: That's one model, yeah. These are aircraft mounted, in the door with a swivel.

George: Big old fucking belt? Jesus!

Bill: Pop pop pop pop pop pop pop pop! [laughter] That'd tear up a grizzly bear. Can you imagine that? Have to shoot the wildlife with a machine gun before you can work on somebody?! [laughter]

Bill's final comment is perhaps the most interesting. Frequently, medics joke about working as a "tailgunner," as if the ambulance were a World War II bomber, with one of the medics manning a machine gun in a turret:

Mark G.: Weren't you a tailgunner in New York?

Lars: Oh yeah, New York. They have big units, so in the back, there was a turret.

In narrative terms, there is a connection between Bill using a machine gun to "shoot the wildlife" before treating a patient, the jokes about working as an ambulance tailgunner, and the constant anxiety faced by medics while working in dangerous settings. The metaphoric link between animals and patients is rather clear. Thus, to some degree, many of the stories about treating animals can be understood in conjunction with the medics' use of storytelling as a means of negotiating their position vis-à-vis unpredictable patients and a hazardous environment.

The distinction between animals and humans also blurs in medic stories about obese patients, who are frequently dehumanized in narratives, at times compared to animals, and often held up as objects of scorn and ridicule. Medics comment frequently on their patients' weight, since it is an environmental factor affecting their work. After all, they are expected to carry critical patients down stairs, up stairs, through narrow halls, and across barriers. Injuries from lifting are among those most frequently incurred by paramedics, and such an injury, which commonly involves the lower back, can easily end a career.[3]

In American culture, weight and sexuality are closely linked. Popular magazines, television, advertising, and film all connect weight to sex appeal. While media images and diet marketing would lead one to believe that this country is full of people with lithe athletic bodies, numerous studies show that a large percentage of Americans are overweight, revealing a significant discrepancy between the media-fueled ideal body image and the average person. Inevitably, such a discrepancy between a hypothetical norm and reality produces anxiety. In their stories, medics struggle both with the general cultural uneasiness associated with weight and with their more job-specific concerns.

Between calls on a sunny afternoon, while "people watching" at a downtown park, Bob tells a story in which a man refuses to aid his obese neighbor:

Bob: So this 320-pound guy had been stuck in this tub since yesterday morning and he'd been pounding on the wall. And someone had answered this pounding and yelled through the wall and said, "What's wrong with you?" And he answered "I'm stuck in my tub." And the guy answered back to him, saying "Well, you big fat man, you should know better than that, I've been telling to you to lose weight, and I'm not going to call an ambulance for you." That happened last night that the man told him that. Then this morning someone else answered to his pounding on the wall and called 911.

We got there and he couldn't get out of the tub. So we helped him out of the tub and his blood pressure is really high, but he refuses to go to the hospital. So we asked him why and he told us that he was a Christian Scientist and refused to go to the hospital and he said he'd stay at home. He had a blood pressure of like 230 over 120 and this man is three hundred pounds! Just overweight. Really bad. So we left him. Had him sign the appropriate papers, we called the hospital, told them what was going on, they talked to him. We left him there. It happens all the time.

Here, the neighbor gives voice to the general public perception that the obese bring their problems upon themselves. In this story, the patient seems to confirm this stance, refusing to help himself by accepting medical treatment.

George and Bill V. both tell typical stories of the problems that accompany responses to calls for obese patients. Bill's story also makes clear the connection between sexuality and weight:

George: This was an odd call. We had this man who weighed over three times what an average person weighs. And the second amazing thing of that call was that he was on the ground floor, thank God! You know as well as I do that the cardinal rule of obesity is that they don't live on the ground floor, they always live upstairs. But anyway, this guy, I don't remember what his complaint was.

But what I remember is him getting on the gurney and the gurney not being able to roll! I mean, the wheels were skidding on the ground, and we got him out to the ambulance, and he was too big for the side rails, so we couldn't lock the gurney in place. We had to put the gurney upside down on the bench seat, put him actually on the floor of the ambulance, and hold him to keep him from rolling around the back of the rig. When we got him to Stanford, took him into the bed, rolled the gurney back out, he had somehow— I'd never seen this before—but he had blown all of the ball bearings in all four wheels. Just totally smashed them. Disintegrated them. The wheels were totally loose! The gurney was just destroyed because of the ball bearings. I've never seen that, you know? And I've had heavy people.

Bill V.: I had a six-hundred pounder, I had a six-hundred pounder once, and it was crazy! I mean you couldn't lift her, you couldn't use her extremities to lift her up, 'cause you'd break something. She was in a house and, there it was, two paramedics, two firefighters from a squad, four firefighters from an engine company and four firefighters from a truck company, to move this gal. And she was dirty and stinky! It was sad, the poor woman. What she needed was to be taken to the hospital to have some bed sores taken care of.

Anyway, it was two paramedics, two firefighters off a squad, four firefighters off the engine, and then four firefighters on a truck company, and we had to use a salvage cover [a giant sheet of canvas with handles on it used to carry loads]. We rolled her onto the salvage cover. We had to get a saw and cut out the door, so she not only could fit through the door, but so that all of us could fit through the door carrying her, and we had to call in a flatbed truck, put her on the flatbed truck and took her to the hospital. Then she spent a week in the hospital and it was on the news. Her family lived in Washington State and when she went home, they took her in a truck to March Air Force Base, and they put her on a cargo plane and flew her to Washington.

George: Big lady!

Bill: Six hundred pounds. Six hundred pounds.

George: That is a biiiig woman!

Bill: I wanted her!

In George's story, the destroyed gurney acts as a metaphor for the threat of physical injury the obese man poses to the medics. The gurney is an integral part of the ambulance and, by extension, of the medics themselves. In Bill's story, the patient is so large that she can neither fit through her door nor into the ambulance. To underscore his evaluation of the patient, and to situate the call firmly in the realm of the disgusting, Bill mentions that she is "dirty and stinky." The obese patient becomes a dangerous agent of destruction, requiring a small army of paramedics and firefighters to cut through her door with a chainsaw to extract her from the bedroom. Once outside the house, her size begins to assume absurd proportions. Unable to fit her into the ambulance, the medics call a truck to transport her, and, when she finally needs to fly to her family, she is shipped by military cargo plane. In his final evaluative comment — "I wanted her!" — Bill makes a clear, albeit ironic, connection between obesity and sex.

Most calls concerning obese patients are surprisingly alike. Generally, the person is not within the realm of normality (a typical aspect of medic stories) but is "six hundred pounds!" or "really huge." They often live on the second floor, with George even suggesting that it is a "cardinal rule" for these patients, so that the medics have to carry them down (the rule likely applies more to the stories than to the patients themselves). Also, in most stories about obese patients, their personal hygiene is questionable. Undoubtedly, this characterization stems from the culturally predominant belief that inability to control one's weight stems from general incompetence at taking care of oneself. In some stories, the patient, unable to fit into the ambulance, is transported by horse trailer, a clear example of the dehumanization that marks these accounts. Finally, the patients leave destruction in their wake—doors and walls are cut down, banisters are removed, fire equipment fails under the stress, and ambulance gurneys break. These patients are a danger not only to themselves but also to the medics and the environment.

A callous disregard for the patient's condition is apparent in many stories involving obese patients, although in real life the medics do provide the patient with the needed care. Perhaps the most heartless of these stories concerns a patient who, because of medical conditions associated with his obesity, had to have several amputations:

Mark: Notice how light Mackie was today? He lost a leg. And he was like, "Whoah! This guy's light now!" That leg must have weighed about a hundred pounds!

Bob: Each leg's about a hundred pounds.

Mark: Can't wait for the next one to go, he'll be real light! [laughter]

Mark G.: [laughing] You're a fucking sick bunch of fucks. You're all laughing about it!

Bob: Oh, and you're always so serious!

Mark G.: I take my job serious here!

Bob: Then you ought to send in to William Shatner and get on *Rescue 911*! You know, then you can make visits with his family every weekend and—

Mark: Barbecue with him.

When Mark G. protests the callousness of his fellow medics, they immediately turn on him and undermine his comments. First they remind

him of his own storytelling—replete with similarly cruel remarks—
and then they suggest that he write to the much-derided television
show *Rescue 911*.

When asked about weird things they have encountered, many paramedics also tell stories about calls involving sexual dalliance, strange
sexual practices, and sexual ambiguity. Called into people's bedrooms
late at night, medics get an immediate, intimate glimpse of their lives.
Tom R. notes, "It's not often you walk into somebody's bedroom at
three in the morning if you're not in this profession. Can't really get
much more personal than that." Medics also strip their patients when
there are injuries, and, as a result, develop an intimate knowledge of
those bodies in a very short period of time. Medics frequently tell stories of startling discoveries made while stripping or examining the patient. Other stories involve "walking in" on compromising scenes or
seeing the aftermath of intensely personal, sexual activity gone awry.

Darryl mentions that "girls ask if you've ever had sex in the back
of an ambulance before. And I've been asked that multiple times. I
don't know what that is—maybe that's some Freudian thing, or something." The deviant use of an ambulance as a rolling motel is, in a
way, appealing to medics (otherwise they would not tell the stories);
on the other hand, it is seen as inappropriate behavior. Numerous
stories refer to the existence of a "Code 3 Club," the members of which
have all had sexual encounters in an ambulance. One afternoon in
the emergency loading zone of Summit Hospital, four medics stand
around discussing various "gorgeous" patients they have treated. At
some point, the conversation turns to the "Code 3 Club,"

George: The Code 3 Club. [laughter] You know that, right?
  Tony: I don't know what the Code 3 Club is.
  George: Liar!
  Patrick: Is that like the Mile High Club?
  Tony: I think so.
  George: Yeah, Tony, "Mr. Innocent!" [laughter] Gee!
  [laughter]
  Tony: I have no idea what it is.

George: Gee, you don't know about that stuff!

Tim: So, George, what is the Code 3 Club?

Tony: Yeah, what is the Code 3 Club?

George: I think Tony can, uh, better inform you. He's the president! [laughter]

Tony: I'm not sure what the Code 3 Club is. I think the Code 3 Club is like making love in the back of a rolling ambulance, is that what it is?

Patrick: Don't ask me, I've never heard of it.

Chris: I don't know. I heard rumors about it once, but I heard they said, "See Tony."

Tony: Yeah, right!

The medics dance around the issue, all aware of the initiation rite of the "club" but positioning it in the realm of "rumor." The back of an ambulance is considered to be ridden with germs and infectious agents from the many dead and dying patients. In addition, the gurneys are often used to transport patients covered in filth; given these conditions, it is hard to imagine that an ambulance could have any allure as a rolling motel with lights and sirens.

A number of the stories medics tell involve people who die while engaged in sexual activity. Sometimes the cause of death is odd, as in the story of the man crushed by the piano. Far more frequently, though, people die from heart attacks. Lisa tells a story of marital infidelity that ends in death:

Lisa: I had heard this story—I wasn't involved on this call—about a call that the paramedics that I was driving for at the time had went on. And apparently it was at an office building. A vice president, or whatever, his office had like a suite. And they walked in, and his secretary was in this lingerie and she was hysterical, crying. Well, during their lovemaking, he had coded. [laughter] And his wife didn't know about their little affair yet. And so, it was a little bit— how should I say?—compromising for the secretary. Because, you know, she thought she had killed the poor man, which wasn't the case at all. [laughter] That was pretty funny.

In this case, the adulterers are both punished: the man dies and the secretary's secret dalliance is exposed. While such stories are common

in nonmedic storytelling, and have even formed the premise for numerous commerical films, medics can present the story with greater
immediacy. Even though Lisa starts with a degree of narrative distance
(she was not, after all, one of the responders), as she tells the story, she
identifies with the medic crew, which is apparent in the shift from third
person to first person—"how should *I* say." She then offers comments
about the discomfort evident in this scene of sexual misbehavior.

In other stories, masturbation results in death. Masturbation is certainly a taboo subject in American culture, as the removal of Jocelyn
Elders from the post of United States Surgeon General attests.⁴ Subjects that cannot be discussed openly are sometimes broached in com-
municative forms such as jokes and stories. Matt tells one story that
focuses just as much on his own mistakes as on the "mistake" of the
man who goes to an adult bookstore and masturbates:

Matt: We got a call about ten miles from here at an adult bookstore and I
walk inside—we're real cocky—my partner skids up to the store—literally
skids up—and leaves the siren on for about two seconds after we had parked.
I get out, all cocky, thinking, "No one who collapses in an adult bookstore is
going to want to go to the hospital with us." So I walk in with nothing in my
hands. [laughter]

Go to the back room, my first time in one of these places and they have
these little booths where you go and sit on this half bench, watch your movie
and do your thing—you put tokens in. So I walk in and look at this guy laying
on the ground, I look at him again and I go, "Hmmm, is he breathing?" No!
[laughter] "Does he have a pulse?" No! [laughter]

So as this is happening, the firefighters are walking in. So I have my partner, 'cause he wasn't in yet, bring everything in with him, and we started working on him. And they were all jokesters, the firefighters. The poor guy's name
was Jack and he was back in this little booth doing his thing, he had his penis
out. [laughter] He had obviously been in there for a couple of hours. The guy
at the counter said that he didn't remember when he went in, and he was flatline to the monitor, but he had a pacemaker, so he had little spikes.

So we started an IV and intubated him and gave him a couple drugs and
we ended up leaving him in there for the coroner. But you just wonder, I mean,

it would be terrible to get that call, you know, "Ma'am your husband, Jack, has died," "Oh, that's terrible!" "But there's more bad news!" [laughter] "He died in an adult bookstore in a booth!" We never did look and see what movie he was watching, but it was probably a good one.

Matt adopts the typical, sardonic, wisecracking manner found in most medic stories. Here, his laughter is directed at the embarrassing nature of the call. With death, the patient's actions are no longer hidden from view, as social norms dictate, but rather become the object of public (or at least paramedic) scrutiny. Now the embarrassment no longer accrues to the patient but to his wife, who receives a hypothetical phone call in Matt's story. The death makes public what should be kept private and thus resonates with the medic stories about accidents, in which what is usually hidden (internal organs) is brought into the open.

Perhaps the most startling of the calls concerning sexual activity involves autoerotic asphyxiation[5]:

Lars: Okay. The other night, our last call. We had a wicked slow day. We had about three calls—I mean one was for a scraped knee. The other two, I don't even remember what the other two calls were. But we're sitting around, falling asleep. And we got a call, Code 3, for the unconscious. Sort of a far, far East Oakland, almost San Leandro kinda suburban area. So we're, you know "woo woo!" come flying up there and we pull up right with the fire department at the same time. There's a couple of cop cars there.

Cop cars? God! Actually, there was like two or three of them. I'm like, "For an unconscious? What, overdose? Suicide, something? So we walk in and the fire department's like, "Err, I don't know." And they're all half asleep. We walk in, and the cops are like, "Yeah, back here, in the back bedroom." I'm traipsing in with my equipment, and there's a guy laying in there, face down on the floor. Head's all purple and I look at him, and there's blood coming out of his ear. And I'm like, "Wait a second. This guy's got blood coming out of his ear!" I touch him and he's ice cold and stiff as a board. I'm like, "Wait a minute. This guy's dead!" And my partner, by this time is in there and the fire-fighters, and the cops are kind of like, "Well, hey, you gotta look at the big picture here."

And I look and I'm like, "Hey, wait a second. This guy's wearing a bra and panties!" [laughter] Crotchless panties, nonetheless. This guy's lying there, face down on the floor, dead. Last seen at three-thirty, purple from the head up, and he's got the sash from a bathrobe around his neck about four times and tied wicked tight. It was autoerotic asphyxia! So he was strangling himself, and he was jerking off to heighten this. The idea is you hang yourself or you strangulate yourself just to the point of asphyxiation, and it's supposed to totally heighten the orgasm, you know?

So this guy's laying there, jerking off, in bra and panties, asphyxiating. And there he is laying there, dead and cold, face down with one hand under him, clutching—you know, he's jerking off. Right next to him is a big jar of Vaseline. And clutched in his other dead, cold hand is a magazine called *Big Bazooms*! [laughter] This man died with one hand on his dick, and the other hand clutching *Big Bazooms*. Laying there, you know, in his bra and panties, like as if he wants to confuse everybody. And there's a note on the door: "I'm at Kim's." I couldn't help but think, I guess Kim wasn't home. [laughter]

So, there we are, like three or four firefighters, two paramedics, bunch of cops, and we're all like, "Ha ha ha." And just to top it all off, in the background he's got the radio on. I guess to cover the noise of autoerotic asphyxia. I imagine it's a noisy process. But he's playing the radio, and just as I walk in, there's this Donovan song playing. I don't know if you're familiar with Donovan, but it's that weird, kinda sixties, far out there music. And I'm like, "Now this is just weird." [laughter]

So we put him on the monitor. And he's dead. This guy is so dead. He's just stiff and cold. Cops are like, "Don't roll him over! We're just going to call the coroner." And we're all surmising, when we roll him over is he gonna have two purple heads with blood leaking out of them? [laughter] I don't know. But we're trying to be very subtle and calm because, you know, the family's there. And I'm walking out of the house, and this family friend's behind me, and he's like, "So, is he gonna be okay?" [laughter] "No. He's dead." And he's like, "Well, what, was it an overdose or something?" And I'm like, "Yeah, in a manner of speaking." [laughter] Too much *Big Bazooms*. [laughter]

So we're out there on the front lawn. I'm filling out my paperwork. And they have this one rookie female cop that they've got doing all of the report because she was one of the first people there. And the other cop's like, "Well, get in there and write down everything you see." But we're all standing out there, "What is this called? What the heck is the name for this? [snapping] Something asphyxia? Something, something asphyxia." It was like a game show. I'm like, [pause] "Autoerotic asphyxia! That's it!" And they're like, "Oh yeah," writing it down in their paperwork. And so that's what the paperwork says. It says 10-5-5, which is the code for dead body [in formal voice], 10-5-5, secondary to autoerotic asphyxia. But he was dead.

What a way to go. I can just imagine this guy having a big-time out-of-body experience, just before he dies, going, "No, no, no! Let me back for just a minute! Let me get the goddamn bra and panties off! I can leave the *Big Bazooms*." [laughter] What a way to go. At least he died happy.

In typical fashion, Lars injects the scene with absurd humor and adds a coda in which he imagines the man having an embarrassing "out-of-body experience," caught not only with his pants down but with his bra and panties on.

Earlier in the story, Lars mentions that the responders are attempting to be tactful, since the situation will undoubtedly cause the family embarrassment. Lars's intense attention to detail at the scene further heightens the narrative comedy, and underscores the "weirdness" of the call. His mention of the strange music on the radio, possibly playing to cover the noise of the act, provides a soundtrack for the scene. The note on the door—"I'm at Kim's"—and Lars's sarcastic comment suggest that the victim would have been alive if he had been able to find a "normal" outlet for his sexual needs. Notably, the "rookie" cop sent in to write a detailed report of the scene is a woman, and the police and medics have fun exacerbating the embarrassing aspects of the situation. As in many of Lars's stories, the scene becomes a burlesque, culminating in the "game show" atmosphere on the front lawn where the responders try to provide a name for the event. Lars, the medical authority on scene, is the first to remember the official term, and his authoritative pronouncement enters the police record.

Transvestism and transsexuality appear in numerous other paramedic stories. The person's sex is one of the first items in a patient report and is generally not speculative. While age, height, weight, and medical condition are often subject to interpretation, the patient's sex is usually easily determined. The confusion associated with sexual ambiguity is apparent in Steve R.'s story of a transsexual patient:

Steve R.: We had this call for this one lady, that wasn't really a lady, it was a guy. And she said that she got beat up by her boyfriend. My partner at the time, she didn't even know that it was a he or she-male. So we were supposed to do these complete physical examinations and write this whole thing on all our findings, and I said, "Well, did you check the pelvic area?" And she says, "No," and I say, "I think that patient is a guy, I don't think it's a girl." And she says "No, I don't believe you." I say, "Yeah, well, I think that he is." And then the patient tells me later on, we're in there, we're in Highland here, and he says, "Oh yeah, I've had a penile inversion, and I've had this sex change," and blah blah blah. And he says, "I fooled your partner pretty good, didn't I?" And I say, "Yeah, but you didn't fool me!" You know?

And then she's explaining to me how much the operation costs and all this. Just bizarre, too bizarre. And my partner, we're supposed to write down the name. Well, of course, this guy has a female name, 'cause that's what he identifies with. But it's kind of troublesome to fill out the paperwork saying whether the guy is male or female, so we identified him as a female, 'cause that's how they say to do it. Bizarre.[6]

Steve takes pride in being able to discern the gender of his patient, while at the same time commenting on the abilities of his former partner. Bill V. quickly picks up on the theme, and offers a similar story:

Bill V.: About two months ago, we got this call, this guy got in a fight with his roommate—female roommate—he had some disk problems, and a history of back surgery, and tweaked his back. He's got a full beard, you know, the whole nine yards. Took him down to St. Rose, he's got his shirt off, he didn't have a shirt, he's just wearing shorts. Took him to St. Rose, put him on the hospital gurney, and then I start doing my paperwork. And the nurse comes in and she goes, "Could you help me get this woman you brought in off the backboard for me?" I said, "I didn't bring any woman in!" "No, you brought in a woman." So I went back there, and she says, "Look at her crotch." And she had her pants pulled up tight, and it was a woman who was mid sex change to become a man. She was waiting for her operation. She had her boobs taken off, she'd been on steroids and hormones to grow hair, facial hair and chest hair. She had more hair on her back than I have on my head! And [laughter], and she was waiting to save up the thirty grand to have a penis added to her!

Here, the sex change is from female to male, but the patient's ambiguous nature still leads to confusion. In the first case, Steve uses the story to emphasize his extraordinary diagnostic abilities—the operation cannot fool him. Bill V., as a more experienced medic, rarely uses stories to support his own competence. In fact, here he derides his diagnostic abilities, admitting that he received a lesson in basic human anatomy from no less an enemy than an emergency room nurse.

The confusion present in encounters with patients of ambiguous gender is evident in Mark G.'s attempt to tell a similar story. While Mark tries to incorporate the confusion precipitated by the patient's sex change, he mixes up his pronouns, with the result that the story, rather than the scene, is confusing. His narrative emerges as an unintelligible attempt at humor:

Mark G.: We got a call for a person who fell off a ladder in West Oakland. So we get there, you know, and this person had fallen off this ladder. And it was a legitimate call with the ladder. And there he was, laying on the ground, complaining of agonal left foot pain. Okay, so we find out what happened.

So, throw her in the back of the rig, turn on the—throw *him* in the back of the rig. I'm going along, doing the blood pressure and everything. Didn't even question this. Took him in, "twenty-six-year old man," you know, whatever. It was at Providence, down there.

And a couple of days later, my partner goes, "Hey, did you know that guy was a girl?" And I said, "You're kidding me!" And he said, "No, you see, he had to go to the bathroom, took his pants off, and there it was—a penis." We never even questioned it. We were certain it was a guy. I mean, he said he was a guy and everything. [pause] Or was it he said he was a girl? That's the fucking main part! [laughter] Guess my story doesn't make any sense now. It was a girl, man! Had long hair! But it had a penis, and it had breasts! That's where I was going with the he, and then it turned out to be a he, but it was really—

Lars: It was a he and it turned out to be a guy?

Mark: It was a girl.

Lars: And it turned out to be a guy?

Mark: It was a guy. It was a woman with a penis.

Lars: It was a woman with a penis?!

Mark: She had breasts, she had long hair. The guy said, "It's my wife." And you know, I'm going, "What the fuck!" So the technique is to ask, "Do you have a penis?" if you're in any doubt or anything like that.

Lars: He asks all the patients this now: "Do you have a penis?"

Mark: No.

Lars: "Are you having any trouble breathing? Do you have any chest pain? Do you have a penis?" And the system seems to be working out pretty well.

Lars picks up on the confusion, and, while Mark tries to talk about the medical anomaly of a woman with a penis, Lars teases him about this obvious narrative lapse. The story then dissolves into good-natured banter reminiscent of Abbott and Costello's well-known "Who's on first" comedy routine. Lars and Mark's storytelling styles and senses of humor mesh extraordinarily well, and they entertain themselves as they extend the comedy of Mark's narrative gaffe.

Interestingly, stories of masturbation and transsexuality are seldom told by women. The focus on the penis in these stories—its "abuse," its removal, its reattachment—may of course be linked to classic male anxieties concerning castration.[7] Lars tells one story of an especially hapless shooting victim who is hit in the groin:

Lars: I didn't get the full story, but I did hear that it was a case of mistaken identity. This guy came down to this guy's apartment and bangs on the door, and the guy in the apartment opens the door, sees a guy with a shotgun and closes the door. And the guy shoots him right at groin level through the door with a shotgun.

And so we get there, and I'm walking behind this apartment building, and this cop comes out, "In here, in here! Quick! It's real bad! It's real bad!" And so I go walking in and I expect to see some guy with his head blown off. And I come around the corner and, there in the kitchen, is this guy sitting up against the kitchen counter. And he's all sweaty and pale and he's moaning and I'm looking, "No, nothing in the head, nothing in the chest, stomach." Get down to about groin level and his whole groin is just soaked in blood. And I'm like, "Oh, that's gotta hurt!"

I get him on oxygen, cut off all his clothes, and all he can say is, "Is it shot off, man? Is it shot off? Is it still there? Is it shot off?" Well, I cut off his pants, and I say, "Well, it's still there, but it's got a lot of holes in it." And I get him all packaged up and we start out to the trauma center. And we get to the trauma center and every male in the trauma room is just wincing.

Lars makes it quite clear that the focus of the story is the victim's wounded penis and the anxiety this injury produces in the male medical attendants at the hospital.

On a sunny afternoon, in the parking lot of Children's Hospital, a group of medics and several interns take a breather from a hectic day. In a far more innocent story of threatened genitalia, Steve K. tells of a young boy whose penis gets caught in a bath toy:

Steve K.: We got this call one time, not long ago, for this unknown medical. And it's a couple streets away from our station—we beat the fire department. So we go into the house and as we walk in, there's this little seven-year-old boy laying on the floor in the hallway, totally naked and he's holding his hands over his groin and he's crying. And we're kind of going, "Okay, what's going on here?" And we talk to the mother to get her to explain a little bit of what happened and she said, "Wait a minute," and she told the kid to take his hands away.

And he moved his hands and he had this little plastic fish toy where it's got a little bug on a string in its mouth and you pull it out and you let it go and the fish swims in the bathtub until it gets to the bug and it eats it. Well, he was playing with this toy in the bathtub and, for some reason, he got the string tied around his private parts and he wasn't able to grab the fish before it came like a Pacman, whacka whacka whacka, on his privates. And it was stuck there, and the string had wound around and you couldn't pull it out any further and it was jammed.

So, we're kind of looking at each other, "What are we going to do?" And this poor kid is in pain, he's got this toy stuck and we don't know how we're going to get it off. So I ask one of the firefighters to go out to their fire truck and get their little tool kit that they carry. So he brought it in, and I got a pair of vice grips, we were gonna try to see if we could disassemble this little toy and see if we could get it off of this kid's privates so he could do whatever he had to do. So we finally got out the vice grips and as soon as he saw those vice grips coming out of the tool box, his eyes got about this big around when they started heading for his private parts. So we had to reassure him, "It's okay, we're not going to do anything that's gonna hurt you."

So we were able to get the vice grips around the toy and crack it enough where we could get inside and loosen the spool of string and finally we extricated this kid's privates from this toy. And he was grateful, Mom was grateful, there was no lasting ill effects, and he was able to go to the bathroom fine. He ended up not wanting to go to the hospital, and neither did his mother. But to this day every time I see one of those toys I think of that little kid laying on the ground holding himself.

In the evaluative coda, Steve mentions the impact the story has had on him. As in most medic stories, Steve is the one who controls the scene, ordering the firemen to get their tools. The extraction is successful, and the boy remains a boy.

Steve's story immediately sets off a round of narrative brinksmanship. The stories now stray into the realm of homoeroticism. A well-known series of stories about homoerotic acts involving gerbils has been documented by folklorists.[8] In these tales, a celebrity is admitted to a large hospital suffering from the ravages of a rodent introduced, during sexual play, into his rectum. A noted element of many of these stories is the claim to medical authority that narrators include, attributing the story to a nurse or doctor whom they know.[9] In the paramedic stories, the narrators allude to either transporting the patient themselves or hearing the story from a medic who had transported such a patient. Sara, a new intern, recounts one such story. Here, however, the object inserted into the rectum is an apple:

Sara: When I was doing my internship in the ER in San Jose, a gentleman came in claiming that he had a whole apple stuck up his rectum. And he did. Apparently this gentleman had been masturbating and had taken this apple and soaped it up and while he was masturbating, was rocking back and forth on this apple. And because it was lubricated, as he rocked backed on it, it proceeded to go up into his rectum and get stuck.

So this gentleman comes into the ER kind of waddling in, and he had to run himself in, it had been up there for a couple of hours before he realized that he was not going to be able to get it out himself. So they took him in and they checked him out and did our patient assessment on him and took the X-rays. What the doctor ending up having to do was take a pair of hemostats [small, pointed forceps] and stick them inside the gentleman's rectum and into the apple, and then proceed to break the apple up into pieces and then remove it piece by piece. And that's really it. He went home.

George: Ha! Lessons learned.

Sara: It's really embarrassing though for this poor gentleman to first of all have to explain how this happened and then to have to come in and then endure. It was fairly humiliating for him I'm sure, but stuff like that happens. It was quite humorous. It was very hard to go in and speak to this gentleman professionally without laughing and ask him what happened, how did it happen, how long ago did it happen and so on? It was hard on both ends of that particular patient.

Why does someone stick a toothbrush into their rectum? You know, you hear all the stories of any kind of foreign objects getting stuck — light bulbs, Coke bottles, gerbils, hamsters. Dildos are definitely a big one.

Tim: You've heard ones about hamsters?

Sara: Nothing that I've heard that I could confirm, just the typical rumors. Yeah, I was gonna say about the big jokes, about the gerbils. But you can't really say for sure, but, yes, the gentleman with the apple was definitely very much alive. He was a young man, married, he came in by himself and was very adamant that we didn't call his wife, and to tell her that he was in the ER and why. He just wanted to get in and have us take the apple out and get out of there quickly. I'm sure he sat funny for a couple of weeks after that.

Sara makes direct reference to the "rumors" about gerbils, but dismisses those in place of her more authoritative version of the apple story. Since the apple gets lodged in the man's rectum during masturbation, this story makes a link to the other medic narratives about masturbation and the resulting embarrassment for the patient.

Tom B., however, gladly tells a story of a small rodent caught in someone's rectum, using the story in large part as a comment on what he obviously considers to be sexually deviant behavior:

Tom B.: Okay, this friend, she's a nurse and she works as a paramedic part time. And one day we're coming back from a call and I ask her to tell me the weirdest call that she's ever been on in her entire life. And she said that they went on this call for a high fever. Well, what happened was, these two guys, these two buddies [laughter], one of them put a gerbil up the other guy's backside. And the gerbil cut through and got into his abdomen and stuff. Well, all the toxins and stuff spilled out. Of course, the guy had a fever of like 106 in about two minutes. She said that when they got there, they were trying to find out why his fever was so high and they were asking. Well, finally they got him to tell, "Well, there's a gerbil inside." She said she didn't even know what to do. It totally threw her for a loop. [laughter] Loop!

As in the stories of transsexuality, the situation is so confusing that the medic does not know how to respond. The story, most likely an example of one in the well-developed complex of gerbil stories, comments on sexual deviance and also, as Dresser points out, on fears of homosexuality and AIDS.[10] Medics' anxieties over AIDS are reasonably well founded, given their frequent contact with HIV-positive patients and members of high-risk populations.[11] Needle sticks, while rare, do occur; inserting an IV into the arm of a combative patient in the back of a moving ambulance, for example, can be a fearful exercise.

Sexuality constitutes an area of human interaction that provokes nervous laughter, averted glances, and feelings of anxiety. It is rarely addressed openly, and discussions of it are frequently marked by joking. Among paramedics, stories at times reflect a sense of "locker room" banter, with joking allusions to sexual prowess (to wit, the comments on the "Code 3 Club"). Paramedic stories also tend to focus on sexual taboos, particularly marital infidelity, masturbation, and homosexuality. The Bay Area is known for its large gay and lesbian population, and this fact no doubt informs some of the paramedic stories, in which the medics comment directly on this population, using their first-hand credibility of being responders to calls for emergency assistance to support their evaluations of sexually aberrant behavior.[12] The stories of bizarre sexual behavior attributed to homosexuals may be linked both to conservative medic views on sexuality and, by extension, medic anxiety over AIDS.[13]

Paramedics often respond to calls involving patients and situations that fall decidedly out of the bounds of normal experience, and the adjective "weird" appears frequently in their storytelling. Examples of sexually aberrant behavior and the public exposure of hidden behaviors are a significant presence in paramedic stories. Obesity is also a common subject. While certainly motivated in part by the general cultural fixation on weight, the stories are also informed by the threat such patients pose to a medic's physical and economic well-being. Like other groups of patients, obese ones are sometimes compared to animals. Stories about providing medical help to animals are also plentiful. At times, the medics respond compassionately to calls for animals in distress, treating them with the same care and expertise that is available to human patients. In other instances, the animals are handled callously or even emerge as an environmental threat. The stories about animals thus reflect the same degree of ambivalence that is shown by medics toward human patients and the environment.

# 5

# 5150s, SUICIDES, AND ALL THE OTHER CRAZIES

One of the most commented-on groups in paramedic storytelling is the mentally ill. These patients are so thoroughly unpredictable in their actions and behaviors that medics never know what to expect when answering a call for a "5150," the standard designation for a mentally unstable patient. Although the majority of 5150 transports are performed by EMTs on a nonemergency basis, paramedics often respond to calls which eventually result in a 5150 assessment. Bill V. and George, sitting on the patio of Bill's regular south county coffee shop, discuss some surprising experiences with 5150s:

Bill V.: I had an ambulance stolen one time. A 5150 broke out of the hospital and stole our ambulance.

George: Makes you feel kind of naked, doesn't it?

Bill: Oh, I'm sitting in the hospital parking lot with the rest of my buddies laughing at me and this guy's driving all over town with his lights and sirens. He's got out the microphone, singing, "It's just a love machine." He's driving around, woo woo woo woo, "It's just a love machine and it won't work for no-body but you," and he's driving around all over Riverside, cops are chasing

him. He finally just parked and got out, didn't break anything, didn't hurt anything.

George: That's hilarious!

Bill: We never used to lock the ambulances, you know? It was funny, driving all around, "It's just a love machine!" I got my ambulance back about an
hour later, it was funny!

Most paramedics characterize their experiences with 5150s as "funny."
At times, however, the 5150s become more than a simple source of
amusement. The 5150 psychiatric hold is intended not only to protect
others from the sometimes violent actions of patients but also to protect the patients from themselves. In many cases, paramedics encounter
patients who are suicidal or are called to the scenes of suicides or attempted suicides.

In America, as in many cultures, people who suffer from mental
illness are marginalized. Mental illness does not seem as "legitimate" as
other illnesses, and people generally speak in hushed tones about relatives or friends who suffer from such afflictions. While Cousin Bobby's
appendix operation is discussed openly, Uncle Stan's manic depression
is alluded to with euphemistic circumlocutions. Employers are suspi-
cious of job applicants who admit their mental health problems, and
health insurers are reluctant to provide significant coverage for treatment. Many people suffering from mental illness, particularly the poor,
in addition to being ostracized by society receive woefully inadequate
treatment.

During the 1980s, a policy of "deinstitutionalization" obtained in
many states.[1] The goal of these programs was to help mentally ill patients begin a transition back into mainstream society. While many of
the programs had noble ideals, the movement was in part economically motivated. Institutionalized patients cost the states an enormous
amount of money. By "deinstitutionalizing" these patients, the state
mental health authorities could cut their costs and simultaneously endorse a progressive program that would do away with the dreaded
mental health institutions. In the best-case scenario, the deinstitutionalization programs would assist patients with the lengthy transition

process back into society through limited stays in halfway houses and other supervised care programs.[2] The patient would develop the skills necessary to become a fully functioning and contributing member of society and would also have easy access to continuing care.[3] However, as the programs gained in popularity, patients were forced more and more to fend for themselves, and had less and less supervision in their transitional care. Simultaneously, the availability of mental health care for new patients was eroding.[4] Many of the patients who were supposed to be slowly reintegrated with the mainstream population found themselves out on the streets. California's stagnant economy during the early 1990s further contributed to a significant rise in homelessness in Alameda County.[5] Bill R. comments on the implications for the paramedics of these deinstitutionalization programs:

Bill R.: Mental health. That's one of the greatest crimes in America, what goes on with mental health people. Because they used to be taken care of once. It's just that they're the first people that you cut back on, you know? I mean, it's the first cut now. Most of the people walking the streets are actually looney-tunes. I mean, they obviously can't take care of themselves, but, you know, Sam doesn't have the money anymore to take care of them now. And, again, it all leads down to us. If these people had just warm shelter, a little bit of food, a clinic every once in a while for a visit—you know, a dentist clinic or something—they wouldn't need to call us. When you see them in the emergency room, you're dealing with the nine problems they have plus neglect and you're paying for it.

Bill R. makes the economic argument repeated by many medics that emergency care for the indigent mentally ill is far costlier than other preventive programs.

Lisa echoes a similar economic concern in a story about assisting a particularly down and out homeless woman:

Lisa: It's kind of sad. Certain homeless people you see all the time. Then they disappear and you wonder, "Did somebody kill them?" Or maybe they just took off or maybe they even got out of it.

There was a lady on Grand Ave., her name was Elle-Marie. And she had the worst cellulitis [a diffuse, acute infection of the skin and subcutaneous tissue] on her feet. That was when I was working with Diane. And we just happened to see her on the street, she was all huddled up—it was probably October, it was a little cool, not too bad. And she was so sick, she had a fever, she hadn't eaten in probably like a week, and we came up to her and asked her if she wanted to go to the hospital.

But she absolutely refused to go to the hospital because apparently another paramedic crew had told her never to go by ambulance unless she could afford it. We pretty much told her, don't worry about paying. We made up some name, some address, some social security number, put it down on the paperwork, so she wouldn't ever get a bill for it. Took her to Highland. Stopped off at the store, got her some food. [laughter] But I didn't say that!

Melinda: There are a lot of homeless people, who you just get over and over again, and you just can't figure out, what do they want? There's this one woman who you get in Hayward a lot and she seems really sort of together when you talk to her, when she's not really drunk. She had gotten hit by a car so she had been in a home for a while in Livermore and she left it because it was too hard to take a shower and it was too hard to go to the bathroom or something like that. She thought she'd have an easier time on the streets of Hayward. And I mean, I could understand that she'd rather be in Hayward or something, but I just don't understand what she wanted. We were in the Safeway parking lot and she saw us and she told her friend to come over and get us and give her a ride to the hospital so she could get some dinner.

Lisa: That's what she wanted! [laughter]

Melinda: No, but, I mean, I just don't get it, you know?

Lisa: You mean, what she wants out of life in general?

Melinda: Well, yeah, why she keeps walking around Hayward.

Lisa: Well, actually, Judy—I know she hangs out with a bunch of other homeless people and they hang out behind this one liquor store and underneath the Grove Overpass. And they're just this little community there, hanging out.

Melinda: I guess it's true, she has friends and all.

While Lisa expresses dismay at the other medics who have told the homeless woman not to seek care unless she can pay for it, Melinda brings up the problem of habitual abuse of the system by the indigent.[6] In this short conversation, Lisa and Melinda address several of the points regarding the homeless and the mentally ill that occur time and again in paramedic discussions about these patients. On the one hand, the medics view them as being in need of assistance and are often willing to break company rules to help such people, who obviously cannot pay for their own treatment.[7] Lisa thus clearly expresses the generally compassionate attitude of most paramedics, though these feelings are usually masked by the bravura of their storytelling. Melinda, however, voices the simultaneous concern that the emergency system is frequently taken advantage of by noncritical patients. Stories of "frequent fliers" (those who habitually abuse emergency ambulance services) abound, and usually the abusers incur the narrative wrath of the medics. Melinda also expresses a fundamental consternation with the plight of the mentally ill and the homeless, saying, "I just don't get it." In large part, the storytelling acts as a means for "getting it." Organizing and commenting on experiences in the narratives gives the medics a way to fit these patients into a conceptual understanding of the environment. As such, the storytelling allows Lisa and Melinda to humanize the homeless, in sharp contrast with the dehumanizing descriptions found in other medic storytelling.

A significant proportion of the stories concerning mentally ill patients includes criticism of other first responders who are reluctant to approach and treat such patients, thus underscoring the prevalent attitude that these patients are marginal, only barely human. One night, while waiting in the desolate lot of a south county hospital, Steve and Stephanie swap stories about calls for 5150s in which the police improperly assessed the situation:

Steve Y.: My old partner Bob Wilson was telling me this story, him and his partner were both telling it to me. A 5150 is a psychiatric hold that the police department put on people for violent behavior toward others because they're a danger to themselves or others or if they've taken an overdose or something else along those lines. In this particular instance, my old partner got a call

Code 2 for a 5150, the Oakland police on scene. And they get there and they ask the cop where's the 5150.

Stephanie: First the EMTs get there.

Steve: Hunh? No, no, no, they were there first, this is a different one. And they're all, "He's over there against the tree, he's not talking to us, he's not saying anything and he has a history of being a psychiatric patient and so we're 5150ing him."

Well, we go over and this guy's got his belt kind of hung up on the tree and he's propped up but his head's down. And we go to touch him and shake him and he falls over and he's stiff as a fucking board! [laughter] And these cops had put this guy — a dead guy — on a psychiatric hold. [laughter] Somehow in the middle of the night, he'd just kind of leaned up against the tree, just wedged himself up there, and died. And then the cops came along and knew him and thought he was just not talking and put him on a psychiatric hold!

Stephanie: Oh yeah, they got real close! But that's not the first time that happened, there's a recent story where that happened.

Steve: Oh, I haven't heard the recent story.

Stephanie: I think it was at the Sutter Hotel or some hotel in downtown Oakland.

Steve: Oh, yeah! That's the call. We were on that call!

Stephanie: You guys were on that call? Oh, see. I heard that story. And so the EMTs get there first 'cause they usually transport the 5150s. So this guy is in the room and he's not letting anybody in. They're trying to open the door, "Let us in! Let us in!" and he's not letting them in. So finally I guess the EMTs get in there. The cops had already 5150ed him, wrote up the green sheet and everything. And the EMTs kind of barge their way in there, and what he had done was died against the door. He'd wedged himself against the door! [laughter] So then they called for the medics to come and work this guy up, so that's another dead 5150 call.

Steve: Yeah, I'd forgotten all about that one.

Stephanie: And you were there?!

Steve: Yeah, they dragged him out in the hallway. He was an overdose, he died, and they 5150ed him. And they were there fifteen minutes before the

EMTs got there to pick him up as a 5150 and then it was another seven minutes before we got there and he still had agonal heartbeats and stuff. So basically if they had called us as soon as they found him, he might have had a chance of living. We never did get a pulse back but we did get a rhythm. Yeah, he was a junky with no family so nobody was going to sue them or anything. But it was a major fuck-up. I still like the 5150 propped up against the tree though. That's great.

The narrative shifts apparent in these two stories are worthy of consideration. Steve positions himself in the first story as the narrative authority, even though he openly admits that he was not on scene. In the second story, even though Steve had been on scene, Stephanie positions herself as the primary narrator. As is often the case with long-term partners, one partner feels sufficiently versed in the other's call to claim it as her own. Thus, Steve tells a story of a call that his former partner had run, while Stephanie tells of one involving her current partner. In both cases, the medics emerge as the incredulous authorities. Interestingly, the victims are not accorded much weight, the first being "a drunk," and the second a "junky." This narrative marginalization undoubtedly lessens the emotional impact of their deaths.

Many medics find the behavior of the mentally ill to be amusing, and often their antics are a story's focal point. Lars recounts an involved story of responding to a call for one such patient:

Ken: Remember we had that guy who'd end up looking in the cabinets and start screaming at himself? [laughter] He'd just look in the cabinets and go "arrr arrr arrr" and start screaming at himself. Then he'd hit the cabinet and he'd stop and turn around.

Lars: Was he yelling at the cabinets or at his reflection?

Ken: He was yelling at his reflection in the cabinets 'cause we had one of these new units.

Lars: Oh, that's like when you hold up a dog or something to the mirror! [laughter] A little puppy who's never seen a mirror and you hold them up, and they go "arrr arrr arrr arrr"! 5150s are the same way, you hold them up to a mirror and they see themselves. And if they've got a split personality they start arguing! They can carry on an argument with the other side of themselves. "You're wrong!" "No!"

Ahhh, 5150s. Where would we be without 5150s? Oh, man, we got a great one in West Oakland! They gave us the call for the naked man sitting on the corner! [laughter] He was a young guy, like in his early twenties, and he was sitting in the west Oakland housing projects completely naked, sitting on a stoop, smearing himself with shit!

Ken: What? Oh, my God! [laughter]

Lars: He was great. He was smearing himself with shit!

Sarah: Oh, God. All right!

Lars: Just sitting there — apparently he'd been sitting there for about half an hour doing that — and we walked up and PD's all standing around, Fire is standing way back going, "Ununh, not us!"

Ken: I'm surprised they didn't stage!

Lars: Whoa. And we walk up and they're trying to figure out who the guy is and they're talking with him and they were asking about him. Somehow someone came up with a name, I don't know if they heard it from a bystander or what. "Is your name so-and-so?"

Ken: Shithead!

Lars: Yeah, shithead! They're like, "Is your name so-and-so?" and he's like, "Oh, yeah, yeah my name's so-and-so." He was just agreeing with everything, they were like, "Oh, great. Great." And they're writing down this name! [laughter] I'm like, "Wait a second!" [radio traffic] Oh, is that us? Is that us? Are we clear?

Sarah: Yeah, we are.

Lars: 5-2-8, was that for us?

Dispatch: 10-4, 5-2-8, this is in front of the admission building there.

Lars: Okay, 5-2-8, go ahead. [to other medics] Or no, they gave us the call, we should go ahead! [laughter] See ya!

Ken: Next they'll ask dispatch for an ETA.

Dispatch: Cancel 5-2-8.

Lars: 10-4. Score! Oh, do you want the rest of the 5150 story? [laughter] As long as I'm into it, they asked him his name and he was like, "Yeah." So they're all like writing down on the 5150 and they guess, "Oh, is your last name so-and-so?" And he's like, "Oh, yeah, yeah." [laughter] And I say, "Wait a second!" I walk up to the guy and I'm like, "Are you a fire truck?" And he said, "Yeah, yeah, yeah!" [laughter] I was like, "All right, if that's his name, he's a fire truck!"

Ken: So did you transport?

Lars: Yeah, we put him in the back of the unit, we had him all restrained, he's all happy. It was really good that we restrained him because I'm back there and I start talking to the guy and he's all happy and suddenly he looks up at me and goes, "Your momma sucks my dick!" And he just starts going off on me, yelling and screaming [laughter], "Oh, man! Your momma sucks my dick!" I look at him and I say, "Ah, only for a price!" [laughter] And then he went ballistic, he went totally nuts. He was great.

Despite the untimely interruption by the radio dispatcher, Lars is able to continue his story without missing a beat, a narrative ability that reveals an interesting aspect of medics' work experiences. Emergency medical calls are, by nature, unpredictable and can come at any time. As a result, medics are constantly being "interrupted" while doing paperwork, running errands, talking to coworkers, catching a few minutes of sleep, or eating. Once done with their call, they can return to what they were doing. While most people would be unable to pick up where they left off if interrupted by a medical emergency, medics have adjusted well to such interruptions, an adaptation clearly evident in their storytelling.

At times, mentally ill patients can be physically threatening, and medics have to restrain them. Bill L. says, "If they're violent 5150s, they're a hassle. You have to wrestle them and tie them down and they're a hassle." During the transport of a rather benign 5150, Lisa tells the story of a far more threatening call:

Lisa: Oh, boy, 5150s. They all seem to kind of blend together. I remember this one, she was a very nice lady when we first got there — she was being cooperative, and this was like way in West Oakland. We had to take her out to John George. And she started talking to me, she was very pleasant at first, and then she started singing gospel songs. And I was kind of trying to sing along with her, 'cause she wanted me to sing along with her.

All of a sudden she started getting a little bit more agitated, and talking about Christ, and God, and the Devil! And she started to get even more agitated. I was starting to get a little bit worried, 'cause we hadn't put her in restraints, 'cause she was being cooperative. So, we get to John George, and by this time she's got this like wild look in her eyes. [laughter] And she just keeps looking at me. So we took her out of the back, and we're wheeling her up. All of a sudden, she just like lunged across the gurney and went for my neck, and she starts screaming, "Lucifer! Lucifer!" I was like, "Arrr, get her off of me," you know? [laughter]

Thank goodness there was a sheriff's officer over there, because he just grabbed her and slammed her back down onto the gurney. But she really scared me. That was the first time that anything like that had happened to me. That was one of the more memorable 5150s, anyway.

In Lisa's story, the police are presented as helpful protectors, able to thwart the unexpected attack of the 5150.

Standing outside an emergency room entrance, dripping with sweat from the chase described in the following story, Darryl offers a counterexample in which he, rather than the police, is able to thwart the threatening escape of a 5150 from a medical facility:[8]

Darryl: All of a sudden this black man, this buff black man runs out with this wrap on his head and takes off, right? And security is right on his tail from ER, right, running after him and yelling "Stop!" And he yells to these two Berkeley cops standing across the street, "Stop that man!" And one Berkeley cop jumps out of the way and the other tries to stop him. But he like gives a head fake and—whoosh!—he's down the street. So he takes off running. Well, I'm thinking, "Oh, I'll go back the cop up," right?

So I'm running down the street, and I'm running down the street, and all of a sudden, we get to the end, right there where it comes into Telegraph, you know? We're running down the street and the cop's totally winded—wheeze, wheeze—stops right there, gets on the radio. I said, "I'll get him!"

So across we go—boom!—I'm running across the street, dodge a couple of cars just like the movies and everything. Over the curb and stuff, right through the parking lot into this picnic area. I jump the fence right after him and everything. We run like about a quarter mile down on Ashby. And I'm right on this motherfucker's ass and everything. So, Dooks—I hear sirens in the back coming—and Dooks comes jamming down Ashby with the siren on, cuts in front of him. I go, "I got backup there!" Boom! CRASH! Fuckin' all over that motherfucker!

Derek: Bulldog that boy!

Darryl: Took him to the ground and shit and everything. Got a little scrape there and everything, but you know, hooked him up. Then all these cops fly up all over the place. It was so cool!

Nurse: What did he do?

Darryl: He was a 5150.

In Darryl's story, the escaped 5150 becomes the focal point of a scene "just like the movies." The dramatic chase, however, has a paramedic in the lead role with the police dropping back winded, and only appearing again after the dirty work has been done. The patient himself is marginalized, and Derek's telling comment, "bulldog that boy," adopted by Darryl in later retellings of the story, reveals a dehumanizing view of the patient. The story reveals a great deal about Darryl's attitudes—the patients are animals, the police are incompetent, and only medics can bring order to the scene by removing a dangerous psychiatric patient from the streets.

Medics also tell of turning the patient's tenuous grip on reality into a weapon to counteract their assaults. Tom B. narrates the most outrageous of these tales:

Tom B.: About six, seven months ago, and we get a call for a 5150, way up in North Oakland, on the Oakland-Berkeley border, in the Claremont area. And it's just this guy. He's a schizophrenic, okay? And he's got this cut on his forearm. And he says that he was reaching into a trash can when he cut himself on a bottle. But OPD isn't sure whether or not he was a victim of an assault. So, nonetheless, they write a green sheet, 'cause he's got a little bit of alcohol in the blood and he's schizophrenic. And he just got to tell you this, you know, "I'm a schizophrenic." It's like, "Yeah, yeah, yeah."

So we put him in the ambulance, and he's going, "I'm a schizophrenic, and you don't know what that is." I'm like, "Yeah, I do, I'm a paramedic." "No, you don't. I'm a schizophrenic and you don't know what that is." So, he gets on this tangent: "I'm a schizophrenic and you don't know what that is. I'm a schizophrenic, you don't know what that is." [laughter]

So, it's in the middle of the day, I'm working day shift. I've got my sunglasses on. We're sitting in the back of the rig. And I've got him semirestrained because of he's so animated. So, I get right in his face with my scary sunglasses on and I'm like, "Well, you know what? I'm a homicidal maniac and I like to fuck with people until I kill them!" [laughter] And this guy, he doesn't know what to think now, right? So I restrain his arm up over his head, because now he's getting a little too animated. So, I've got one arm up over his head, one arm straight down, got his arms in the gurney straps. And I bring the oxygen out. Put the oxygen on and I go, "This is poison gas! It's gonna make you numb all over!" So I put the $O_2$ on him and I turn it up to six liters so he could feel it flowing in his nose. And he's trying to get it off, he's struggling around. I go, "Don't struggle, man, it's not gonna help. You'll be numb all over here pretty quick." And he's going, "Oh, man, you're crazy! You're crazy!" And I'm going, "It's just starting."

So, I take his blood pressure, it's like 130 over 90 and he's got a heart rate of about 90, you know? So I'm telling him, "Just chill out, you know." And he's getting more animated, going, "You're crazy! I'm a schizophrenic and you don't know what that is." So, I go, "Okay, man, that's it. If you don't calm down, I'm gonna give you electric shock therapy! You know what that is?" He gets all quiet. And I pull out the heart monitor. Put on lead two, turn the volume down. Stick it on him. "Now, if you don't shut up, I'm gonna burn you with this electric shock therapy." And so he's all quiet for about two and a half minutes and then all of a sudden, he's all, "You're crazy." And I said, "Be quiet." And he's all, "You're crazy." And I said, "That's it, man!" I said, "I'm gonna fire this thing up, man." And he's all, "No no no no no!" "Okay. Be cool then."

Next thing you know, he starts in again. I'm, "That's it." I turn up the volume, and he's thrashing around going, "Wheaaaaah!" All of a sudden, he realizes he can't feel nothing. [laughter] And he's sitting there, "I don't feel anything." And I said, "Do you hear that beeping noise?" "Yeah." "Every time you hear that beeping noise, that's fifty thousand volts going through your body!" And he's going, "I don't feel anything!" And I go, "That's that poison gas in your nose!" And he's all, "Blwaaaaaaahhh!!!" And he's screaming and yelling and I'm going, "Oh, shut up."

So, then we're getting to the hospital, and my partner's up in the front barely driving, he's laughing so hard. And right as we're pulling up, I go, "George! George! I think I killed him!" And he's going, "I'm aliiiiive! I'm aliiiiive!" So, I pull the heart monitor off him, I pull the oxygen off him, 'cause we were backing it into Highland, you know? And I start giving him a sternal rub, "Hey! Hey! Come back, man! I didn't want to kill you! Come back!" He's sitting there screaming, "I'm aliiiive! I am aliiiive!" So now, I take off my Gargoyles,[9] get out of the back of the rig, pull the doors open, lower the gurney. And he's screaming, "You're crazy! I'm alive!" And I'm all pretending like he's dead, you know. And he's just going crazy, man! That was great. Brought him into the ER, "Oh, no, man, dude's just losing it." [laughter]

In this story, Tom narratively punishes one of the numerous patients who question his medical authority and threaten physical violence. He may also be engaging in the game of narrative chicken, using the story to express how far he has gone, or perhaps how far he would like to go, in transgressing the rules governing medic behavior. It is important that he is able to punish the patient without being caught. In an amusing twist, he appears in the story as being even more psychologically unstable and dangerous than the patient, an image reminiscent of the frightening final sequence in the film *The Twilight Zone,* in which a paramedic turns into a monster.[10]

Many stories illustrate a contemptuous attitude towards the mentally ill that is similar to the general public's. But the medics' attitude is tempered by frequent interaction with people desperately in need of substantial, long-term psychiatric care. In large part, medics express frustration with a system that forces these people to fend for themselves. They also hint that the extraordinary stresses of their jobs could lead to their own psychological collapse. In the previous story, Tom counters his patient's continued questioning of his medical authority by taking on the persona of a mentally ill person himself—a "homicidal maniac." In another story, Bill V. tells of a police officer who lands on the streets:

Bill V.: I've picked this guy up once before. And I picked this guy up in Hayward, he'd been sleeping behind this dumpster—fifty-five-year old man—you could tell he had been drinking, you could tell he was educated. We picked him up in the back of the ambulance and I'm treating him for chest pain and difficulty breathing, we're taking him to Eden and he says to me, he goes, "You paramedics are the only ones who care." And I said, "Well, you know, I imagine that if I was in your boat I'd hope that somebody would do the same for me." And I said to him, I said, "I'm sure you've done the same for other people." And he goes, "You know my story?" And I go, "Yeah, I know your story." We continue on to the hospital.

   This guy, his name is Dave, I can't think of his last name, but he was a sergeant in the CHP, and fifteen years ago, I guess, he was in some crazy shooting or something that was out in the valley. And apparently one of his men got killed, it was pretty nasty, it was before the days of critical debriefings, and apparently after the episode he fell apart. Started drinking, lost his job, lost his family, lost his house. Kept drinking 'til he became homeless, sleeping in dipsy dumpsters, you know, hating life. It just goes to show, like you were saying earlier, George, we're walking a fine line. [laughter] Between where we are now and living in the gutter, you know, it just goes both ways.

In his story, Bill mentions the caring nature of paramedics, but does so cleverly by having a former police officer provide that evaluation. He also underscores an underlying anxiety, namely the possibility that medics themselves could become 5150s. The story thus echoes his earlier story of the Cerritos air crash and the importance of debriefings after difficult calls. Perhaps the stories that he and other medics tell, and the sometimes aberrant behaviors and attitudes expressed in those stories, can be better understood in light of his remarks. As noted earlier, storytelling in large part serves as a continuous Critical Incident Stress Debriefing. It also allows the expression of otherwise sanctioned opinions, as well as providing an opportunity to laugh about tragedy and suffering, in an established forum.

I have been riding with George in his supervisor truck for the better part of the afternoon. We have been "jumping calls," meeting with medic crews at various hospitals, "sightseeing" down by the Oakland docks and in the public housing projects, and visiting scenes to assist the medic crews. Throughout the day, George has kept up a steady chatter, a nearly endless flow of story after story. Sometimes, other medics are present, and they join in, while at other times it is simply George, in the front seat of the truck, driving and talking. On the way to the scene of a fatal stabbing, George brings up the topic of suicides and attempted suicides:

George: We go on a lot of suicides, attempted and successful. And probably the worst successful suicide that I've ever seen was a gentleman who basically put a shotgun in his mouth and blew his head off. I've seen a couple of those, but the thing that made this one kind of weird was it was in a bedroom that was decorated with Old West paraphernalia. Wagon wheels and stuff like that. Old pistols and stuff on the wall. But there was stuff dripping off the ceiling from his head and all that. That's not uncommon in the gunshots to the head. But the thing that really sits with me is that the bookshelf—it was about a three-shelf unit full of Old West books, Billy the Kid and, you know, old stories like that—on top of the bookshelf was that famous picture of Butch Cassidy and the Sundance Kid from the movie, making their break out of that building with their guns drawn where they both ended up getting shot to death. And this picture—the glass on the picture frame—was just splattered with the blood from this guy. With everything considered on that scene, it was the most strangest, most eerie, suicide gunshot to the head that I've ever seen. It was in that most strange category.

Medics often comment on the strangeness of the scenes of suicides and attempted suicides. Here, George continues with the frequent analogy between the work environment and the Wild West. His detailed description of the scene, rather than of the patient, becomes the main focus of the story. Indeed, the patient is almost absent from the story, his presence indicated only by the allusion to "eerie" splashes of blood. Brain matter clings to the ceiling, and blood splatters the photograph of the two ill-fated movie gunslingers; the entire room takes on the feel of a tableau. This style of description is quite common in medic stories, particularly those that concern horrific events; the scenes, like movie stills, are static and full of surprising detail. Time stands still, interrupted only by the blood dripping from the ceiling.

Late one night, outside Children's Hospital, Kathryn describes the scene of a murder-suicide that likewise left her with an indelible mental image:

Kathryn: We've had weeks where it just seems like everyone dies. Either they've been shot, stabbed, hit by a car, or just died for medical reasons. In fact I think I was off work because I injured my thumb on a call, I tore a ligament in my thumb and I was off work for two months, came back to work and my first week was like that. Everyone just died. I think I had a couple of codes a day and they were all really, really nasty. Like domestic violence, you know? You go in and it's just horrible. And finally I just had to take some time off, I just couldn't deal with it anymore.

I think perhaps the worst call that I've ever had was when I was working out here for a different company. I was working with a paramedic unit when I was an EMT because one of the paramedics had injured her knees, and so I was doing all the lifting for her, and we got called out for a hostage situation. We must've been there like three hours. And what had happened, I guess this woman wanted a separation from her husband, and she had been in her apartment visiting with an uncle and her husband came in with a shotgun. Her uncle snuck out the back door, went and called police. Well, the police finally arrived and—oh, we got a call.

Mary: Go ahead.

Kathryn: Anyway, police finally arrived and they heard two shots go off, and so they figure that the woman was probably dead, you know? But they're worried about the two kids that were inside. One was eighteen months and the other was five years old, and they kept seeing movement inside the house, so they thought it was the man walking around. So they called the SWAT team. This must have been like two, three o'clock in the morning. Seems like everything that happens that's really bad, happens at two or three in the morning. And you could just see all these like police officers on the tops of roofs in the nearby neighborhood. They were just waiting there, 'cause they thought he had like killed the children, too.

Finally I guess somebody got up close enough to notice that it was just the children who were moving around and got the children to come out. And they were just covered in blood, and they didn't know why. So they sent us in. The cops had finally gotten in and noticed that there were two people down. It was the man and the woman.

We go inside and it's upstairs in this apartment building and it was just this really eerie feeling, like you could just feel like the evil. It just hung in the air. It was just really heavy, it was really oppressive. And you walk in the door to this bedroom and there was a man laying on the ground with his hands behind his back like he'd been handcuffed, a shotgun laying in front of him with cartridges that had been used laying on the ground. And then a woman laying on the bed.

The bed was long and she was laying back and there was a window above her head with a police officer looking down at her. Her mouth was open and she had the worst look on her face that I'd ever seen in my life, it really frightened me. It was just a look of pure of terror. Her mouth was open, and it was filled right up to the teeth with separated blood. And she was already stiff. But at that time, which was quite a few years ago, we still had to check everyone out and call it in, and make base contact and make sure we could leave them on scene. And she must have had a hole that was as big as my hand right in her chest from him shooting her. And then he just put the gun right up to his chest and shot himself. So it looked like he was handcuffed but I guess what it actually was, he was holding on to the gun and then pulled it out of his hands and put them behind his back.

But that call, I had nightmares for weeks. I imagine this woman coming down my stairs after me. Just the look on her face was really frightening. I think that was perhaps the worst call I've ever been on. We'll see what this next call is.

Like many calls that become an experiential yardstick, this one occurred during Kathryn's early training as an EMT. Although the story is interrupted by a call, Mary urges Kathryn to continue. The story is engaging, and Kathryn builds a certain suspense. Even Mary, who has heard the story before, wants to hear about the gruesome discovery the medics make when they finally enter the house. Kathryn's description of the scene is reminiscent of George's, but here she narratively follows the gaze of the police officer down to the bed, to the gunshot victim whose face is frozen in terror. Kathryn's description of the murderer offers additional punishment to his suicide, with the man seemingly "handcuffed" on the floor.

The unexpected nature of the scenes, the incongruities, and the sometimes inappropriate responses of others all emerge as common elements in medic stories about suicides. Taking one's own life is so fundamentally antithetical to the work of paramedics that they situate suicide victims in a space far removed from the world of normal human existence. In George's story, the suicide takes place in a fantasy world of the Wild West, while in Kathryn's the bedroom is frozen in time and reappears in the dream world of her nightmares. In a similar story, Lars highlights the actual physical distance that separates the suicide from the medics' normal environment:

Lars: We were in Castro Valley and we get a call for a possible suicide. It came in as a possible shooting, it came in as a shooting. And it was way up at the end of Crow Canyon — Crow Canyon or Cull Canyon? There's two up there. I guess it was at the end of Cull Canyon — way, way out there. So, we get the call, we get the address, "Woo woo woo woo!" Drive all through Castro Valley and drive and drive and drive and drive. Finally we stop and say, "Wait, where are we? We're driving a long time, where is this?" We're way out in the middle of nowhere, we get on the radio, and we're like, "Where exactly is this? 'Cause we're driving out here in the middle of nowhere." They're like, "Well, take Cull Canyon, follow it all the way to the end. It's a very long road and at the end you'll hit a dirt road. Follow the dirt road up, follow the right fork, and go all the way up. It's up behind a nudist colony." So, I'm sure all anyone heard was me going, "All right!"

So, we're driving and driving "Woo woo woo woo!" you know? Finally, at one point, this sheriff's car goes by us — whoosh! — rocketing down this road which is all curvy, and we go driving all the way out there. We get on the dirt and we drive up the dirt road to the end. And we get there. The fire department's going up this dirt path in a four-wheel drive and the East Bay cops and the sheriffs went up there in a Bronco. And we get our equipment, go walking up there and go walking up this trail, I've got the heart monitor. And we get up there, and one of the sheriffs, she's like, "Unless you're planning on doing miracles with that thing, I don't think it's gonna help this guy at all." And we're like, "Why?" And they're like, "Well, he's over here. Come on over, take a look."

And we get there and there's spotlights and there's headlights pointed, and this guy's laid out on the grass, and he's curled up around a shotgun.

Steve Y.: There was steam coming out of the top of his head. I mean he looked like a little smokestack that had fallen over. It was real *Night of the Living Dead* shit.

Lars: He had put a double-barrel shotgun in the back of his mouth and he had just blown the entire back of his head off! It was — blam! — blown out. There was no brain in the skull. I mean, we didn't even see where the brain was. We couldn't even find brain bits. They were somewhere — he was up against a hill, a wooded hill — and we assumed his brain was somewhere out there on the hill.

Steve: Yeah, everything from his forehead back, kind of in a concave, had mushroomed over and there was nothing inside. [laughter] And he's just sitting there like this with a shotgun in his hands flat on his back and his head, everything was gone. It would've made a nice salad bowl! [laughter]

Lars: But yeah, he must have hit the Pearly Gates at about a hundred miles per hour. He was dead. And you know, he's laying there, he's all curled up around the shotgun and his hat is sitting right there on his chest. And someone was saying, "Oh, he just got his hair cut today." You couldn't tell. [laughter] And then there's this crowd of guys there. And one of them's got this little cordless phone, he's the one who called 911. There's a bunch of guys living in this trailer. And the other guys are like, "Oh, why'd you even bother calling 911? He's dead. We would have just taken him out and buried him somewhere up here in the hills." It got us kind of wondering, "I wonder how many people have died way out here and they just brought them out and buried them out there in the hills!" But he was really quite dead. He'd really done himself in. He took both barrels, right through the back of the head.

The scene's remoteness stands as a major element of the story, while the mention of the nudist colony offers some humorous relief. Lars notes that he and his partner feel compelled to "see for themselves," reserving final medical judgment, despite the dismissive attitudes of the other first responders. While Lars mentions the thoroughness of the man's actions, Steve dwells on the wound and the surprising physiological repercussions of being hit with a shotgun blast at close range. His evaluative comment, *"Night of the Living Dead* shit," underscores the common attitude concerning suicides, as well as the frequent appeal to popular movies as a device for categorizing the images of an emergency scene.

Despite the horror associated with these scenes, self-inflicted wounds and efficient methods for committing suicide hold a surprising fascination for paramedics. In a lull between calls, Tony and Patrick discuss various suicide and attempted suicide victims they have encountered:

Tony: We had a suicide on BART. This guy, he like, laid across two rails and then reached over for the third rail. When he touched the third rail the only parts that got really burnt badly were his genitals that were laying on the track, and his upper chest, which was also on the track.

Patrick: Where he grounded himself.

Tony: Yeah, where he grounded himself. I heard that he blew his nuts off! [laughter]

Patrick: Oh, wow.

Tony: But he's alive, and I'm sure he's regretting it now! [laughter] There was another suicide story, right after the earthquake. The hanging! This guy, he hung himself in a garage, from a beam that was maybe four feet off the ground. He tied the rope up there, got on his knees, put a bucket down underneath the beam. Put the noose around his neck, got on the bucket with his knees on the bucket. Held his feet behind him, and then just jumped off the bucket. The guy was maybe like two inches off the ground. That's all he was off the ground. His feet were bent, that guy held his knees. He was holding his legs up until he died.

Patrick: Wow.

Tony: Or maybe he went from paralysis, that happens, broke his neck. But that was incredible. And the knot was about here, it was just strangulation, the knot was here on the side. A young dude.

Patrick: Yeah, sometimes they don't even break their neck when they do it. That's why like in the Wild West days, there were books on the best placement for the knots.

Tony: On the side.

Patrick: Yeah, they either put them on the side, or right underneath, so it snaps his head backwards, and breaks the neck, like first thing.

Tony: Yeah, see, that's strangulation with the knot right up here in back, 'cause there's no crack. That guy didn't reach out. I would have. I would have stuck my feet in!

Patrick: Yeah, I would have too. I would have stood up and rethought it: "Maybe I'll do something with pills."

Tony: Oh, that hurt! [laughter] Yeah, I'm not doing that anymore.

Patrick: Yeah. Sleeping pills!

Tony: Yeah, I would have thought of something else. But that guy was determined to die. Sometimes they put a gun in their nose or in their head, and they just like blow their face off, but they live! [laughter]

Patrick: Yeah.

Tony: It's like, "Put it in your eye!" That's a sure shot.

Patrick: Yeah, really.

Tony: There's nothing but brain that it goes through after that, and there's already an opening in the back, so no skull to have to go through.

Patrick: I guess you're not thinking too clearly though, when you're about to put a gun to your head.

Tony: Plus you think — "In my eye?! That would really hurt!" [laughter] In your head, you can do this, but you can't do this to your eye! [laughter]

Tony's and Patrick's short exchange infuses the discussion of suicides with humor. Rather than dwelling on the grim aspects of the call, they instead focus on the physical ramifications of failed suicide attempts, as well as on the persistence of some suicides. Their final, speculative musings on the thoughts of a potential suicide seem to mock the decision-making process.

Lars offers one of the most dramatic stories of an attempted suicide. In it, he describes the results of "improper" gun placement:

Lars: Oh, it was beautiful! We got a call for shortness of breath, Anton and I, last call of the night. And we get there, right with the fire truck and there's this woman out in front of her house and she's just like freaked out. I'm like, "Oh, okay, must be really short of breath."

So we come out and we're like, "Well, what's wrong and where is he?" "It's my husband! In back." She leads us into the back yard, it's pitch black back there, we're going, "This is weird. Shortness of breath out in the back yard? It's two in the morning? It's dark as hell out there, what the hell?" So we get back there and none of us brought a flashlight 'cause we thought we were going inside. And there's her husband, laying face down on the ground, but he's propped up on his arms. Now he's completely naked except he's got this quilt over him. And we're walking up going, "What the hell?" And he's kind of moaning and we're like, "Hey, what's going on, sir?" And he moans and groans and we get a little penlight out, we flash it at him and there's— there's blood all over him!

We're like, "Oh, shit! Look for the gun. Someone get a flashlight," you know? And there's a .38 laying in the grass right next to him, and we're like, "Christ, what is all over him," you know? We're trying to get out equipment and stuff and finally we get a couple of flashlights, and shine it on him. He'd taken the .38, put it up to the side of his head and pulled the trigger. And the bullet went through and it popped out one of his eyes. His right eye had popped out completely and was hanging there. And the bullet came through, came out the left eye and took the eye out with it. So it was all hanging down, deflated and all. There's the vitreous humor [a semigelatinous transparent substance] and stuff all just sort of leaking out of the eye and just blood coming out of his sockets and there's just blood all over him. And we're like, "Whoah, I'd be short of breath, too!" [laughter]

And the guy is conscious and he's talking and he's alert and oriented. He knows where he is and what day it is and stuff, so I'm like, "I'll go set up the unit for a trauma." So I go up to drip the lines and Anton is trying to deal with the firefighters. He's trying to get them to help him load him up. Well, finally they do, they get him on this gurney and stuff.

I don't know if you ever saw *Total Recall*,[11] when their space helmets break and their eyes bulge out — it looked exactly like this. I mean you got one eye here and one there. We get him in the back of the ambulance and I'm driving Code 3 to the trauma center. And in the rearview mirror, all I can see is this guy laying there, I can see his eyes hanging there, and I can hear him talking. And it's just the weirdest thing, to look up in the rearview mirror. And Anton's back there starting IV's on the guy and he finally asks him, he goes, "So, sir, why, why did you do this?" And the guy said, "Do what?" [laughter]

Now we're like, "Okay, full-blown denial here." He's like, "Well, shoot your-self." He's like, "What are you talking about? I didn't shoot myself." We're like, "Okay. Right." So we get him to the trauma center and the guy's like, "No, no, nothing like that's happened," you know? "Oh yeah, well how many fingers do I have up?" [laughter] "Or should I put them over here?" [laughter]

So we get to the trauma center and we're wheeling the guy through the doors, and this is the first time I've seen a trauma surgeon look at a patient and go, "Ugh!" 'Cause that's what he did. He looked down and went, "Oooh, jeez. Ugh." And we brought him inside. The guy lived. I mean, his brain wasn't damaged at all — just his eyes. Really disgusting. Actually, that's the second time I've seen somebody shoot themselves through the head, through and through with a .38 caliber and be alert and oriented. It just affects the eyes! What happens, they blow out the optic nerve, the bullet travels behind the eyes. But whatever reason this guy wanted to kill himself before, now he's really got a reason to be depressed, you know? I mean, God, his face is all messed up, he can't see, gonna be blind for the rest of his life! Whoosh! [laughter]

Like Tony and Patrick, Lars speculates that the victim of a botched sui-cide is in worse condition, both emotionally and physically, after the attempt. His reference to the film *Total Recall* resonates with Steve's characterization of a suicide victim as being reminiscent of another movie, *Night of the Living Dead*.[12] It is indeed interesting that medics appeal to popular film, particularly horror movies and science fiction thrillers, as a means of organizing their experiences. No longer do these experiences occupy the real world but resemble the fictive world of motion pictures.

Suicides and attempted suicides are, of course, an unavoidable part of the emergency calls medics receive. Paramedics, trained to save lives, find themselves in a slightly contradictory position at the scene of a suicide. Here, a person has deliberately taken his or her own life, undermining the basic premise of the paramedic's profession, namely the sanctity of life. Thus, suicides pose an interesting contradiction for the paramedics. On the one hand, the medics need to treat people whose attempts at suicide have failed. Generally, they express amazement at both the victim's persistence and his or her bad fortune. On the other hand, they cannot help but deride the person. It is an odd situation indeed to be called to save the life of someone who has attempted to end it.

The policy of deinstitutionalization, the cutbacks in government-funded treatment facilities and programs for the mentally ill, and the long-term California recession in the 1980s all contributed to the explosive rise of the homeless population in Alameda County. Most paramedics note that hardly a day goes by when they are not called to assist a person who, in their opinion, is in desperate need of substantial psychiatric care. Although the goals of deinstitutionalization were indeed noble, the lack of commitment in many communities to provide continued care means that many patients do not receive the outpatient attention they need. Without care and supervision, some of these people become a danger to themselves or others and, at that point, become subject to categorization as a "5150."

Paramedic stories about these psychiatric patients are, like many other medic stories, replete with sarcastic remarks and sardonic observations on human life. The unpredictability and the inherently violent nature of many of these patients make the 5150 a difficult call. While the medics all express amusement with the patients' "weird" antics, these stories reveal the anxiety that accompanies dealing with people who can become inexplicably violent or react to innocuous queries in unexpected ways. As in the stories of transsexuality, sexual deviance, and obesity, the psychiatric patients emerge as a population apart. While the medics are undoubtedly drawn to those who unabashedly mock social conventions, they also ridicule such people.

Although the stories are good-natured and told with great humor, some, such as Tom B.'s, in which he terrifies the patient with his uncouth actions, show the 5150s becoming dehumanized and appearing as animals — little puppy dogs who can easily be manipulated. Bill V. suggests that the propensity of medics to laugh at psychiatric patients comes from anxiety about their own psychological frailty. One call can easily send a person into an emotional crisis.

A suicide or attempted suicide represents the ultimate failure of the system. Patients are placed under a 5150 hold specifically to protect themselves against their own self-destructive urges. In stories about suicides, the medics develop even greater distance between themselves and the victims. Although they joke about the physical condition of the victims, the bodies do not correspond to those of real people but are linked to the fictive world of movies, dreams, and the legendary past. Thus the people stop being human beings and become simply images in the ongoing motion picture in which the medics find themselves. Like the comments on internal tourism that medics make about their work environment, the frequent references to popular films help them situate their experiences outside the realm of "normal" life. The vivid images culled from the silver screen bolster the medics' presentation of their work as extraordinary and make the medics seem larger than life. At the same time, the references also remove the emotional weight of the scene. After all, the gunshot victim's eyes look just like those in *Total Recall*.

# 6

# CAN YOU SAVE
# THE BABY?

Usually, babies are delivered in hospitals; however, when a woman cannot get to one in time, she has the baby wherever she happens to be. As a result, babies are delivered in airplanes, taxis, buses, restaurants, theaters and at sporting events. Births take place in grocery stores, office buildings, courtrooms, second-floor apartments, public restrooms, and parks. In these cases, someone usually calls 911. Since the arrival of a baby is generally considered to be a joyous occasion, newspaper reports of these unexpected deliveries are accompanied by photographs of mother, child, and paramedic, grinning and doing well. In their storytelling, however, paramedics present a very different picture of these calls.

After dropping a pregnant patient off at Highland Hospital late one night, Tom B. begins to tell stories about delivering babies:

Tom B.: So my partner and I get Code 3 for the O-B Boy [a delivery]. So we're fruit-rolling it over there and on the way they go, "Yeah, Paramedic 24, the baby's been delivered." And we're like going, "Greaaat," because this particular fire department at the time wasn't really pleased about doing medical calls, you know? So, I'm thinking, "We better hurry because they're not real good at suctioning airways on a newborn." So, we blaze over there, I come bailing out of the rig. We used to keep an OB kit [obstetrical equipment] behind the driver's seat. That way we wouldn't have to climb all the way back into the cabinets to get them.

And so I get out of the rig, you know, and the fire department's going, "Up here, up here!" And I'm going, "Greaaat." Well, it was dark and there was a chain slung across the driveway on this apartment complex. So, I'm like my normal self, I decide to run over there. Didn't see the chain — wham! — paramedic to ground action! So I get up and I continue on. And it's like, you ever been working a chest pain and you bump your knee on the coffee table? You know, you get this wracking pain and your face is kind of all cinching and you're going, "And just exactly what were you doing when this pain started?" I know what I was doing when I got my pain!

But I get up there, and my knee's starting to swell, I can feel the blood running down my leg and I'm thinking, "Damn!" And here's this lady, in this tub — I'm standing in the doorway, thinking about myself at the time — and here's this lady, sitting in this tub, bathing in this bloody bath water! And here's this infant and the cord and the placenta, all on the floor. And I'm thinking, "Fuck! Pick the baby up and bring it over here!" You know?

So they scoop the baby up and the placenta and the cord, and they bring him over and then Darryl walks in. So I hand off the baby and I'm like, "Take care of the kid." So now I'm like, "Ma'am? Can you step out of that tub?" And she's going, "I don't wanna get out of the tub." And I'm going, "Ma'am? You know, you could be bleeding to death and you wouldn't know it. Could you at least let us take a look at it?" "No! Go away. I don't want you! I didn't call you! I don't want you! It's an ugly baby, you can have it." And I'm thinking, "Oooh." Yeah, she's going, "It's an ugly baby, I don't want it." And I'm thinking, "Man, I ain't seen nothing like this before." This lady looks like she's about fifty-five.

So I keep going, "Ma'am, please, could you get out of that tub? You could be bleeding." "I ain't bleeding to death, just go away! Get the hell out of my house!" And I'm going, "Ma'am, please." And then, Fire gets a call for a fire, so they're like, "We're outta here!" They left all their equipment upstairs, they go running out of there and out to their engine. Left all their medical gear.

And Darryl's dealing with the baby—and the baby's fine. Clamped the cord, cut it, bagged the placenta and everything's pretty good.

Anyway, I ain't getting anywhere with this lady. Finally, I tell her, "Look, get out of the tub!" She's like, "Get out of my house!" So on top of that I wasn't feeling too good, my knee was all swollen, I was like, "Fine!" So I tell Darryl, "I'm going to grab all of Fire's gear, see if you can't get the lady out of the tub." So I bring the gear down to the rig. Big mistake. Now I have to walk back up two flights of stairs with my knee. I'm like, "Shit."

Well, I get back up there and Darryl's standing in the doorway, he's going, "Lady, you're under medical arrest. We're the paramedic police, you're in violation of paramedic code six-oh-two dash seven. Get out of the tub!" "Yes sir, officer!" [laughter] She gets right out of the tub, man, bloody bath water and all! So we get her all wrote up and bring her down, tell her she has to go to the hospital, put her in the ambulance, you know? She didn't want nothing to do with this kid, which was really sad. She's saying, "Oh, I didn't know I was pregnant, and the baby fell out of me when I was cooking dinner!" And I'm thinking, "Ugh!" So, we assessed the baby really good, take her out to Alta Bates.

So, we're standing in the doorway of Alta Bates, Darryl's holding the baby, I'm standing next to mom and the labor and delivery ladies come down with their isolette and go, "Give that baby back to its mother! It's, it's missing an important bonding process!" Darryl goes, "Oh yeah? You give it to her." So she takes it and goes, "Awww, here ma'am, here's your baby." And she's going, "Take it away! It's an ugly baby! I don't want it, you can have it!" And the nurse is going, "Oh! Oh! Oh!"

The idyllic vision of a mother bonding with her newborn child is undermined by the unsettling vision of her bathing in a tub filled with bloody water and her hostile rejection of the child. The woman's surprising claim to ignorance—that she did not know that she was pregnant—is, in fact, a common refrain in stories about deliveries.

In contrast to mothers such as this one, who bear the brunt of medic narrative disdain, young children are the epitome of the innocent victim. Medics often mention that they work "extra hard" when a child's life is in danger, and many acknowledge that the most psychologically draining calls that they have run involve children. Most of the stories about pediatric patients are not told with the same acerbic wit as other stories but with a degree of solemnity. But while children generally make it through the narrative with their innocence intact, their parents are frequently the subject of typical medic scorn. In stories about out-of-hospital deliveries, the parents are derided for their irresponsibility and their stupidity. In other stories concerning pediatric calls, the parents are criticized for dangerous lapses in judgment.

When the call for a delivery comes over the radio, the dispatchers distinguish it as an "O-B Boy"; thus, the medics will not confuse the call with one for an "O-D David," or overdose. Very few medics enjoy these calls, as Darryl and Derek note:

Darryl: Alone, probably, I've done, I don't know, I stopped counting. At Allied we tended to do it a lot, because that sector of the population tends not to have good prenatal care. So, twenty-seven of them or something or other. And a bunch with Dooks. Me and Dooks, we've done two or three together. We be aces!

Derek: You know, the first time's great because you're giving birth. [laughter] I mean you're birthing somebody and you don't know whose it is. Well, I mean you know whose it is, but you don't know the person really well.

Darryl: The majority of all our calls is dealing with human suffering and everything, and death. That sort of thing. But with these, you're giving life. Except it's—

Derek: A mess.

Darryl: It's a mess and it's an extra PCR, 'cause now you have twice the paperwork, one for the mother, one for the baby. So I'd rather get them to the hospital, personally and everything. Plus, typically, the population that doesn't make it to the hospital are ghetto people I guess, or "underprivileged" or what have you. And they're sick—no prenatal care, a lot of crack babies.

Derek: A lot of crack babies. Drug abuse.

Darryl: And they come out and they're very ill. Kids that are young enough—neonates, newly borns that are ill—are way tougher to deal with than any ill adult patient. Except they're a lot easier to carry—like a football. [laughter] Like a nerf ball!

Derek: Oh, man, too much.

Like many medics, Darryl and Derek point out the added work that the delivery of a child requires. The ambulance is a mess, they are required to fill out extra paperwork, and the children often have complicated medical problems.

In addition to containing an expression of disdain regarding what is considered a "messy" call, most of the paramedics' stories about deliveries involve patients suffering medical complications. Typically, it is the medics, more than anyone else on scene, who have the ability and cool-headed competence to deal with the situation. As in many other stories, firefighters are often the object of criticism. Tom B. tells a story of arriving on the scene of an obstetrics call, only to find that the firefighters have initiated the delivery:

Tom B.: My old partner Darryl, he has baby karma, okay? This guy probably delivers more kids than any paramedic I know. So when I worked with him, I delivered maybe four in the field and, by the time I was done with him, I had delivered like fifteen in the field. And I don't count the crack babies, you know, premature, Code Blue, basically dead babies when they deliver. You know, these are live viable births.

One time, we rolled on this call, and Oakland Fire was there with one of their truck companies, I think it was Truck One. And they're there, and there's like one firefighter who says, "Oh, we got it, we got it, she's gonna deliver, you know." So, we're kind of kicking back. They had some new firemen they wanted to break in, you know? So he's down there getting ready to deliver this baby, and all of a sudden—boop!—out pops a foot! Man, you should have seen that fireman jump! Whoa! "It's all yours, man!"

So I jump in there, it's like, "Oh, shit, now we're in trouble." But it was present breech and she just kept pushing.[1] We're trying to tell her, "Hold on, hold on." But we're on the second floor and we're kind of compromised. She was like, "I can't stop! I gotta push, I gotta get this thing out of me!" So she kept pushing and the butt started coming, the other foot came out, and the body came really easy, both arms came out. And it's just the head still in there. I was like, "Whoa shit!" This is the worst part of deliveries, passing the head, everything else is easy!

So I was like, "Damn, man!" So I'm trying to get some fingers in there, because usually once the body presents, they'll try and breathe, you know? And

I didn't want him breathing amniotic fluid. So I'm trying to get a finger up in there and I'm just like, "We're here now, man. Start pushing, lady!" So it came pretty easy, we got that baby's head out and suctioned him out really good. Go ahead and clamped the cord. Cut it. You know, give mom the baby and we extricated it down.

But you should have seen that fireman's face, when that foot came out— boop! "It's all yours, man!" He jumped out of the way. I'm going, "Oh ho, great, you want the glory when it's easy, but when they come out hard, it's like, it's all yours!" So that was pretty cool.

This story is one of the rare instances in which an account of a delivery is told with a positive resolution; the baby is healthy, despite the difficult delivery, and the mother gets to—and wants to—hold her child. Tom makes a disparaging evaluation of the firefighter's ability to deliver the child and, simultaneously, voices a more general critique of the firefighters, who, in the eyes of many medics, are "hungry for glory."

Tom continues in this same vein, telling another story of firefighters' surprising, if not naive, incompetence at the scene of a miscarriage:

Tom B.: Hey, man, this is the real world here! So we show up to this address, right? It's a sixteen-year-old female. And the father meets us at the door, he says, "Yeah, the paramedics are in the back with her now." It's San Jose Fire, right? So we're like, "Hey, wait a minute, man, we are the paramedics! Can't you read?" The guy's like, "Oh, okay" So he directs us to the back bedroom.

And here are these two firemen. One's got this OB kit laid out, all over the bed. She's wedged between the wall, the bed, and the dresser. And this fireman, right down between her legs. Sixteen years old, okay? Vaginal bleeder. He's got this OB kit laid out all over the bed. We walk up to the bedroom door, and the mother's talking to the firemen, going, "Can you save the baby?" Well, she's six weeks pregnant, man! Darryl looks over and goes, "You got a red top?"[2] [laughter] So we ended up transporting her Code 3 back to Kaiser Santa Teresa, with a blood pressure less than 90 and a heart rate of 150. Bleeding like nobody's business! But these firemen got this thing laid out, man! All ready to deliver! What were they gonna deliver, man?! [laughter] Oh, man, it's too much!

In addition to noting the firefighters' incompetence, Tom offers a critique of the patient and her family. He voices consternation over the youth of the patient, derides the husband for improperly identifying the firefighters as paramedics, and dismisses the patient's mother for her absurdly optimistic question concerning saving the baby. Interestingly, Tom attributes the tasteless comment about saving the miscarried baby in a blood tube to his partner, Darryl; thus, he is able to make the remark without having it reflect directly on him.

At times, a delivery's environmental challenges, rather than the medical ones, become the focus of these stories. Steve M. narrates an extraordinary call involving the delivery of a child after a car accident:

Steve M.: We had a call one time where this woman was in a car. She was driving down the road really fast, had a blackout. So she passed out and rolled into a canal upside down. So they thought she was in the car, obviously. So we go down, look in the car, and she's nine months pregnant, her water had broken, she was crying, the canal was filling with water, and she was screaming bloody murder, trying to get out!

So we had to deliver the baby at the same time. It took like twenty minutes just to get the car open to where we could get her out. In the meantime, we had delivered the baby, we hand the baby up to someone else, and then we're trying to get the mom up, and she was really mashed, her chest was mashed, her pelvis was mashed, and all that. So we brought her up here and she lived to breed again!

This was like her sixth kid, she was nineteen years old. Man, I've had three deliveries as a paramedic and two as an EMT, but that was the most memorable one cause you're upside down in the water and you've got all this water, and you think, "God, I could be out windsurfing instead."

Here Steve is confronted with a call that, if for an accident victim alone, would probably have been remarkable enough to be classified as a "cool call" and thus warrant retelling. Because of the complication of the woman's pregnancy, the call becomes even more memorable. The clock works against Steve and his partner as they scramble to deliver the baby before the canal fills with water. Not surprisingly, they manage to deliver the baby, extricate the woman, and save her life. Steve, however, adds a sardonic evaluation of the woman. Medics often comment on what they feel is irresponsible behavior on the part of their patients; in this case, the number of children a young woman already has becomes a topic for derisive commentary. Like many other medic patients, she is compared to an animal—in this case, she "lived to breed again."

Among the most alarming stories that medics tell about deliveries concern women who are unaware of their pregnancies:

Lars: It was on the Fourth of July like two years ago, we got a call for childbirth. And we got there and the firefighter is holding the baby in his arms, the girl's laying on the couch and there's blood everywhere, on the floor, coming out of the apartment, in the bathroom, and we're like, "What the fuck? What happened?" And the firefighter's like, "Well, she gave birth—in the toilet!"

And the story was that this fifteen-year-old girl said that she didn't know that she was pregnant. She just thought that she was gaining lots of weight. And that day her stomach hurt her all day long, and it felt like she had to go to the bathroom. And she went into the toilet, and she was pushing real hard, and she heard a splash and she looked down in the toilet. And there was a baby floating around in the toilet.

So this girl, rather than pulling the baby out of the toilet, ripped the cord, leaving the baby in the toilet, went traipsing out of the apartment to her neighbor's place and banged on the door, and said, "Oh, something's wrong." Well, she brings the neighbor back in, and the neighbor looks in the toilet bowl and there's a kid doing the backstroke or something. Pulls him out, calls 911. And so we get there, "Oh, great!" So this kid's been floating around in the toilet for a while.

So we rush him over to St. Rose hospital and they had a pediatrician who came in. So we're telling him the story and he's like, "Is this girl stupid and ignorant?" I mean, how do you go for nine months and not wonder, "Hmmm, what's up here?" I mean, how do the parents not wonder? But I was talking to a nurse at Children's, and she said, "Oh yeah, that happens all the time, we call them splashdowns."

Mark G: Sounds like a fucking ride at the water slide!

In the story, Lars uses the voice of the pediatrician to ask the question on everyone's mind, namely how a woman could not know that she is pregnant. The girl is old enough to know better, and no longer considered worthy of empathy. Instead, she is considered to be tragically uninformed.

Lars's story, as suggested by the nurse's "naming" of the call, is not a unique one. Other medics tell markedly similar stories:

Mary: I was working with Dawn and we had an OB call and this gal had delivered — it was probably a twelve-week gestational fetus — in the toilet. And she wouldn't open her legs and I asked if she was bleeding, and she told me she didn't know. So I said, "Well, stand up," you know, "let's see what's going on here, let's check you out." And she wouldn't open her legs, so finally I got her to stand up and the fetus was still attached to the umbilical cord, floating in the toilet. That was, like, really tough 'cause that little guy had been dead since day one probably. And we had to take him outside and he wasn't perfectly formed and things they just weren't right on him. But I mean that was really, that was tough. It was weird, it was different and I never want to have it happen again.

In this case, the baby dies, and Mary makes none of the sardonic comments found in Lars's story. While one could speculate that the women's stories of obstetrics calls reveal an attitude that is significantly different from those held by the men, it is not clear that this is the case. Women medics also express the sentiment that OB calls are messy and problematic. Neither do they always show empathy for the pregnant women, particularly in cases where they feel that the child's well-being is unnecessarily jeopardized. Perhaps Mary's narration is subdued because of the child's death — generally, when children die, the stories are far more restrained than usual.

Parental irresponsibility plays a major role in many of the stories about deliveries. Medics mention that if parents received proper prenatal care and were concerned about their children, last-minute calls for obstetrical emergencies would be rare. While they generally express disdain for those who allow their pregnancies to progress without consistent prenatal care and for those who ignore the developing fetus's well-being by continuing to abuse drugs or alcohol, they also criticize people who call for emergency transport when they are not at all close to delivery:

Tony: I was gonna tell you about Darryl. I wasn't working with Darryl, I was riding along with him and we responded to a call. And when we get there, it's a lady and she's pregnant. She's telling us that she's having some contractions, but really spread apart. She's not due for like another month and a half. And she's there with a guy, with her husband. And Darryl's like, "What's going on here?" And she tells him that she's having some contractions, she's seven and a half months pregnant, she wants to go to the hospital.

And Darryl's like, "Who's this fellow?" She goes, "That's my husband." He's like, "Do you have a car?" And he's like, "Yeah." He's like, "Well, why aren't you taking your own car?" The guy says, "Well, I don't got any gas." So Darryl reaches into his pocket, "Here's a dollar. Get yourself some gas." He goes, "Oh, well, I'm off to work, too." He's like, "Oh, yeah, how are you getting to work?" "My car." He said, "Well, your car doesn't have any gas. How are you going to take your car?" He's like, "Well, I don't work far." And he's like, "Well, the hospital is really close. If it's any closer than that, I'd walk to work!" And the guy's like, "Well, you know."

So Darryl says, "Dang, I can't believe this — this is your own wife, with your child! She's pregnant, and now in labor, and you won't take her to the hospital! You're a good husband." He says, "Let's go to the hospital." And then the guy wants to come along with us! [laughter] Darryl's like, "You — you're dreaming, right?" Shuts the door. We leave. He was an idiot. That was too funny. Darryl was gonna give that guy a dollar to get gas! [laughter] That was cool. I mean, you should take your own wife. She was in no distress. She was walking, waiting for us. She had like one contraction while we were en route to the hospital.

In this case, the lazy husband suffers Darryl's scornful wrath. The mother-to-be, in fact, is not the story's focal point; Tony's narration becomes a comment on the irresponsibility and lackadaisical attitude adopted by many patients toward an event that the medics value highly (as long as it does not happen in their ambulance).

Stories about obstetrics calls and deliveries are filled with ambivalence. On the one hand, medics admit to their feelings of awe when delivering children for the first time. Rather than dealing with people in life or death crises, or witnessing their patients die, they can feel the delivery of a child as a life-affirming event. However, numerous encounters with drug-abusing parents and pregnant children, as well as the medical complexities of dealing with sick neonatal patients and the mess a delivery entails, sour them on these calls. While presenting themselves as the only ones who can competently perform these duties, they suggest that their efforts are not worth the end result. These stories certainly challenge the media reports of paramedics joyously delivering babies in unexpected places.

No such feelings of ambivalence exist regarding calls for children in crisis. Paramedics unanimously express a willingness to take extraordinary measures when children's lives are in danger. Stories about these calls are devoid of the sardonic witticisms that characterize much of their other storytelling, since pediatric patients do not show the bad habits, attitudes, and "stupidity" that make other patients objects of scorn. Instead, the narrations are solemn performances—usually other medics sit silently and listen to the story, rather than interrupting with amusing rejoinders, stories of their own, or laughter. Instead of establishing significant distance between the medics and their patients, the stories do just the opposite, giving full weight to the tragedy of pediatric fatalities. Because of the innocence of the patients and the sadness of having a life cut short, these stories offer medics an opportunity to express emotions openly.

Medics often mention that, when treating pediatric patients, they are willing to perform procedures that they otherwise would not consider. Lisa narrates one such call:

Lisa: It was about a year ago. We had an unknown medical. I was working with Mark at the time. We arrived on scene, Fire was not on scene yet and we were first on scene. I was driving, so I pulled around to the side of the ambulance to pull out the cart and Mark was on the other side getting equipment out. All of a sudden, I see this woman running across the lawn, screaming,

"My baby! My baby!" So, I grabbed the baby and it wasn't breathing, I felt for a pulse, so I started CPR. And by this time, Mark had all the equipment out, and I just laid the baby on the gurney and right at that point Fire rolled on scene and they started helping. And we did all of the ACLS procedures and we took the baby to Children's.

But the next day, I was at home and I get a call from Tom R., he's our director of operations, and he wanted to know what had gone on on this call. Apparently, the woman called channel seven news and told them that she came up to the ambulance and was banging on the side of the door, and we refused to get out of the ambulance to help her. Even though I had gotten out and was doing CPR and mouth-to-mouth on her baby. She basically accused us of not trying to help her in what we did—and we did more than some people would do. But that was a horrible experience, being accused of something like that. Especially when I had—

Melinda: The only time that you had done mouth-to-mouth on somebody.

Lisa: Yeah. I would never ignore somebody when they were asking for help. And to be accused of something like that, it was pretty devastating at the time.

In this case, Lisa goes to extraordinary lengths to help the child; yet the mother accuses her of professional irresponsibility (it is perhaps the mother's misperception of what constitutes proper response that provokes her complaint). The media representation of paramedics creeps into the story as well. In their commentary, Lisa and Melinda both criticize the mother for her lack of appreciation of Lisa's efforts. Protocols governing the extent of paramedics' intervention for pediatric patients limit the steps that they might otherwise take. In Lisa's story, despite her willingness to perform a procedure—mouth-to-mouth resuscitation—that lies in a murky area of medical interventions, she still stands accused of not taking the proper steps.

Medics express frustration over pediatric calls that, due to their medical complexity, afford them little chance of success. This frustration contributes to their general uneasiness about pediatric calls. They are annoyed by frantic parents who overstate the severity of a child's condition, but they are equally irritated by review boards that question their medical abilities when, despite their best efforts, the child dies.

Lars voices both of these concerns while sitting in the ambulance zone at Highland Hospital one blustery summer evening:

Lars: A lot of parents, there's something called NMS—new mother syndrome—and their first baby. You see, babies can't really control their breathing or swallowing. They have trouble synchronizing the two. So they're feeding them and they start to gag and gurgle and cough and it looks kind of like they're choking. If I were a new parent, I'd be all nervous, too! But the kid starts to gag and cough and mom freaks out and calls 911! I don't mind that. I tell parents, you know, "I'd rather have you call me a thousand times and have it turn out to be nothing rather than not call 911 one time when the kid turns out to be choking."

The only kid I ever had who was really choking, it didn't come in as a choking, it came in as a seizure. And the fire department thought it was a seizure, until they got there and realized, "Oh, my God, the kid's not breathing!" They're trying to bag air into him and it's not going in and we managed to find out that the kid was choking. What happened with it? The kid didn't live.

That was probably the worst call I've ever done. Nothing we did worked. We couldn't get what he was choking on out, and it just turned into a disaster. And it came back to haunt my partner and me, it came back to haunt us. A year after we're still hearing about it from the company. I mean, as far as I'm concerned, we did everything we could to get the thing out. It took two doctors working together twenty or thirty seconds to get it out. And they had good lighting and their suction was powerful and it worked. Our suction didn't work so hot. It was just a disaster.

Here Lars deflects his frustration away from himself and toward the usual suspect, namely the firefighters. He also offers a stinging critique of the equipment supplied by the company. How, he asks, if it takes highly trained doctors thirty seconds to remove the obstruction in a controlled setting with functional equipment, could he possibly be expected to achieve the same results with malfunctioning equipment, improper information, and a difficult environment? Lars evaluates the call as a disaster, and refers to its haunting nature—no doubt it continues to bother him emotionally, and the company review board's constant reexamination of the call prevents his forgetting it.

In other situations, the paramedics simply become witness to tragic accidents involving children:

Steve Y.: We got a call for an auto-ped. This would probably be the most heart-breaking story we've ever come across. It was an auto-ped and we're coming into the scene in this little court and we see the fire department kind of scrambling around. We just know something is really wrong — you have that sinking feeling — and we get there and find a three-year-old, or what was it, a two-year-old?

Stephanie: I think it was three.

Steve: Two and a half, three. Anyway, sprawled out on the lawn, looking pretty lifeless with a lot of deformity to him.

Stephanie: I remember green, green grass. It was really a manicured area — a little area of grass — and this death white child laying on the grass.

Steve: Yeah, he had a real weak pulse in his neck and he wasn't breathing. So the fire department, we get them going on bagging the kid and get a good airway for him and start checking him out and then his heart stopped. And he just had multiple trauma to his head, his chest. So we put a tube in him and intubated him, started CPR and going to the hospital, we had these IO lines going. So we get there to the hospital. Anyway, what had happened, apparently a lady was baby-sitting this kid, she'd taken her eyes off the kid and he'd gone next door.

Stephanie: He was on the tiniest little horse with wheels, it must of been about half a foot tall, it was the tiniest little thing you'd seen. I guess he was sitting on it though, so he was sitting on it and then a car, her car —

Steve: No, the neighbor's car.

Stephanie: The neighbor's, she didn't see him and she backed out of the driveway over him. Stopped, didn't know what had happened, and pulled forward over him again I think.

Steve: Yeah, ran over him twice.

Stephanie: When I was setting up the rig and everything, as I came around to go inside, there was an old lady and she had a bucket of soapy water and a broom, and she was just kind of methodically cleaning the blood off the sidewalk, saying, "This is gonna really upset the kids to see this. This is really gonna upset the kids to see this." And of course I have three hundred things to do so I didn't think to say, "You know, you need to stop, the cops aren't here yet." But we finally stopped her from doing it. We worked really hard to get him back.

Steve: Yeah, we got a pulse back for a little while and then he died and it was just—

Stephanie: It was tragic.

Steve: Yeah, basically there were like six people's lives totally ruined out of that whole thing. You had the kid who died, the baby-sitter who's responsible for this kid, the baby-sitter's husband who was totally devastated, the lady who crushed the kid and the mother and father of the child, totally ruined for life. And that was probably the single most tragic thing we've ever witnessed unfold.

Stephanie: The thing that touched me more was the medical code where we had that eighteen-year-old guy.

Steve: I wasn't on that.

Stephanie: That one upset me a lot more. It was just terrible, it still kind of haunts me, I had nightmares about it for a while. It was a late-night call for shortness of breath and we get there, and there's a family and they're pretty hysterical. We go down the hall and their teenage son is face down on the carpet in the bathroom with a history of asthma and he was purple. I mean, his respiratory was eight and it wasn't moving any air at all. And he was brady-cardic and he was cold and unresponsive and there just wasn't that much we could do for him. We intubated him and we gave him epi and alupent and the whole works and rushed to the hospital and by the time we got to the hospital he'd coded.

Steve: [radio traffic] Oh, shit, 10-4.

Stephanie: Where? Back to our call?

Steve: Back to our call, for abdominal pain.

Stephanie: Come on. You know, he was seventeen or eighteen years old and there wasn't that much we could do for him. It just really upset me and the family was all in denial and he had a bunch of brothers and sisters who were around and watching us work him up in the kitchen. So they worked re-ally hard in the emergency room and got his heart started again but he had dilated unresponsive pupils, and he died in intensive care about ten days later. It was just really terrible. It was just terrible that we couldn't do more for him. That's all. Now we have to go back to that place.

Steve and Stephanie express remorse at not being able to "do more" for their patients. The general attitude among medics, despite what might come across as heartlessness in many of their stories, is a willingness to do whatever it takes to save a patient. In both of the cases above, they simply cannot reverse overwhelming circumstances. Steve and Stephanie also draw attention to the emotional distress wrought by the untimely deaths of the children. The importance of family and the impact of death on families are recurring themes in many of these stories. Family members undoubtedly feel the emotional impact of the deaths the hardest; by incorporating these people into their narratives, Steve and Stephanie allow them to stand as surrogates for their own emotional distress.

Violent crimes involving children also figure prominently in paramedic storytelling. Bill V. and George discuss one such call, and express relief that they did not have to respond:

Bill V.: I've never missed a call.

Tim: I'll bet you've wished you missed some calls.

Bill: Oh, absolutely! [laughter] Abso-fucking-lutely! There's a lot of calls I wished I missed. Like those kids got their throats slashed a couple of weeks ago? We were driving by that apartment when it went down. I mean, I'm sure we were driving by that apartment complex when someone dialed 911. Someone was modified to Tennyson, and we were dragging our feet leaving Tennyson, and then they gave us a post on Southbound 880 in Livermore or something. We were just getting on the freeway when it came down — child full arrest. I'm going, "Fuck! Glad I missed that!" By the time we got to post, the unit on scene is asking for two more units. Oooh. And a supervisor. Man, I'm glad I missed that one.

George: Yeah, that was MacGregor's call.

Bill: Yeah, I wouldn't want to be on that one at all!

George: Yeah, I could do without that call.

Because of the emotional nature of calls involving children, incidents that would normally be considered "cool calls"—shootings, stabbings, and trauma—are gladly passed up.

Lisa tells one of the most shocking stories of responding to a call, only to discover that one of the victims is a small child:

Lisa: Tragic, and sad. I was working with Mark—I know the exact date. It was May 21, 1992, at 4521 Gilbert St. in Oakland. [laughter] But we arrived on scene—I don't remember what we were dispatched for—but we came on scene and the firefighters were in front of us, and I was walking behind the firefighters. All of a sudden one of the firefighters came running back, and he just kept saying "There's blood everywhere, there's blood everywhere." Well, what had happened was, a man was stabbing a woman and when the firefighter rounded the corner, he turned onto the firefighter. And that's why the firefighter retreated and we just basically all went out.

Well, PD had arrived at that time and they went in, caught him stabbing this woman. They told him to stop, he didn't stop. So they shot him three times in the chest. And he turned around and nearly decapitated himself. Well, we were finally cleared to go in, and when we went in, we found a man. And he was kind of slumped against the wall and nearly decapitated. And then the woman was laying next to him and she was stabbed several times. And I just remember thinking that this doesn't seem real, this seems like something out of a horror movie. It just seemed so grisly.

But we started working on the woman, and Mark went to go get more equipment and to call for other units, when one of the neighbors came up and started screaming, "Where's the baby? Where's the baby?" And everybody just stopped. Because we couldn't imagine that there was a baby involved in all this. Well, one of the firefighters ran into the house and started screaming that the baby was stabbed. So I yelled back to her, "Well, is he breathing?" and she said, "No." And I asked her if she had a pulse and she said, "Yes, he still has a pulse." So, I said, "Bring the baby out here." So, she brought the baby out and he was a three-year-old little boy. And he was stabbed left chest and it almost looked like his chest was flayed off.

So we started working on the boy. I had him intubated and pretty much packaged when the other unit came on and they just took him. Then another unit had come on at that time and they took the man. And then we took the woman. But that was the worst call I've ever been on. Because it was so grisly and because there was a baby involved and just 'cause it was so violent. That was what got me, just the violence of it all.

We found out later that they were boyfriend and girlfriend and they had broken up or something and she had actually moved out. And he kept constantly coming over to the apartment and trying to bug her. And that day, he had come over and he knocked on the door, and was screaming at her. And she opened the door and, at that point, he grabbed her and pushed her out into the hall and locked her out of the apartment while he went in. That was his son, that he killed. And he went in and killed his son. At that point, she ran next door to call for help from the neighbor and then when she came back, he came out after her. And that was pretty much when we came on scene. But that was sad. Nicholas, that was his name.

As others do in medic stories, Lisa draws a connection between the violence of the scene and horror movies. Although laughing at the start of the narration, amused with her remarkable recall of the "exact date" and the precise street address, she quickly becomes somber.[3] Melinda, who has heard the story before, remains silent, so that Lisa is uninterrupted; unlike some of her other stories, this one is related in the past tense despite frequent appeals to direct speech at dramatic moments. Thus, she keeps the events at a narrative remove. Unable to explain the viciousness of the attack, Lisa recounts what she "found out later" as a summary, adding the evaluative coda "it was sad." By this point in her narration, her eyes were filled with tears, and Melinda stared resolutely out the window; what had begun as a good-natured narration of a memorable call had become an exploration of the emotions produced by a vicious attack on a child and his mother. It was the closest to tears I had seen medics during my fieldwork. However, moments after the narration, they received a call, and Lisa dissipated the emotionally oppressive force of her story with a laugh—"Oops, we got a call."

Certainly stories about pediatric traumas and fatalities are not completely devoid of the medics' typical humor. Firefighters, nurses, doctors, and other first responders are frequently ridiculed, and medics show no compassion for adults who endanger children. Accordingly, narratives about pediatric calls can be filled with sarcastic evaluations of adults' dangerous behaviors, just as long as no children have been seriously hurt. Lars tells perhaps the most amusing of these stories, concerning an event that he refers to as the *Pediatric Apocalypse Now*. None of the children is seriously injured and, thus, his humor does not seem misplaced:

Lars: We got a call up in Robert's Park for "possible multiple children with heat exhaustion." And we pull into the park, there's like five fire trucks — there's three from East Bay Regional Parks and a couple from Oakland — and there must be about three hundred kids all spread out all over the parking lot and all over this field. There's like all the parents all running around, all kinds of people with walkie-talkies and stethoscopes and stuff.

And we get out of the ambulance — we're the first ambulance there — and suddenly everybody hones in on us! And they're like, "Oh, you've got to come over here! Oh, it's terrible." So they pull Mark over and they've got all these poor kids who are hyperventilating, all hot and tired, and they've got one pediatrician there and a bunch of firefighters and some rangers. There are some other people who pull me over to a station wagon and they're like, "Oh, you've got to check out these kids!" And the kids are fine, you know? Then this one ranger is like, "You've got to come over here!" "No, you've got to go over there!" "You've got to come over here!" "Across the parking lot there are two children, they're very critical."

So I go across the parking lot, meanwhile Mark here, he's on the other end of the parking lot with this other group of kids. And I get there and there's another pediatrician with these two kids there. And I start trying to find out what's going on and the kids are hyperventilating and this pediatrician is like, "You know this girl, she's very tachycardic, and her pulse is 120, she needs an IV." "Okay, what's wrong with her?" "She's been out in the sun too long." And I'm like, "Well, is she dizzy, is she A/O times 4, is she alert?" And the pediatrician's like, "I don't understand your terminology!" Like, "Is she conscious, is she talking?" "Oh yeah, she needs an IV." "Well, what is it? Heat exhaustion? Heat stroke?" This doctor, she's like, "Uh, I don't know." And I'm like, "Well, we'll take her to Children's."

By this time somebody else has called for other ambulances and finally we're like, "Yeah, keep the other ambulances coming." [laughter] Finally one of our supervisors shows up, and I'm like, "Great!" 'Cause now everybody was coming up to me and saying we've got this and we've got that and I just said, "Oh, go to talk to the supervisor. Go talk to him." And so I sent everybody over to him. [laughter] Then I said, "We've got two kids, we're going to take them to Children's." And he was like, "Fine!" So we were happy, all "Bye!" and then we took off.

It turns out that what it is, is that it's a choir thing. They got choirs from all over the country, all over the world—they've got like four hundred kids—and the big culmination of this is that they're going to film public service announcements like, "Be nice to your kids," or something. And they march four hundred kids in the blazing sun to this park here. And that was the extent of it. They flew over these kids with a helicopter and filmed them walking up and down hills in the blazing sun, sort of like the childhood version of *Apocalypse Now.*

In his story, Lars draws attention to the ill-advised ideas and poor planning that end in the mass casualty. He makes slighting reference to the doctor on scene and takes delight in manipulating the situation so that his supervisor is forced into the unpleasant position of calming hysterical parents and treating dehydrated children. The irony of the story lies, of course, in the intention of the event—the filming of a public service announcement about children. At the end of his story, Lars cannot resist the temptation to refer to a film, Francis Ford Coppola's chaotic vision of the Vietnam war.

Stories about calls involving children best reveal the ambivalence that many medics feel toward their work and their patients. While delivering babies is presented in an idyllic light by the popular media, most medics have a far more cynical view of these calls. For them, the calls are messy affairs that force them to do more paperwork. The women who do not make it to the hospital in time to deliver are generally those who have not received adequate prenatal care and, in extreme cases, are drug abusers. Teenage pregnancy figures prominently in many of these stories; medics who tell of young women giving birth much to their own surprise make an implicit commentary on both the failings of sex education and the breakdown of the family. Parents of these teens emerge as unconcerned, so distanced from their children that they do not even recognize a pregnancy.

While stories about obstetrics calls suggest a surprisingly cynical attitude on the part of the medics, other calls involving children reveal the depths of empathy and compassion they feel for their patients. (Although the medics may have these feelings for patients in other situations, the callous jocularity found in their stories helps them build an emotional barrier against the sometimes horrific scenes they witness.) In cases involving children, the barriers come down, with the stories openly expressing the emotional toll inflicted by emergencies involving fatalities. Since children are nearly unanimously presented as innocent victims unable to fend for themselves, medics who reveal emotion in relation to these calls do not become the target of their coworkers' derision. The stories about calls involving children are unique in that they are solemn performances. While a medic's usual self-presentation is that of a person able to handle even the most horrible events with a sardonic smile, in these stories it is one of a compassionate person doing a job based on the inviolate importance of life.

# 7

# WHAT'S THE GROSSEST THING YOU'VE EVER SEEN?

Lars leans forward, mumbles something into the radio, readjusts his chair, sits back, and smiles:

Lars: The other night, at some scene, I was standing there — my partner was in back with the patient — and this cop and I were talking. I don't know what we were talking about, but he reaches into his uniform and he pulls out this Polaroid picture which he shows to me. And I look at it, I'm like, "Blah! What the hell is that?" And he's like, "Oh, this is what I went to last night."

It was a picture of this woman laying on the floor and this was like early October. And I figure she had died sometime in late September. So it had been like almost two weeks since she died. And they don't know if she was murdered or committed suicide or what, but they found her in her apartment, and she's laying there dead.

And she had a cat. And apparently the cat had gotten hungry. And had started eating, chewing on her face — it had eaten her eyes, her eyeballs, her nose, her lips. There were these sockets and there was no nose and you could see all the teeth, sort of like that skeletal grin, you know? And all the flesh around the edges was sort of rotted, it was kind of blackened. And the cop was saying that all around this woman were these little bloody paw prints.

It was really, really disgusting. He said he had a rookie partner who almost puked. And he'd gotten this Polaroid. I mean, he was just like zipping it out and showing it to people. I was like, "Blah, God, what is that?" [laughter] He said they rolled her on her side to check her back out and all kinds of stuff just—blah!—splurged out of her eye sockets! Really disgusting! The picture was disgusting. I can only imagine how gross the actuality was.

Lars's story, by his own admission, is filled with horrific images. He is not himself one of the responders to the scene, and his impressions of the call are all derived from a photograph. Thus, his story offers an interesting view of the vicarious nature of medic storytelling. In many medic stories, surprising things suddenly emerge in the narration, and, in this case, Lars himself is confronted by the abrupt appearance of an appalling scene. The shock of seeing an especially ghastly picture, coming from an unexpected quarter, constitutes the visual punch line of the story. The police officer then becomes the primary narrative voice, and characteristically relates how his "rookie" partner was unable to handle the call. Lars, like his audience, can only "imagine" the gruesomeness of the actual scene.

There is a fascination with horror in American culture. Mutilation and violent death occur frequently in popular cinema. In a standard film image, yellow police tape flaps in the wind, as the flashing lights of police cars and ambulances play off the brick facade of an apartment building. Blood pools at the feet of the detectives who huddle around a radio car and discuss the crime, while, in the background, paramedics load a dismembered body onto a gurney and drive away into the rain-swept night. (Actually, paramedics do not transport corpses, but representations such as this feed the pervasive belief that paramedics have "seen it all.") However, "righteous, gnarly, mashed-up-brain calls," as one medic refers to them, constitute only a small fraction of most medics' storytelling. When medics do discuss the sometimes disturbing condition of their patients, making light of anatomical incongruities, they are generally doing so for purposes other than to provoke disgust in the listener. But nonparamedic audiences want to hear stories that make them recoil in horror.

Medics find themselves in an odd position when confronted with nonmedic audiences who want to hear stories about traumatic injuries and horrific death. While telling stories allows medics a chance to present their profession to the public, they are aware that the audience's expectations may not be realistic:

Darryl: Or how about this. The three questions most asked in the ten years that I've been a paramedic and stuff, and the number one would be — my favorite — is, "What is the grossest thing you've ever seen?" I mean, everybody always asks that. So I just say, "Your face!" I have no idea. I lie, you know? I mean, what is gross to you? I don't know. That's what people ask. "What's the grossest thing you've ever seen?" I'm glad I have some pictures, though, that I can show people and everything, that they go, "Ugh!" You know? [laughter] "That's gross!"

Darryl's reaction to the question is, in fact, common among medics. By answering as he does, he is able to criticize the voyeuristic tendencies of the nonmedic, while also suggesting that he has seen and can handle scenes that would disgust most, a claim substantiated by his book of photographs. Indeed, Darryl even carries a small camera with him to document his calls:

Darryl: Yeah, I have a 35mm that I carry with me at all times. It's got auto-focus, and a flash and stuff and everything. And every time we have bad wrecks and I'm not really doing anything and, you know, everything's basically under control, I go ahead and take pictures of what's going on.

This is the home of gallows humor, I think, probably, you know? You are truly a warped individual sometimes, and my mom thoroughly thinks she raised a completely warped person, I think, when I tell her stories or show her pictures that she'd rather not see.

We have this one picture where this chick had hung herself in a closet and she's like, errr. And she'd been there probably for a day, and she was stiff—

she was dead, dead, dead! And we took a picture of her hanging there with like me with my arm around my prom date [mimics action]. And I think that that's generally warped but I think you develop that as a mechanism to deal with all this craziness that you see. You know, you see all kinds of stupidity. Humanity at its worst and at its best sometimes. That's probably the best part about our job.

It is intriguing that Darryl feels compelled, as many other medics do, to keep a "scrapbook" documenting memorable scenes of human suffering.[1]

The public fascination with stories about violent and traumatic death is related to the phenomenon of people slowing down to catch a glimpse of an accident on the highway. While the images will undoubtedly be disturbing, it is hard to look away. Similarly, in a movie theater, members of the audience peer out between their fingers at the horrors playing out on the screen, not wanting to look, but at the same time not wanting *not* to look. The window of a car can act as a screen, making it hard to believe that the scene outside is real. The same analysis can be applied to police tape at accident scenes, the police line forming an inviolate boundary between the spectators and the spectacle. Thus, through their stories, paramedics can act as intermediaries, allowing others to observe vicariously the carnage of an accident scene.

In medic stories, horrific scenes are usually situated in the distant past or at great physical remove, which underscores the extraordinary nature of many of these calls. Bill V. tells an involved story from his days in the air force, a common setting for many of his more startling stories:

Bill V.: I was in the air force in 1980 when Mt. St. Helens blew. My pararescue team was there from Southern California supplementing the rescue team up in Portland. We were there four hours after it blew. For the first seven days, we were flying rescue, pulling people out of Mt. St. Helens. Then we had a day off and we were just hanging out. And our boss asked us if any of us wanted to go fly with the army, go pull bodies out of the area.

So this is what we were doing during Mt. St. Helens: we were flying in — we got tips from family members who had family in the area who were either fishing or loggers or something like that — we'd go in where the family was supposed to be and look for survivors. So we'd hoist out the helicopter, go down and check a building or check a car, or a tractor coming from the logging camps. And if there were bodies there, we would mark it with a yellow streamer — a twenty-five-foot yellow streamer — and the army was coming in behind us. If they saw a yellow streamer, they'd mark it on a map and come in and pick up the bodies.

Well, our tenth day there, we're bored, so we ask the boss, "Hey, can we go fly with the army and pick up bodies?" "Yeah, sure!" So my team leader and I, we go fly with the army. You ever see in *Life* magazine back then there was this picture from Mt. St. Helens of this hand sticking out of the ash? You ever see that one? Well, anyway, we picked up that guy and his buddy. It was Hand Man and Running Man. That's what we named these guys. Hand Man was this guy who was buried in this ash and all that was above this ash was his hand.

George: He almost made it out.

Bill: Yeah. So we're digging him up and we got down to his head and shoulders and it's like — he's been cooking for ten days in this hot ash — so he's like, you know, pot roast! [laughter] He was like — sloop, sloop — you know? And then there was Running Man. He was his buddy. And he was like in a dead run and this big old tree Wile E. Coyoted him. Just went — bam! — you know? He was in the run position with this big old tree on top of him. We had to chainsaw this tree and roll the log off him.

Well, we get these bodies loaded up into body bags and put on the helicopter and I'm on the helicopter, and I'm like, "C'mon, Fred!" That's my team leader, Fred Scantly, and I'm like, "C'mon, Fred!" And he's coming, and he's walking, and he's doing this, you know? Like he's got a chain on his finger and he's like whistling, he's walking over to the helicopter. Thing's spinning around his finger and back around his finger. And it's like, "Hey, what's Fred got?" You know — na-na-na na-na — he's walking and he gets closer. And he gets up close to the pilot, and he's like, "Whaddaya got, Fred?" And Fred goes, "This!" And it's this fucker's eyeball on the optic nerve! [laughter] And he's — zzzzzzzip — spinning it around on his finger, and our pilot was like, "Whoa!"

He just lost it, man! Throws up all down the front of his uniform! [laughter] It was funny. It was funny as hell, man! I was dying and Fred is just like whistling. Running Man's eyeball. Ugh! Wait, I think that was Hand Man's eyeball, 'cause Running Man was pretty intact.

George: God, that's sick! [laughter]

Bill's narrative success in large part centers on his ability to draw comparisons between the extraordinary and the common. The first man is likened to a pot roast, while the second man's optic nerve is compared to a chain. The nicknames for the victims are also comical, and Bill compares the entire scene to a cartoon, bringing to mind the viciously funny scenes in which anvils and other heavy objects land on the Wile E. Coyote character in the *Roadrunner* cartoons. The narrative punch line, the startling realization that the chain is in fact an eyeball on the optic nerve, catches the audience—and the pilot— off guard. The story is undoubtedly intended to shock, and George's evaluative comment is the expected reaction.

Smell is one of the characteristics that medics time and again mention in these "disgusting call" stories. Their vocabulary for describing smells tends to involve food, and they frequently make comparisons between odors emanating from bodies and vaguely similar smells associated with eating. Perhaps because the calls are so unappetizing, the medics like to draw attention to their ability to "stomach" even the worst ones. In Lars's opening story, a rookie police officer nearly gets sick, and, in Bill's story about Hand Man and Running Man, the army pilot throws up.

Surprisingly, stories that medics consider "disgusting" generally do not include trauma. Derek says, "Blood, blood, you just work past that. The only thing that bothers me with patients is vomit, you know? When they start puking, it's like I'll be right next to them, throwing up in the ambulance!" While stories about blood and trauma are the ones that most nonmedics expect to hear when they ask "What's the grossest thing you've ever seen?," the scenes that medics find particularly disgusting, and which can make even the most self-assured vomit, involve decaying patients who smell bad. The patients in these stories are old, indigent, or sick, or have not received proper medical attention over a long period of time, and sometimes their bodies have been infested by insects. As such, they represent the most extreme cases of many of the common problems medics face in their work. While sitting at post in a quiet park, Mark and Lars exchange a series of stories about such calls:

Mark G.: I always tell this to people. I picked up this guy one time in a park. He was sitting on a bench. So this guy was sitting on this bench, the lady across the street called, and I was kind of upset at her for calling, because this guy was just sitting on this bench, he wasn't doing anything wrong.

So I went over to him and asked him, "What's the problem here?" And he says, "Nothing, I feel fine, everything's cool, I don't need any help." And he seemed like he was together, he seemed to know where he was and what day it was. He was about fifty years old. So I started looking at him and I looked down at his feet, and he didn't have any socks on. And he had these black plastic leather shoes on — you know, those fake leather shoes? And I looked down at his feet and I see maggots crawling out of his shoes.

So I get him in the back of the ambulance and I take off his shoes, and his feet were infested with maggots. His toes — he had about three toes that had rotted off — and apparently what he'd do, instead of pulling down his pants to go to the bathroom, he'd just go right in his pants, and the urine had drained down into his shoes. And he'd been sittin' on this bench for about three days, with no food or water or anything. The people across the street had been feeding him. The flies, man, they just infested him, and his skin was just sloughing off. I never did find out if he made it out of the hospital.

Lars: This guy in Hayward had been laying on the ground, he was in a wheelchair, and he fell over. And he was just laying there for like two days, and he was just laying there. And there was that ammonia smell, you know? And the urine and the edema on the side of the face, you know, like they start getting bedsores on the side of their face, and stuff? This guy didn't have any maggots. But he had ants. He had ants just crawling all over him! It was great. [laughter] As a matter of fact, we had ants in the unit for the rest of the day. And it smelled great! He was like covered with feces. And the cops were great, too. They all walked in and said, "We'll be outside."

Mark's initial annoyance at a suspected abuse of the 911 system turns to horror when he discovers the condition of the man's feet. In Lars's story, the police react in expected fashion—only the medics are able to handle the scene. Even after the patient leaves the ambulance, there is a reminder of his hideous condition. Most medics consider the back of the ambulance appallingly dirty, a suspicion confirmed by stickers warning that the area is legally considered biohazardous. Thus, the remaining ants can be read as a clear representation of the microorganisms left in the ambulance after the transport of an ill patient.

In other stories, the patient suffers not only from insect infestation, but also from untreated, complicated trauma:

Lisa: This one call, fuck, this must have happened at least two years ago. But we came on scene and right when we came on scene, the firefighters were leaving the house and throwing up outside. And we walked inside and there was like feces everywhere in different stages of decay. And there was a man sitting in a wheelchair. He said that his mother had fallen. But his mother was lying on just this box spring mattress in the middle of the floor. No sheets, nothing, just lying in feces and urine. And she had a bilateral femur fracture. And her skin was just rotting, basically. And there was this trail of ants leading up to her legs and carrying pieces of her flesh away.

This man who was in this wheelchair was her son, and he's supposedly an invalid and can't take care of her. And he says that she just so happened to fall. But it's obvious that she had been like that for a long time. She was completely emaciated and malnourished and just not doing well at all. Well, we ended up trauma activating her and taking her to Highland, where she died, three days later. But just the most disgusting part of this whole call is that they were talking to neighbors, and the neighbors said that they have seen him walking around and that he's not an invalid. And that he's the one that did that to his own mother. That's disgusting.

Melinda: So she had been lying there for a long time with a femur fracture?
Lisa: With two femur fractures. And he did it. To his own mother.
Melinda: Crazy people out there.

The mother suffers at the hands of her son, a shocking breakdown in family integrity which ultimately leads to her death. For the medics, the horror resides not only in the physical scene itself but also in what it represents. All of the crime and violence of the inner city seems to be represented here, along with the breakdown of the family, the neglect of the elderly poor, complicated trauma, and infection so extreme it is best represented by swarms of ants eating the victim's flesh.

Paramedics ascribe a great deal of the blame for the startling condition of these patients to neglect at the hands of other family members.[2] Just as the medic stories describing obstetric and other pediatric emergencies emphasize the need for family cohesion and responsible parenting, these stories strongly endorse the position that children are responsible for their elderly parents. With an elderly patient in the back of the rig suffering from malnutrition and a host of other ailments, Stephanie tells a story of horrific neglect:

Stephanie: Yeah, I guess this is about the third or fourth time that I've seen this kind of thing where there's an old person at home not being taken care of very well. Mostly I see neglect more than any kind of abuse. One woman—the caretaker—was adamantly saying that she gives her a bath every day and she takes real good care of her, and she's just eaten, and that she always cooks for her and all this stuff. Just really adamant about it. But the woman had roaches crawling in her bed, on her, there were roaches everywhere! We had to climb over things to get around to where her bed was, and she had maggots on her sores and stuff like that. Totally incontinent and she'd been laying like that for god knows how long. It was just scary.

And then you meet the people that live alone—in their eighties and nineties, reaching a hundred—and they have two or three dogs and lots of cats. And one lady we went on, the house was beautifully taken care of on the outside. The lawn, she must have had a gardener, took beautiful care of the house on the outside. On the inside, though, there must have been a foot and a half or two feet of garbage. Newspapers and dog shit and all that kind of stuff piled all along the stairs, everywhere. All the way up to the ceiling and every place that you could imagine. Just piles and piles and piles and piles of junk mail and newspapers and food and all sorts of stuff like that. And what the problem was, about five years ago, she just couldn't bend down anymore. So she'd drop something and she couldn't even pick it up because she had a bad back or something. [laughter] I thought that was kind of interesting.

We went on a call. Or we heard about this call. This guy had fallen and he couldn't get up. The medics got there and he was up saying he was okay and everything. But there was this stench coming out of the house where him and his wife lived. Just decrepit old, old, old, old people. And so there was this stench and the medics went inside and they had like two or three dogs, but there was a big German shepherd dead on the living room floor, rotting. We don't know how long he'd been dead. But he was there, rotting in the middle of the living room floor. [laughter] Kind of interesting. But you know, to a certain extent you need to respect these people's independence. Yeah, we turn them in, and then they go through the care system and they lose their independence. So if we just got these people some help in their house, I think that would probably be the best thing for them. 'Cause for the most part, the ones that I've met were pretty able minded like this woman we just ran was. She was just really old.

Steve Y.: It's time to run that one from the front lawn. "Hey, are you okay in there?" "Yep, I'm fine!" "Okay! See you later! We'll come back when your house is disinfected!"

While Stephanie turns the stories more towards a commentary on the lack of consistent care from which many elderly people suffer, Steve brings the story back into the realm of humorous commentary on the disgusting elements of the call. In his scenario, the house is so filthy that even the medics are hesitant to enter, preferring to run the call from the lawn.

Tony and Patrick provide the best example of a series of stories clearly intended to disgust. Interestingly, they begin to tell these stories on a ride to a local "roach coach," a lunch truck, and continue to tell them while waiting in line for service:

Patrick: We got this call, it was a guy who was 10-5-5 in his apartment. And this guy had been dead, this guy had been dead probably at least—at least—seven days! He lived by himself, he had cancer and he was fairly young, he was like in his forties. And the neighbors called, they smelled like a rotting garbage smell. And we got up there, and the homeboy was dead in his room. He was really dead.

Tony: That's not the stink call though. This stink call was, we went to an apartment in Hayward, and there was a really nice apartment, but it stunk. And Uncle Mark [laughter] was on the couch, on a sleeping bag, and it looked like he peed on the sleeping bag. But it wasn't pee, it was pus that secreted from an abscess.

Patrick: He had an abscess on his butt.

Tony: An abscess that developed on his butt. And in like two days, they said it was huge, like a softball. And then it blew! Hoooo!

Patrick: It smelled like dead tissue. Like, have you ever smelled a dog that got hit on the train tracks, or something, you walked over it when you were a kid?

Tony: We're talking nasty! Really, really, really stinky.

Patrick: Rotting flesh. That's what the smell was, it was just rot.

Tony: Rotting flesh, it was just dripping pus.

Patrick: When I walked in, I had to turn around and walk out, 'cause the smell was just awful. It was terrible. I skedaddled out of there.

Tony: The nephew of Uncle Mark was vomiting. He had to leave, because he started vomiting, he started gagging on this smell.

Patrick: He was like, "Uncle Mark, I love you but you smell bad!"

Tony: "Dang, man, you smell!" he kept telling his uncle. Poor Uncle Mark! That was the stinkiest call I've ever rode on. [laughter] That one and the good GI [gastrointestinal] bleeders, those ones are really stinky. But, you know, that cyst one was really nasty. I've never seen a cyst that bad in my life before. Oh, and the other call, the woman at the apartment complex! This lady had ants coming in and out her eye and ear, all her orifices — nose, mouth — just roaming around. She was dead for days. That was really gross, having ants and stuff.

There was another one, for a young girl. Were you with me? Oh, that was Jason. We went to Hampton, there was a very young girl who was a marathon runner. And she was a Christian Scientist, and she didn't want anything to do with doctors, or with medication. She developed a cyst on her chest. And we got the call because of a possible dead body. And it was definitely a dead body. It smelled! It was really bad. And we walked in, I noticed she was young and still very fit. But on her chest, she just had a big black necrotic, open-tissue sore. Nasty thing. She died of infection. Just 'cause she wouldn't go to the hospital to get that taken care of. And she died and she was like thirty-five years old and a marathon runner. She'd run four marathons before this last year. That was very sad. So, yeah, it was on top of her breasts there. That was sick. Flies must have sat in that, I think, while she was alive. [laughter]

There was another one, she wasn't dead. No, she wasn't dead, she was a 5150 call. This lady living in a house right here in Oakland by herself. Her children called from wherever they lived and said, "Mom, are you okay? You sound strange." And she says, "No, I'm fine, I'm fine, I'm fine." And they just heard something weird in her voice, and they hadn't seen her in like two months. So they went to the house, they walked in and they found the house was a mess. Garbage all lined up against all her walls, like she didn't take it out. There was a dead dog in the middle of the living room. And then they walked into her room, which was pretty immaculate. Her bed was made, everything was in its place, it was very clean, except for the walls and the floor—it looked like they were moving. And we got a good look at it, and what it was, it was just all fleas. Her house was infested with fleas. The walls, the floor, it just jumped. And we told her that her dog was dead, she says, "No way! I heard him barking this morning, and I feed him all the time." And the house had dog shit all over the place. Just piles of dog crap.

There was another call in Richmond that I ran, that had dogs that lived in the house and there was dog shit all over the place. The house was a mess, it had newspapers piled chest high, dog cans, everything was in the house. The kitchen table was stacked with garbage! Just like little coves made out where they sat and ate. Above the table was one of those bug lamps? So it illuminates light, but at the same time you hear, "bzzzt! bzzzt!" [laughter] It was zapping bugs at the same time.

Patrick: A little bug zapper?

Tony: Yeah, that was really gross. And she thought nothing was wrong. We ended up having to 5150 her. I don't know how we got the call, but we went there Code 2. And we got the 5150 out of her. She was too much. That was a nasty house, that was a really stinky house. And the bug zapper was too much.

Patrick: Just about from the first time I ever smelled a dead body to this day, it just makes me ill. There's some people who can get used to that thing. It's like the smell really doesn't bother them that much, but not me!

Tony: The burning flesh smell is the other really stinky one.

Patrick: Mine is the necrotic tissue smell.

Tony: Necrotic dead?

Patrick: Yeah, the gangrenous stuff like that. Oh, man, I cannot handle that smell at all. That thing gets my gag reflex every time. And it's like I interrupt our call and walk out of the room.

Tony: That burning hair, flesh smell is really nasty.

Patrick: It doesn't really bother me that much. Ha! We had this one guy. [laughter] It was really funny. It's this Indian guy. And he was working on his car, he was playing with the carburetor with a cigarette hanging out of his mouth. And the carburetor just blew up! And he looked like Yosemite Sam in the Looney Tunes cartoons. His hair going straight back. This guy's beard was burned off, his eyebrows were burned off, his eyelashes were burned off. His hair was totally singed. All the front of it where his hairline was, was burned off. But as it went back, it was just sort of singed, and it was less and less singed on the way back. He was actually a great guy, a really nice guy, he had a really dynamic personality. He was just a talker and everything. But it was just so odd, because he was like really in your face when he would talk to you. I was trying not to laugh at him, because he just reminded me so much of the cartoons. [laughter] You know, like when the bomb goes off and his hair goes straight back and his face is all black?

Tony: [laughter] That's funny. Speaking of burns, there was a pretty nasty burn we took. It was a guy, he had a cushion in the back of a truck. The truck wasn't running, but it was in the back of a building. And he put a cushion back there. And I don't know whether he was homeless or that was just his hang-out, but he was smoking a cigarette back there and fell asleep. When he fell asleep, the cigarette fell and must have caught the mattress on fire. He caught fire, and when we got there, he was still in the bed of the truck. The water had doused everything, including him. And we all went down to pick him up out of the truck and he was still alive. And just in pain. I went down to pick him up, and I had an arm and another person had an arm. And when we both grabbed the arm and pulled up, all we did was take the charring right off his arms. Ugh!

Patrick: Oh, nasty.

Tony: That is one of the sickest feelings I've ever had. That, and digging into some warm blood are pretty much the nasty feelings on the job.

Patrick: Or like when you do CPR on someone who's just died, especially an old woman? And you start doing the compressions on her chest and as you push down, you can feel the ribs cracking. And it's like—

Tony: When your knuckles crack?

Patrick: Yeah, when you crack your knuckles, it's like that feeling, yeah. The crack, the popping, every time you go—pop! pop! pop!—push down on it. That's one of the gross things. That is kind of a gross feeling.

Tony: I don't know. Just pulling back the skin—the charred skin—and seeing fresh flesh. You know, red pink flesh?

Patrick: All the subcutaneous tissue.

Tony: Yeah, yuck! That's pretty bad. Oh, here we are. This is where we come to eat.

Patrick: We had this older man who was probably in his seventies. And he lived alone in Oakland. He had his own house, just this little old house that he used to stay in. And his son would come and check on him periodically, like every couple of months. I believe his son was a truck driver. He'd go and be gone—like he would go across the country—and be gone for long periods of time.

So, the son came back to check on his dad, and he couldn't get the door open. They're all knocking at the door and stuff and they thought that maybe dad had died. Banging on the door, banging on the door. They called the police, the police showed up, one of the cops went in through a window. And they found dad, on the ground in the kitchen. He'd fallen, and he'd been down for like a couple of days and hadn't been able to get up. So, we get there, we're doing our thing, talking to him and stuff. And this guy, he just smelled like necrotic tissue. This guy, he smelled horrible. We didn't know really what was going on. And he'd like peed all over himself and crapped all over himself, and he had some food stuff around him, 'cause he had fallen in the kitchen, so he had access to the cupboards. But he couldn't really move around a whole lot.

And we were in there, doing our assessment stuff on him, trying to talk him into going to the hospital. But this guy was adamant, he didn't want to go with us. And we finally figured out what the necrotic smell was. I guess he had poor circulation or something in his feet. But his feet had these huge holes, huge open sores down there that had never healed. And they had eventually taken over his entire feet. It was really disgusting. He had these slippers on, and a pair of socks that we could tell. And the feet were just gangrenous. And the tissue from the feet had like meshed in with the fabric of the sock. So it had become like this messy stinky feet thing. It was really disgusting.

So I took off my trauma shears and I was going to try to cut these things off, so I could get a look at his feet, try to see what was going on. I started to cut, and as I peeled away the top layers of the slippers, it was peeling away layers of skin that had like just got mixed in with the fabric of the sock. So I had to give up on that. Eventually, what my partner and I ended up doing was wrapping his feet and transporting him like that. Just the smell that came out was unbelievable. I could not believe how horrible this smell was. So we had to seal that up and took him into the hospital. We finally wound up talking him into going, because we'd convinced him that his feet were infected bad enough that he could die from it. And he was a pretty sick old guy.

The narration covers an extraordinary range, and reveals the links Tony and Patrick make between stories. From describing a call in which a patient suffers from a pustulant abscess, memorable because of the smell generated by the infection, they turn to a call of a woman dying from a similar abscess. Here, her refusal of medical treatment and unwillingness to compromise religious ideals are resoundingly condemned, as her actions are so fundamentally antithetical to the medics' mission. Tony then narrates another call as a commentary on neglect. This story leads to an exchange concerning unappealing smells and then to a discussion of a series of calls involving burn victims. Tony and Patrick next describe the unpleasant sensations they have experienced during the treatment of patients, including the cracking of ribs and the sinking of one's hands into badly charred flesh. (There is no possible way for nonparamedics to contribute to such a conversation.)

The session ends with Patrick's story about a call for another elderly patient who has fallen and is suffering necrosis of his foot tissue. Thus, the storytelling comes full circle.

Asked by nonmedics to tell stories, the medics are frequently glad to comply; yet sometimes they hesitate to tell stories that they tell each other. Lars and Mark discuss this paradox—hesitance to tell stories to outsiders—one evening behind Highland Hospital:

Tim: Why do you think paramedics tell stories?

Mark G.: Shit, I don't know. I guess we find it exciting. It's almost like, I don't know, "I had a better call than you did." I don't know.

Tim: One-upmanship?

Mark: Yeah, it could be that. Could be just, you know, that's all they have to talk about. No lives outside.

Lars: Think about it. If you work, if you work as many hours a week as you do, you run out of other things to talk about. "What do you do in your life?" "Well, I drive around in an ambulance," so I might as well tell stories. And then, people to an extent want—that's why those shows are so popular—they want to hear about it. That's why when there's a car accident, everyone wants to come out and look.

So if you go to a party, or something, people want to hear, you know, "Oh, what's the grossest thing you've ever seen, man?" People want to hear it but to an extent, sometimes you want to tell it, sometimes you don't. You get a feeling that either you're just gonna come off sounding like a rescue geek, "Oh, yeah, one time, I remember..." Or, you don't want to come off sounding like an asshole, one of those, "Oh, man, my job's so rough, I don't want to talk about it." So you're caught in a catch-22. You either talk about the job and tell people everything they want to hear, and you run the risk of sounding like some kind of dweeb, whose only real thing in life is, "The time I went Code 3 for whatever." Or you sound like some kind of stuck-up asshole who's so hung on himself that, "Oh, my job's so rough, I can't talk about it." And, in reality, people like that want you to ask about it, they want you to drag it out of them, "Come on, man, share, tell us!" Fuck you, whatever! So, either way, you run the risk of sounding kind of like an asshole.

Among cohorts, there is little chance for sounding "like an asshole." "Hero stories" are immediately derided, and the narrator is forced to beat a hasty retreat into the ironic stance common in most medic stories. With nonmedics present, however, the normal rules of storytelling no longer apply; the medic has fewer constraints. Audience expectations, informed by media representations of the profession and fueled by a general voyeuristic fascination with death, provide the medics ample opportunity to tell tales of their experiences. Since medics are authorities, with access to events that others do not have, people are interested in hearing their stories and, to a certain extent, medics want to tell them.

But, as Lars points out, there is a problematic disjuncture in these storytelling situations. If medics tell stories, they risk misinterpretation by the audience, who may believe that the medic's presentation of self attributes too much stature to the work he or she does. If, on the other hand, they refuse to tell stories, they may be misinterpreted in another way; the audience may believe that the refusal is part of a representation of the difficulties of the profession. Since medics generally enjoy telling stories, and since audiences expect to hear them, the medics develop strategies for dealing with the situation. Some simply avoid telling stories to noncohorts, suggesting that they do not like to "talk shop." Others indulge their audiences, taking the opportunity to tell "hero" stories normally excluded from cohort storytelling sessions, and still others, as Lars indicates, reluctantly agree to tell stories and thus bolster the representation of their job as difficult and emotionally demanding.

A fourth strategy also exists, namely the fabrication of stories which conform to audience expectations but are not based on actual calls. In this scenario, the medic is able to satisfy the listeners and simultaneously undermine their perceptions of the storytelling. The audience is fascinated and horrified, not realizing that the medic is playing a game. Generally, only other medics who are present recognize the manipulation of the storytelling; they thus constitute a secondary, initiated audience. Steve L. mentions this strategy one evening while joking with other medic crews at Highland Hospital:

Steve L.: Yeah, when I started this, I had a bunch of friends and family who always wanted to know what's going on and how to experience what you experience. And, in all actuality, there's not too many people that can handle what you experience. How do I handle it? Drinking helps.

But people ask you, "So, what is the worst thing you've ever seen, man?" So, finally, I got tired of telling them stuff and so I made up this story. And I kind of stole it from a lot of people. Basically, people make up these stories all the time. Well, this one story I made up, and I stick with it, it's pretty cool. And you get people working, get their imagination worked up. And you say, "Well, I don't know if I can tell you. It's pretty gross."

And you start being serious, you go, "Well, it has to do with heavy equipment and machinery, and people getting caught in it." And you see their eyes, and they're like, "Yeah, yeah?" So you go, "Well, you know those tree-limb crews that come along and trim the trees so that they can put up cable wires and stuff like that?" "Yeah! Yeah!" "Okay, well, have you ever seen the machines they use to trim the leaves and the trees? And they throw the whole limb in there. And it's got this giant mulcher and it just mulches things to bits?" And people go, "Yeah, yeah, yeah!" "Okay, well, we got a call one time for the operator of this thing, and he had a long-sleeved shirt, and it caught his arm. And it accidentally pulled him into the machine. And we got there. Oh! What can I say. It was just really bad, you know?" And then these people are all going, "Oh, my God, that's gross! That'd be terrible! Terrible!" And then you realize, it makes little chips of things, man! Can't be real! Nobody gets it. [laughter]

Steve's story includes many of the most common elements of medic narratives. The situation is extraordinary, and the patient suffers from extreme trauma. But the story lacks the frequent commentary on the role of other first responders and the medics' abilities to bring order to difficult scenes. Instead, the derision is reserved for the unwitting audience who are duped into believing a story that "can't be real." The audience does not "get it."

Steve admittedly fabricates the story because he has lost interest in telling stories to this particular type of audience. Quite possibly, telling stories to nonmedics removes several important elements from the storytelling situation. The audience is in no position to provide other stories, and therefore the frequent give and take of medic storytelling is absent. Furthermore, the storytelling loses its didactic and enculturating qualities, since the audience is neither in need of information about possible scenes nor in the process of becoming medics themselves. Finally, these nonmedic storytelling contexts do not provide the debriefing quality of cohort storytelling. Thus, there is little motivation for the telling of medic stories to nonmedic audiences. Steve finds motivation by undercutting his own position of authority — he tells a story about a call that did not happen. By deceiving his nonmedic audience, he underscores their inability to engage in the paramedic storytelling tradition. The deception has little value by itself, but, in relating it to other medics, Steve and his medic audience collectively confirm their group status.

Late one evening on an exceptionally slow shift, I discuss the fabrication of medic stories with Mark and Lars. As an experiment, I ask Mark to invent a story. He smiles at Lars and tells the following story:

Mark G.: You ever see those crews that trim trees? You know, in the green trucks?

Lars: Davie Tree? They're all over the place.

Mark: There was this job at the corner at my house — this is when I was a little kid. This is how I actually ended up being a paramedic and getting into this kind of stuff. This guy, he was up trimming one of these really tall trees. I forget what kind of tree it was.

Lars: Oak?

Mark: No, it wasn't an oak, it wasn't a birch or a eucalyptus.

Lars: Beech?

Mark: Something really large and huge. Anyway, he was up there trimming off some limbs, and he had the chipper going and everything. He was at it for a couple of days. And, fucking, you know, the chipper's going — vroom! vroom! vroom! — you know, that chipper's going on. And fucking one day, I'm playing in my yard, and I hear all this screaming, "Hey! Vern! Fucking! Wah wah!" Apparently, the guy had fallen out of the tree into the chipper. And there was enough force that his whole body was sucked right down in there. And, I'm not sure if it actually spit him out, or what happened, but they just took all the chips away and that was it.

Lars: Did they bring him to the hospital?

Mark: Actually, no, because they really couldn't find him. I think he was just mixed up in the tree chips. It was kind of a weird call. The tree, I forget what kind it was, but it had kind of a reddish bark, too, so it was real hard to tell, you know? And chips, being absorbent.

Lars: Oh, yeah.

Mark: They just pretty much soaked up everything that was happening. So the chipper was a real mess. But they ran a little soap and water through there and cleaned it up.

Lars: Wow. Gnarly.

Mark: You know, there's got to be some kind of safety for those, I mean, Cal-OSHA should be looking into those. Wood chippers. Those things are dangerous.

The story is remarkably similar to Steve's, and confirms his statement that "people make up these stories all the time." At first glance, it is difficult to determine the differences between this and other medic stories. However, Mark's story is situated in a past so distant that he is, in fact, not a medic. Although he suggests that the accident prompted him to become one, there is nothing in the story about the medics' response. The patient, in fact, is so injured that he ceases to exist. As in Steve's story, the patient is reduced to the size of small "chips." Mark's narrative, then, does not include many of the elements of typical medic stories. While the story meets the expectations of nonmedics with its description of terrible gore, it does not include references to the common evaluations of the dangers associated with scenes, the medical prowess of the medics, the incompetence of other first responders, or the stupidity of the workers. Even though Mark mentions the surprising anatomical incongruity associated with a human being passed through a wood chipper, his story lacks the visceral and humorous descriptions commonly found in medic stories. Instead, Lars asks, with a smirk, if the medics transported the "chips" to the hospital. Mark himself seems more concerned with the cleaning of the machine than with the discovery of the body. Both men have exaggerated their usual ironic stance to the point of absurdity.

Lisa mentions one afternoon that "a lot of the things you hear are half rumor, half true," thus openly acknowledging the fictive element in medic storytelling. Indeed, medics exaggerate, condense, omit, combine, and otherwise manipulate calls in their storytelling. Certain elements, such as lazy fire crews, inept doctors, and dangerous nurses, appear time and again. At the base of storytelling among themselves, however, is the belief that the call actually happened. When confronted by a nonmedic audience who wants to hear about their "grossest" call, medics can respond with different narrative strategies. Not surprisingly, some decide to deceive the audience with stories of fabricated calls. This willingness to make up stories, however, resonates through the entire tradition. The question then becomes to what degree are all medic stories fabricated? While medic audiences are far more adept at catching coworkers at fabrication, it seems likely that storytellers frequently test the limits of how far they can stretch the truth. Thus, when Bill V. refers to medic storytelling with the emic designation "telling lies," he is providing an accurate, albeit ironic, evaluation of the tradition.[3]

What is disgusting to one person is not always disgusting to another. Medics see and eventually become inured to a great many things in the course of their work. When someone asks them "What's the grossest thing you've ever seen?," they find themselves in a difficult situation. Some undoubtedly take great joy in telling stories that will disgust; others hesitate. The query may provoke a sarcastic response, or a medic may playfully undermine the situation by seeming to comply with the request with a fabricated story. Generally, nonmedic audiences expect to hear stories of mutilation and violent death. Indeed, these stories are an important part of medic storytelling. But medics all concur that a bloody scene does not necessarily constitute a disgusting one. Although especially severe trauma, particularly when it involves multiple compound fractures or the extrusion of brain matter, does figure prominently in some of these stories, most tend to focus on necrosis and infestation.

Storytelling among cohorts highlights the relative nature of what is "gross." Medics do at times attempt to tell stories that their coworkers will also find disgusting. In these cases, the competitive, or additive, nature of storytelling becomes apparent. Most of the stories detail horrific decay, with smells, rather than sights, constituting the primary cause of disgust. Since smells are difficult to describe and impossible to reproduce in the story, the medics resort to physical descriptions of the scenes. The stories function in part on a metaphoric level as well. All of the problems that medics usually face become accentuated in these calls. Environments are decrepit and filled with filth. Patients are truculent to the point of insanity, family support is nonexistent to the point of criminal neglect, public programs have failed to the point of being dangerous, and other first responders are so unable or unwilling to assist that they vomit, wait outside, or even leave the scene entirely. Infectious agents are no longer invisible but swarm over the patient's body, carrying away bits and pieces. The intensification of these elements tries the abilities and emotional stamina of even the most experienced medics. Consequently, other medics can identify with the story and offer their concurring opinion that a particular call is, in fact, the grossest thing they have ever seen, or, more correctly, ever heard about.

# 8

# YOU NEVER KNOW
# WHAT MANAGEMENT
# IS THINKING

Paramedics work with a high degree of autonomy. Although the Alameda County Deployment Center, commonly referred to as "the barn," is the center for county operations, medics only go there to pick up and drop off their ambulances; otherwise, they are on their own. Field supervisors patrol the county, catching up with units to take care of administrative matters, while dispatchers working from a communications center in an isolated industrial park send the medics to their emergency calls. Many medics consider this high degree of autonomy to be one of the most alluring aspects of the work; they also see the supervisory intrusions as being among the most negative.

Medics make sarcastic comments about their field supervisors and generally deride dispatch. In part, the negative attitudes expressed toward supervisors can be seen as an extension of the frequent commentary on the ability of other medical personnel to evaluate scenes to which they did not respond. In their stories, medics also reveal their suspicion that supervisors are "company men" who care more about profits than about the proper care of critical patients. Similarly, dispatchers are considered intruders on the medics' world, reassigning them from one post to another, sending them on calls with little or no information, and occasionally requiring them to work overtime. Of course, at the same time medics engage in storytelling concerning episodes of preposterous managerial zeal and alarming dispatch ineptitude, managers and dispatchers tell stories of medic irresponsibility and sloth. The stories in this chapter emphasize the internal workings of the company rather than the paramedics' interactions with the public, with hospital personnel, and with other first responders.

Tom R., Director of Operations for Alameda County, has responsibility for the nearly two hundred field medics working in the widely dispersed county. Tom began work as a paramedic with a fire service, eventually finding employment with Regional Ambulance. Once Regional secured the county-wide 911 contract, he helped preside over the merger with Allied Ambulance. Now, in turn, he has helped guide the operations as Regional Ambulance has become part of the national alliance of ambulance companies known as American Medical Response. Shortly after my interview with Tom, he accepted another job in Delaware and left Alameda County. Although ostensibly in charge of all the paramedics and their supervisors, he seems to harbor few misconceptions about his ability to control medics working alone in this far-flung area:

Tom R.: It's very apparent—people are gonna do what people want to do. I've learned a lot in regards to how to manage people, and I've actually identified some different steps. The first line is supervising line employees. What it amounts to, in my belief system, is you go out, you support the people, you get them doing things, because they want to do them and they understand why they're doing them. There's one thing you've got to know about paramedics—paramedics aren't going to do anything they don't believe is right. It's just not gonna happen. They're not gonna do anything that they can't see the worth in. And they're gonna question everything.

You know, the job is to walk into a situation and, in thirty seconds or less, find out everything you can about what's going on. Well, what does that teach you? It teaches you to question everything. Even what you think is true, you need to question, right? Well, that's the way they operate with management, too. They question everything. It's not good enough to just say, "That's the way it is, because that's the way we've done it." They question it. Which is fair. That's an interesting level to manage.

Then, managing supervisors is an interesting level. And then, managing supervisors' supervisors is an even more interesting level. I've gotten to progress up through those different layers. I used to think that the higher up in the organization you went, the more control and power you had. And it's actually the opposite. If you think about it, I've got two assistant directors that I can influence. I can try to get them doing what I believe is right. Obviously, when I'm not there, they're gonna do what they think is right. So, I gotta get them to understand why we're doing these things. They need to buy into it.

Now, one of them's got thirteen field supervisors that they need to get bought into what's right. Those thirteen supervisors have a hundred and eighty-nine full-time paramedics in this division. So, if you start talking about influence and who has control and power, I certainly don't have control over those paramedics. I can't influence those people. It just won't happen. Those people won't look at me and go, "Gee, he's in control." Who's in control? Field supervisors. Those are the people who influence people. They're the one's who know what's going on. And actually, when you really think about it, the paramedics are in control. They have the ultimate control, because they have control over what happens on a call.

Although the home office, under Tom's guidance, sets company policy, it has very little day-to-day operational control over the medics. Instead, Tom draws attention to the role that field supervisors play in management.

Medics, who prefer to run their calls and fulfill their assignments as they see fit, view the supervisors as wielding undue managerial power; however, although stories on this subject abound, they were difficult to collect. While medics were willing to tell the stories, they were reluctant to let me record them, many feeling that the company—particularly the field supervisors—would punish them for voicing criticisms. Some medics, however, felt that their position on supervisors was already well known and, because of seniority or impending changes in employment, allowed me to record their comments. Tom B., a former supervisor, compares occupying the role of field supervisor to "playing a game":

Tom B.: Becoming a supe, man. No way, never again. You know, I used to resist the whole way. But they were just all over me, so finally, you quit. You tell 'em, "Hey, get off my back, and I'll play your game." I'll play your game so damn well I'll make Patton and Komar look like problem children.[1] And I did. Okay? When I came to Regional, I just decided that it wasn't worth fighting them over some of this stupid shit. So I just decided to play their game, to a certain degree without compromising my integrity. But man, you find out you can't do it.

As a supervisor, one becomes a representative of the company and inevitably must relinquish the strong independent stance that most field medics value. Tom also reveals the potential for abuses in the supervisor system. Evidently, field supervisors engage in "games," pitting medics against one another, deliberately singling out some for especially close scrutiny and hounding others into compliance with certain agendas.

Some medics pointed out that field supervisors "pick on" certain crews, not necessarily because of poor performance but because of personality clashes, private vendettas, and "power tripping."[2] Lars tells of one encounter with Tom B. while the latter was a supervisor:

Lars: Oh, what was it? There was one supe once who—dispatch asked us what our ETA would be to some street, and my partner gave an ETA of like six minutes—and the supe drove from the site of the call to where we were posted and he came up to us at a hospital and said it only took him three minutes to drive from the site of the call to where we were posted. And my partner was like, "So?" And the two of them started arguing—just all out—and I tried jumping in and said, "Well, doesn't ETA mean estimated time of arrival?" And the supe told me, "At ease, I'm not talking to you."
    Mark G.: Who was that?
    Lars: What? That was Tom B. He's no longer a supervisor. He stuck his hand up in my face, and said, "At ease."

Mark: "At ease, son."

Lars: So that was the type of stuff we had. Everybody writing each other up—before you knew it there was paper going everywhere.

In the story, Tom assumes the role of a military superior telling a soldier to stand "at ease," a demeanor Lars deems inappropriate for the situation.

In another story, Lars describes what he considers to be an absurd example of a supervisor using his authority to punish field medics:

Lars: Our post was San Pablo and 980, and it was my partner's very first day in the field. And he just drove right past post! So we were driving down Broadway, and we hit Seventh and Broadway, and so I said, "Tell you what, I'll show you Jack London Square before we turn around and head back to post." So we went down to Jack London Square to look around and then head back to post.

Next thing you know, there's a supervisor right behind us. Now at that point I wasn't getting along too well with the supervisor. Well, he got on the radio and said, "Unit at Seventh and Broadway pull over," like it was a traffic stop or something. So we pull over, and he walks up, and says, "You guys are off post." At the time, I thought, "Big deal," so I was like, "Yeah, we were off post, but we were just going to Jack London Square to check out the mermaids in the bay there."

Well, we went back and he met us back at the post. And he didn't write up the guy who was driving, he wrote up me! Well, I complained, I said it was ridiculous because I wasn't the one driving, and he's writing me up for something the driver did. I said it was an accident that we were off post, and I got a response saying that, "It clearly was not a mistake that you were off post, because it clearly states in the write-up that you were checking for mermaids in the estuary."

Mark: Well, it's true.

Lars: Yeah, but come on.

That a flippant comment becomes the crux of a disciplinary matter highlights what the medics perceive to be the supervisors' humorless nature and their willingness to pursue field medics for the most minor infractions. Lars compares the supervisor to the police, saying, "Like it was a traffic stop." Numerous others commented on the ardor with which the supervisors carry out these policing actions, which to the medics is reminiscent of a totalitarian state. For example, as a supervisor truck passed in the other direction one day, Melinda quipped, "There goes Big Brother."

A large number of the field supervisors were culled from the ranks of Allied Ambulance, which had been absorbed by Regional Ambulance when Regional secured the 911 contract for Alameda County. This merging of personnel from two distinct companies, along with an influx of new medics to meet the staffing demands, resulted in the emergence of several cliques within the ranks of the field medics. These groups were generally identified according to earlier company affiliations, with the most clearly defined being the former Allied medics. The large number of Allied medics working in supervisory positions reinforced this perception and heightened the tension between groups. Non-Allied field medics suspected that friendships established in the earlier company influenced supervisors' actions, and saw old Allied medics as being nearly immune from managerial actions.

One day, Bill V., among the most experienced of the medics at Regional and not a former Allied employee, confronted his partner for the day, George, who was a former Allied medic and a current field supervisor, in a revealing exchange:

Bill V.: C'mon, man. Allied. All you guys talk about is how hard Allied days were. These guys in L.A. run twenty-five calls a day. A year is a year. A year is a year. You know, you're good, you're the prince, George, but a year is a year.

George: I disagree with that.

Bill: Uh, that's okay.

George: I don't think to work a year in the valley and work a year in Oakland on an Allied rig is exactly the same. I'd have to disagree with that. We see a hell of a lot more patients in one shift than they see in a whole tour.

Bill: But you still see the same amount of criticals.

George: You don't know, see. You weren't here.

Bill: I was in L.A., brother.

George: Well, that's great. And I don't take that from you, you know? I respect the fact that you were in L.A., and L.A. certainly is busy.

Bill: But it's just a year. Just a year. [George leaves as Roy Z., another supervisor, pulls up to the post.] How can you fly like an eagle when you're surrounded by turkeys? That's it, that's my quote. [laughter] Four years, that's what they say. You know, these Allied guys, they worked in Oakland, they think—I hear them saying—"A year in Oakland is like working four years anyplace else." So you run more bullshit calls than anybody else. Trauma's nothing, all it is bloody and messy. You know? You run a lot of bullshit calls like we've been doing all day in Oakland. Does that make you a better paramedic? I don't think so.

Versus working in the valley where everybody has jobs and the only time someone calls 911 is when they're dying. It's the same. A year is a year. But you can't tell these ex-Allied heroes that. They've got it screwed into their skull. These guys here, man—the supervisors' outfit—they're all like old Allied guys. They're funny guys, man. They try real hard though, they're so into this. Look at them, they're planning, doing all their strategies. It's a funny group. They're so into it, they're so young. [laughter]

In this case, Bill equates youth with inexperience, and the supervisors begin to take on many of the characteristics of interns, including excessive enthusiasm and a tendency toward self-aggrandizement. (It was George who earlier had attempted to tell a "hero story," only to be silenced by Bill's caustic remarks.)

Many of the Allied narratives are considered to be "hero stories," meaning that they focus on individual achievement and lack the ironic and self-deprecating humor of more accepted stories. Supervisors, in fact, tend to be more inclined than other medics to tell hero stories, since as part of their work, they must present themselves as the final authority in the field.[3] Their stories glorify themselves rather than the profession and the greater community of paramedics. From the perspective of field medics, this attitude aligns the supervisors with the "rescue geeks" or "Ricky Rescues" of popular media portrayals. Unable to develop the ironic stance of field medics, the supervisors are seen to be inflating their authority, and challenges to this authority, even if undertaken humorously, result in disciplinary action.

Medics routinely criticize the management style of the field supervisors and, by extension, the entire company. Tom R. mentions his experience with criticism and the strategies he has adopted to deal with it:

Tom R.: I used to take it personal. I used to take this whole job personal. I used to really be into it, and you can still probably see supervisors taking it personal. Somebody comes up and says, "I don't like this about the company," or, "The company screwed up and did this." And I used to take that as, "Gee, the company is me and that's personal and they're talking bad about me," and I don't do that anymore. It's not personal. We're all here to do the same job, we're all working for the same place. It's not personal against me, it's not personal against anybody. If somebody has a complaint, they need to bring it in, let's see if we can fix it. You know?

Or they can choose to resolve it their way. And that, of course, never seems to fix anything. I thought I was in control, and then I realized I wasn't in control of everything. But the power and control style anyway — "command and control," as they call it — is a thing of the past anyway. We're a "command and control organization," and that's the way we're structured, but it's not the best way to run the company. We're trying to move into the QI models — quality improvement, employee involvement, self-empowered — which is kind of a joke, because they're already a self-empowered team out there.

Unlike Tom R., however, most field supervisors do take criticism of the company personally, since it undermines their position of authority. Thus, one finds an interesting stand-off between medics and their field supervisors. As Tom R. points out, the medics' job is to question, and, in the case of supervisory intervention, they inevitably question the supervisors. Once questioned, the supervisors retaliate by invoking their experience as well as their power to discipline. In turn, this breeds resentment among medics. Field supervisors themselves are medics and thus also rebel against those who question their authority. Tom B.'s military response to Lars's protestations is an excellent example of the "command and control" model to which Tom R. refers. In this case, Lars's questioning is met by the invocation of a strict "command and control" structure, namely that of the military. This clear demarcation of hierarchies further fuels the resentment among the field medics.

In addition to having field supervisors, the company makes use of various review boards that examine instances of possible paramedic error. One is the quality assurance board, or QA, which reviews field medical procedures.[4] Medics generally are reluctant to discuss the proceedings of this board because QA investigations question their medical acumen. Since most medics narrate stories to support their image as well-trained authorities in the delivery of critical care, stories about calls resulting in a QA assessment are rare. Although the company's quality assurance board is designed to review paramedic performance and insure that patient care is consistent with county protocols, medics at times feel that the decisions of the board are misguided and ill informed. In the view of most medics, those on the quality assurance board, like the doctors and nurses at area hospitals, do not have the requisite field experience to evaluate medics' field actions. Tony tells the story of a save that, despite the success of his treatment, landed him in front of the board:

Tony: So we got to this Code 3 call and it was a problem breathing call. And we got there and we knocked on the door and the lady says, "Come in, come in. My brother, he just came in from New Orleans, he's having a breathing problem. I know he has a breathing problem, so it's probably what's going on. He was sitting here, and he fainted and I saw him having some kind of problem breathing! Can you check him out?" We're like, "Sure, where is he?" She said, "In the kitchen."

So we walked over to the kitchen, and there he was, flat on the ground. And I looked at him and I said, "Yeah, this guy is definitely having a breathing problem." [laughter] Like, a NOT breathing problem. And so we we're working that up, and we didn't have anyone to help us out. So we were doing CPR and then we started doing one-man CPR on this guy because we wanted to start a line and start the drugs.

At this point, I haven't done anything to this guy, the monitor isn't even on him yet. And a fellow's walking by, and I'm like, "Hey, have you ever done CPR before?" And he's like, "No, but I've been trained." I said, "Great! Let me show you then. Sit down. [laughter] Extend, just like me, stand over his chest and start pumping his chest like this." So he started pumping his chest, I started breathing for him, my partner got everything else set up, put him on monitors, started intubating him.

We ended up doing our thing on this guy and making a save on him. Ended up saving this guy. But I—I got QAed by the company for using a bystander to help with CPR. They wanted me to go find this guy and get a CPR card from him.

Patrick: Afterwards?

Tony: Afterwards! I'm all like, "Yeah, right!" I said, "This guy's a bystander!"

Patrick: I know, you don't even know what his name was.

Tony: Right, don't even know who he is. All I know is, it worked!

Even though the patient lives, the company criticizes Tony for not receiving the appropriate documentation from the bystander. Certainly the company is worried about issues of liability, but laws are usually generous in the cases of "good Samaritans" at emergency situations.[5] Although Tony comments indirectly on training, the story is more a stinging indictment of the bureaucracies of emergency medical care and a commentary on the persistent challenges that medics feel they encounter from all quarters.

The other main review body is the accident review board, which examines accidents involving ambulances. Driving constitutes a major part of the medics' work day and, consequently, many medics consider their driving, like their medical skills, to be beyond reproach. However, they are slightly less protective of their vehicle-handling skills than of their patient-handling skills. Among the most numerous driving stories are those about driving Code 3 to accidents. Often, these stories include humorous mistakes made by the medics. Bill V. tells one such story:

Bill V.: We were doing this call for a pediatric. We were Code 3. It was like midnight, you know? Friday night, down in Riverside. We're hauling ass down the freeway doing a hundred miles an hour, making noise — woo woo woo woo — get off the freeway — woo woo woo woo! We're on our way to the hospital, making noise and blowing red lights and running people off the road. And people aren't pulling over and we're flipping them off and doing everything but throwing shit at them, and we're driving, hauling butt to the hospital. Then we see CHP chasing us, and we're like, "What's this guy doing?" We're hauling ass and he pulls up next to us and goes over the loudspeaker, he goes, "Turn your fucking lights on!" Oh. We'd been going for ten miles like this! God, it's a wonder we didn't kill anybody. I hate it when that happens.

Here, Bill's potentially dangerous oversight is easily remedied, and the inexplicable response of the other motorists is quickly, and humorously, explained. His closing remark is a typically sardonic ending — he details an extraordinary event, pokes fun at his mistakes, and then casts the event in the realm of the routine.

On the way to a scene, lights flashing and siren blaring, Lars offers similar remarks about driving Code 3:

Lars: The great thing about driving Code 3 is that you get to do fun things like this. [Lars crosses the median into the oncoming lanes.] You can get on the wrong side of the road and drive in opposing traffic. Hi, everybody! Hi! If we had a PA system we could get on it and say, "Hey, you! Get out of the way," but they gave us two reasons why they took them out. One was, they said, "Oh yeah, if you tell someone to pull through the intersection and they get in an accident, then the company's liable," and the other reason was they said we'd be abusing them. It's funny, I never saw anyone abusing them here like I did in New York City.

In New York, it was great, they'd get on the PA system and say everything, you know? The first call I did with them, the guy driving gets on the PA system, and says to the guy in the car in front of him, "Hey, asshole, in America we move to the right." Probably offended the hell out of the guy, but it worked, he got out of the way. You'll notice. Some people like to hit speed bumps at top speed, you know? Catch air. Now we need someone to do the nice thing, move to the right and slam into us.

Management appears to be everywhere, even influencing the way the paramedics drive. The public address system has been removed from the vehicles in a gesture designed both to reduce company liability and to prevent the medics from engaging in potentially offensive behavior. Lars offers an example of PA abuse, but suggests that such abuse is a minor consideration if it produces the desired effects and results in a quicker response time. His final sardonic comment draws attention to the danger associated with driving Code 3. Despite sirens, lights, and their skill as drivers, medics do get into accidents.

Steve Y. tells a story about one such accident and his subsequent interaction with the accident review board:

Steve Y.: There's one that I got railroaded on by the accident review board! Bringing home a Code 3 down Market Street in the fast lane on a two-lane street, we come to an intersection and there's two lanes, and we're coming down in the left lane. Well, we stop in the intersection with our lights and sirens on and we need to make a right. So we stop because we're a little confused on which way we're going. So we pause for maybe three to five seconds, some asshole comes around from a side street in back of us, passes us on the right as I'm making my turn, and he hits us, okay? He's totally at fault! First of all, you can't pass a vehicle when you're going Code 3. Second, you can't pass one on the right.

So anyway the police report says I'm totally not at fault at all, there's no way to avoid it. And, in the infinite wisdom of our accident review board, they found that I had made an error in judgment. You know, you tell me what that means. And they said, "Well, you made a right turn from the fast lane," and I said, "Well, sooner or later I'm gonna have to make a right turn, I can't keep going straight until I hit the water!" And he says, "Well, you made an error in judgment." Well, fuck your error of judgment.

Stephanie: They wanted you to go to the—

Steve: Hunh? I don't know what they wanted. Anyway, they gave me a point on my driving record. I should have grieved it. Actually I had union representation there, but it wasn't worth a shit either, the person who was there. And I had to go and ride for three hours at remedial driving training on a Saturday afternoon and it was just the most screwed-up thing I'd ever seen. That was my one experience with the accident review board.

Oh, I also backed into a parked car without a backer once. And knocked the guy's rearview mirror off this 1910 Dodge or whatever it was. And, you know, the thing probably didn't even run, I could have slipped him five dollars and said, "Here, here's for your mirror, go buy a twelve-pack," or something. And then instead, like the good employee that I am, I reported it and said I didn't have a backer. Didn't even scratch the ambulance. Got suspended for two days for that!

Stephanie: Oh, man!

Steve: Can you believe that?

Stephanie: God, well, that teaches us to lie, doesn't it?

Steve's attitudes in this series of stories are markedly similar to those of medics in the tradition as a whole. In this case, an institution of authority, closely tied to the management of the company, questions Steve's decision-making ability. Characteristically, he rebels and uses his stories to emphasize the malicious nature of the review board as well as their incompetence. He also brings to the fore the question of company loyalty, indicating that, since the company does little to protect the interests of their employees, the employees have little motivation to protect the interests of the company. As trust erodes, so do the necessary levels of cooperation among the medics, their field supervisors, and the rest of the managerial structure.

Cooperation between medics and management is essential for the efficient operation of the company, as is collaboration among separate medic units. Numerous medics commented on the lack of teamwork among the medics and their supervisors. Although partners generally work well together as teams, beyond the individual ambulance unit the sense of interdependence breaks down. Solidarity among medic crews certainly exists, although at times there is resistance to cooperation. Stories and the storytelling tradition itself attest to the competition among crews. Crews "jump" each others' calls, manipulate scenes to avoid noisome transports, and delay clearing from hospitals and going back into service. At multiple unit responses, generally coordinated by field supervisors, some crews resist the commands of the supervisors if, as Tom R. suggests, the commands run contrary to the medics' own evaluation of the scene.

In medic storytelling, there is a tendency to compare the current company with other companies. Smaller systems are generally lauded by medics for their laissez-faire approach, while larger ones are criticized for their general insensitivity to medics' needs.[6] A similar comparison obtains regarding public and private providers. Public providers are generally considered by medics to have more equitable work environments, while private ones are seen to place emphasis on contract compliance and revenue generation.[7] Perhaps the most cynical attitude was expressed by Melinda. As I met her and her partner for a shift one morning, she pointed out a series of nylon banners emblazoned with various safety messages and touting the new name of the company:

Melinda: Did you see these banners? Look at them, my God! When I came in yesterday morning and saw them, I swore that the one over the driveway there said "*Arbeit macht frei!*"[8] [laughter] This new thing is scary. It's so corporate.

Melinda's comparison of the new corporation to the extraordinarily efficient killing machine of a Nazi concentration camp at once reveals her cynicism concerning the new company's goals and her deeply sarcastic sense of humor.[9]

On a less extreme note, one evening behind a hospital emergency entrance, several medic crews stood discussing the managerial style of Regional, the earlier atmosphere of Allied, and the impending changes posed by the merger of Regional into American Medical Response:

Steve Y.: You know what's lacking at this company? Teamwork. You can't get people to get together and do that kind of stuff, man.

Tom B.: I know. Well, you know, we just got to talk about it more. And we just don't have the opportunity to talk about it more.

Steve: Yeah, people are afraid to talk here, man.

George: Oh, I know, Allied used to be a small family. It was a small family.

Tom: Yeah, yeah, Allied was a much different animal than this place.

Steve: What are we now, the largest in the world?

Tom: Oh, yeah, so they say.

Stephanie: Spanning from east to west, a vast rising empire!

Steve: They just sucked up another one, too.

Steve: They're getting big fast.

Medics who worked for the much smaller Allied saw the switch to Regional as being at once beneficial and detrimental. Although nostalgic for the "family atmosphere" of Allied, they also criticized the company for forcing them to work long hours with defective equipment for low pay. The switch to Regional resulted in better shift schedules, better equipment, better benefits, and better pay. In exchange, they sacrificed a sense of camaraderie. As the company moved to join an even larger one, medics expressed fear of impending changes. Some felt that the larger corporation would be even less sensitive to their needs than the current company. Others expressed optimism that the new organization would provide greater opportunity for geographic mobility as well as upward mobility.

Tom R. also discussed the changes produced by the numerous mergers and overall growth of the company:

Tom R.: My job's been pretty much the same. In eighty-eight it was different, obviously, than it is now. The growth hasn't been external to the county, it's been internal to the county. All of the growth that I've gone through is because the county's expanding and changing its standards, not because of what the company's doing outside.

My changes are mostly going from a static system to a flexible deployment system. And when you start talking about the management side of things, what I look at is that static systems are twenty-four-hour based systems that cover geography. They say, "Okay, we're gonna put a unit here, here, here, here, here and here to cover this area." Flexibly deployed systems are fluid systems. So it can take into account that people move. Fire departments use static systems, because buildings don't move. But people do move. Meaning that you could have a million people influx into an area, and then at night, that million people may go home. Which influxes into another area. You need to be able to move with those people, because buildings don't call ambulances, people call ambulances. So, we need to be able to move with those, and that's why we have ten- and twelve-hour shifts.

Well, so they wanted a higher standard. Most response systems through-out the nation are usually about a ten-minute standard, that they want an am-bulance, 95 percent of the time in ten minutes. That's pretty typical of what I've seen. They started down this new vein of high-performance systems, which is eight minutes, 90 percent of the time. Alameda County took it even to one more extreme, and put it into communities. So there's actually four different contracts in this area, almost like an exam, that's got four different parts. It's not an average test. You have to pass each part with 90 percent. So, if you were successful in three parts, yet fail one of the parts, you still have failed the entire exam. And that's kind of the way our contract is. If we're below eight minutes, 90 percent in one of the four areas, then you have failed the whole contract. And if you do that for two consecutive months, you no longer have a contract—you're in breach of contract. So very high performance, high performance system. I don't know any higher.

While the medics consider shifts from a personal perspective, the man-agement emphasizes contract compliance. The conflicting concerns—personal versus contractual—inevitably lead to a degree of tension between field medics and management. This tension is exacerbated by somewhat contradictory goals. Although medics shoot for quick response times, they also try to be safe, and, not surprisingly, resent supervisors who second-guess them.

Managers and field paramedics are involved in an uneasy dance. On the one hand, managers are faced with meeting the stipulations of contracts, insuring medic compliance with protocols, protecting the company from litigation, and insuring that revenues remain high. On the other hand, the medics battle to maintain control over their calls, attempt to provide care to their patients within the guidelines of pro-tocols, and react to the demands of their schedules. The link between medics and the main office consists of field supervisors, who at times fall prey to the abuses of power to which Tom R. alludes. Medics tell stories about these abuses as a form of narrative revenge. By describing instances of excessive managerial zeal, they are able to undermine the authority of the supervisors. Indeed, medics generally resist any intrusions into their territory and strongly resent those who question their abilities.

Dispatch constitutes an even more frequent intrusion into the medics' work space than do the occasional visits of field supervisors. Dispatchers' voices crackle over the radio, sending the medics to calls, reassigning them from one post to another, and prodding them to go back in service after a call. The dispatchers can require medics to stay in service beyond the end of their shifts, give them permission to run personal errands or take breaks, and, at times, relay messages from field supervisors.[10] Even though the dispatchers themselves are subject to supervision in their communications facility, and work with far less autonomy than the field medics, medics express resentment regarding the seemingly invasive requests and the surprising authority that dispatchers wield over them.

The dispatchers' work environment is entirely different from that of the paramedics. Sitting in a darkened room bathed in subdued blue lighting, they cluster in front of glowing consoles. Large computer-generated maps showing the location of all the ambulances are displayed on monitors overhead. Jamie, a dispatcher, describes the allure of this environment:

Jamie: It's weird, you know? People always ask me out on the street, the first question that comes out of their mind is, "How many dead people have you seen?" Well, I work in dispatch. Not too many dead people get around. So I always have to say, "Well, I'm merely a dispatcher." Oh, you're a dispatcher. And then, automatically, you got these people thinking, "Okay, let's see. Taxi-cab dispatchers, buses." And they don't know really what you do. I could tell them I'm a systems status controller, and I'm in charge of maybe sixty or seventy ambulances at one time. Or that I've got a laser-tracking GPS—global positioning system—at my hands.

What I like to tell people usually is, "It's like a giant video game that you get to play all day and they pay you to play it. You don't have to put any quarters in it. The only problem is, if you screw up, you screw up!" [laughter] It's a lot of fun. This center is a fun center. It's very hi-tech, I think. We're on the cutting edge here. When people come in and have a look at it, it's really kind of neat, because they automatically say, *Star Wars*, you know? And then you get to show them around and it's all dark and it's cool and you got those map lights there and everybody looks like they know what they're doing. And for the most part they do! [laughter]

Jamie invokes the query that paramedics often hear, a question similar to Darryl's "What's the grossest thing you've ever seen?" He then turns his attention to the high-tech aspects of the center. The center's physical aspects and the large amount of sopisticated computer and communications equipment, more than any particular skills, become the focal point of his professional pride.

Jamie continues, likening dispatchers to other radio personalities, and includes, for a second time, an acknowledgment that dispatchers make mistakes:

Jamie: You know, you're a radio personality, sometimes it's tough because maybe you've had maybe four hours of sleep because you'd been partying too much the night before. Or whatever. Just having a bad day. And you just stammer and stumble over everything. You couldn't give out a call if your life depended on it. I don't know. It's funny. If you had bloopers—I guess that's kind of illegal for our company to do that—but you could probably fill a lot of time with bloopers. Dispatch bloopers and blunders. They're actually pretty funny. No. Only funny to people who know dispatch, I guess. [laughter]

In his willingness to draw attention to mistakes, Jamie is taking a position that is significantly different from the one taken by field paramedics in their stories. While the medics acknowledge making mistakes, they always recover in such a way that their skills and abilities are confirmed. In contrast, Jamie not only calls attention to dispatchers' mistakes but considers them to be a source of amusement.

Roslyn, another dispatcher, cites a different question that is commonly asked, in this case by the field medics:

Roslyn: The one question that people always ask me is, what do we eat? Because people always ask us, "Well, you dispatchers eat all the time." And last week, this one guy tells me, "Yeah, I hear you guys eat pig skins. Fried pig skins." I go, "Fried pig skins? Where'd you get that from?" He said, "I don't know. Someone said that's what you guys eat now." I'm all, "That's a new one. I've never heard that one." But dispatchers are associated with food all the time. You know, like, "God, you guys!" But sometimes we do eat a lot in here.

Christmas time, holidays, everything. The first thing crews bring us is cakes and candies and ice cream and everything. They feed us all the time. But when I heard the fried pig skins, I'm all, "Oh, that's a new one, guys! [laughter] That's a new one!" I had never heard that one before. I'm all, "Shit!"

But it gets really hectic in here at times. It gets really, really bad, and really, really stressed. And you go home, first thing you do is just sit down on the couch and you just sit there. You don't turn the TV on. You just sit there. You veg. Yeah. That's all you do. You know, you don't wanna talk. You don't wanna get the phones. Everything's a hassle. You just veg, like, for an hour. And if people do talk to you, you don't hear them. You don't do anything. You just kinda veg. It's pretty wild. Our shifts are eight hours. But most of us do a lot of twelve-hour shifts, just because there's so much overtime. There's always overtime here. And lately, we've just been really short-staffed, so all of us have been pulling. Like today is my day off, and I've been here four hours. Just because.

Roslyn's description of the job of dispatching emphasizes the sedentary nature of the work, in stark contrast to the medics' portrayals of their tasks as being action filled and physically demanding. In fact, eating plays a major role in the representation of the dispatchers' work. Job stress, for the dispatchers, derives from the high call volume and the difficulties of juggling numerous field units. The stress Roslyn speaks of seems to resemble what is described by air traffic controllers.[11] The physical environment itself is akin to that of air traffic control, and Jamie's representation of the work compares the two as well.

Unlike medics, dispatchers do not have a well-developed storytelling tradition. Perhaps because their work is highly repetitive and their environment is generally constant, dispatchers do not have the opportunity for unique experiences. Furthermore, the dispatchers all work in the same area; they do not seek each other out during down time, nor is there any pressing need to trade stories with other dispatchers, as is the case among medics. Jamie mentions this paucity of storytelling:

Jamie: Now, you asked me originally about any stories. It's tough because now I deal in numbers and times. And I don't even remember things. Things like bad calls don't faze me because I'm on the clock. And of course I'm concerned about the public, and I want them to get help, and as quickly as possible. I also have to look at what I've got to do, and after that call has been dispatched, I have to start positioning other units to ensure that that area is covered. And so weird calls, they just don't stick out in my mind.

In large part, dispatchers rarely encounter calls that are out of the ordinary since, as medics point out, most calls are dispatched as mundane, unexceptional emergencies. Furthermore, dispatchers never actually see the scene; its only visual representation is the computer-generated map with a number identifying the responding unit. In medic storytelling, it is only when the medics arrive on scene that the call acquires its startling characteristics.

Dispatchers, of course, express differing opinions on the work itself, but, because of the presence of supervisors, there was a general reluctance to talk openly about problems associated with the dispatch system. They did not, however, hesitate to comment on their uneasy alliance with the field personnel:

Mary: Gosh, the stress level in here would make you burn out real quickly.

Susan: Sharon, you can see the steam coming off the top of her head. Mmm. But you also don't get the luxury of moving around and being outdoors. You're stuck in here.

Sharon: Being able to do your details.

Karen: I would rather deal with the stress in here and not being able to move around than deal with grumpy RNs and doctors.

Susan: I think I'd rather deal with that than in here, because in here you go through grumpy RNs, you deal with your grumpy doctors, your grumpy personnel.

Sharon: You deal with your grumpy crews.

Susan: Your crews, your irate RNs.

Amy: Yeah, but you've never had a doctor berate you in front of people in the ER.

Sharon: You know what? Not to mention, in here. I mean, think about when a paramedic gets on scene of a call of an auto accident, and it's like, a three-unit response. Everybody's running around, it's chaos. We deal with that for almost eight solid hours some days. Now, that crew gets off that call and they're like, "Whew," you know, "it's over." We don't have that luxury. I mean, you have to actually get up and leave in order to do it.

Mary: Yeah. You know, we're in the middle of doing our paperwork, where they can just say, "Well, we can't handle the call, because . . ."

Sharon: Yeah, "We don't wanna go."

Mary: "We don't wanna go," you know? But we have to, no matter what, keep the call volume going and everything. I use an example of how you catch a huge fish that does not want to be reeled in. That's what it's like getting most of these paramedics and EMTs to go on their calls. You have to fight with them the whole entire way.

Sharon: Although there are exceptions. There are people, there are people who will clear in a second for you.

Mary: Yeah, there are people who will clear, and go on calls.

Sharon: And they will give those other crews who sit in the hospitals and heat up their dinner before they clear for a Code 3, they'll give those crews a hard time.

Susan: We had a paramedic crew come in service and not bother to tell us or to log in with the computer because it was extremely busy. And they were watching other paramedic crews pass by them. For five and a half hours they sat at this one post and never said a thing. Fire departments, other ambulances going by them. They sat there and said nothing for five hours, until they finally came up with a GPS and it's just like, "Excuse me, how long have you been sitting there?" "Oh, five hours!" [laughter] It's like, "Okay, you're clueless! What's wrong with you?" You meet people like that—they have no concern for patient care. How could you sit there while your peers run like that?

And then all of a sudden it looks like something that dispatch might have screwed up on. While in turn, we can't really screw up anything unless somebody fails to pass us the ball. Well, we didn't drop the ball. Nobody handed us the ball to tell us that these crews were in service. And there's those crews that won't go Code 12 when they're supposed to, which is really nice. It means they're responding with the fire department. I like that. Then you can tell the crews that have been working too many years. There's paramedics who definitely need to retire, and there's ones who are really enjoying their job. It kinda goes the same way around here. [laughter]

Karen: Yeah, they're some crews that should be hanging up the old jumpsuit.

Susan: Mmm. The ones that should really hang up their old jumpsuit, know-it-all, 10-4, smart on the radio, and they'll try to argue with you on the radio, and it's just like, "I'm not here to argue with you, I'm just kinda here to pass on information." You can tell they're in no hurry. The good crews will try to be there as fast as they can. They'll go with the fire departments. They'll do exactly what they're supposed to. When they're on scene for twenty minutes, they'll go Code 4 with us, to make sure that they're doing okay. They'll usually advise us within twenty minutes. If we don't hear from them, we in turn have to ask them, are they okay? The crews that love their job will go on scene before the fire department, let you know whether the fire department is needed. They'll say that they're fine, they're Code 4. They'll let you know when they're transporting, they'll go 10-7 to the hospital after going in Code 3 and available in twenty minutes. Whereas some of the ones who haven't are still doing their paperwork and haven't even made their gurney up for forty-five minutes. It's like, what is this? So it goes both ways.

As do the medics, the dispatchers make frequent use of jargon in their storytelling; here, it is the language of radio communications. In part, they use this terminology to present themselves as "systems status management" experts, with these conversations becoming a means of criticizing the medics for not fully understanding the complexity of their task. The dispatchers' complaints also suggest that medics shirk their responsibilities, making the dispatchers' work more difficult and thus creating more stress.

Similarly, medics complain that dispatchers add to the stress of their work. Constant shifts in post assignments and incomplete information concerning calls are two elements that medics cite when commenting on the dispatchers' role in contributing to job-related stress. One afternoon, Bill V. discussed paramedic stress and the link he sees to dispatch:

Bill V.: You know our dispatch is a multimillion dollar communication center. If you go in there they've got computers, it's all dark with this soft backdrop light, it's like something out of *Batman*. I'm telling you they've got big-screen wall maps that are computer generated, they can flip up parts all over the world! They've got all the latest communication equipment, they have this computer system where you can push a button in the ambulance and it tells them what hospital you're going to, what code you're going there. When you get there you push one button, when you leave there, you push another button, when you go on a call you push another button. They've got this satellite tracking thing on the roof of these ambulances, where they can track an ambulance any place in the world and be accurate within like ten feet, latitude, longitude and altitude. How many million dollars they spent for this, and they still ask you, "What's your location?" They'll send one ambulance on a call going north, another ambulance on a call going south, passing each other—you're waving at the other crew as you go by them. Or like we just experienced a little while ago, have us go from a south county position to the farthest position in the county north, passing probably eight other units in between. You know what it is? It's the unknowns that stress you out!

Later in the day, Bill once again brings up stress and the effects of it on his physical and emotional well-being:

Bill V.: There's no sense in what the dispatch does. The best organization in the country and they've got the weakest dispatch that there could be. I mean it's mind boggling. See, the dispatch—the communications department—in this company is a completely different department. While we're operations, they're communications, and if dispatch isn't a part of operations I don't know what is. And they're their own omnipotent little organization. They don't answer to anybody but themselves. They just do their own thing and make their plans, their own agendas. No planning whatsoever has to do with the field, and with no education, and no formal training other than some OJT [on-the-job training], they're given this power over the paramedics. They say where we go, what we do, when we do it. They say when we can go get a sandwich, if we can go get a sandwich, when we can go to the bathroom, if we can go to the bathroom. And, after our twelve-hour shift, we're ready to go home, ten minutes before you're ready to get off duty, they can send you off on a call—whether it's emergency or not—and you'll be gone for another two hours, making the day a fourteen-hour day with no concern, no remorse, with all sorts of immunity, just at their own will. There can be another unit closer, if they give it to you, you don't have any recourse.

George: You have to constantly modify in order to get back.

Bill: Oh, you know, I worked nights—a strike shift—for eighteen months. And we were constantly in depletion, which means there's one or two units available in the whole county. And to describe my job to a friend of mine would be like saying, "I go to San Leandro, I pick up an ambulance and I drive to L.A. and back, every day." And maybe run two or three calls in between. I mean, I came up here to this company by choice, and it's a better gig, but because I'm spending twelve hours in an ambulance behind the wheel sitting on my ass all day, I gained fifty pounds, I came down with what my doctor called stress-induced diabetes and hypertension, because you're at work for twelve hours plus each day. You've got an hour commute each way a day, so that leaves you ten hours in a day left to bathe, feed yourself, sleep, and God forbid if you ever wanted to interact with your wife or children! And my doctor called it stress-induced diabetes and hypertension because there's no history of it on any side of my family ever.

Bill offers a resounding critique of the dispatchers' lack of training and of the authority they have, as well as of management's lack of organizational foresight in separating operations and communications. He places particular emphasis on the control that the dispatchers have over his work day, suggesting that this authority has not been earned. Finally, he presents the opinion of a doctor to back up his claims that the irresponsible actions of dispatchers jeopardize his health.

Bill is by no means alone in his criticism of dispatch. Steve Y. also speaks of the seemingly incessant orders from dispatchers to repost, making clear his frustrations with the flexible deployment system:

Steve Y.: Yeah, that's what kills me, just how stupid people are. Any brains at all, they could sit there and look at their computer screens and evaluate the posts, and say, "Okay. Well, everything is full, 527 is on their way down from Oakland. Oh, here comes 529 back from Stanford across the bridge. Well, let's see. They're off in half an hour so we want to get them close to the barn, why don't we stop 527 at San Leandro and Davis?" No, they wait until we get all the way down to post, and wait until 529 tells them they're back on the other side of the bridge. Hello. Okay, well, fuck, now we gotta send 527 back again. You know, just driving hundreds of miles for no reason. And it's all stuff that could be easily fixed. Fuckin' A. King Steve, I'd like it.

To medics working in the field, the fix seems painfully apparent. Medics themselves prefer a static system, since it gets them out of the ambulance and into a more stable environment. Crews on twenty-four-hour shifts, particularly in the eastern sections of the county, do have the luxury of station houses, and these shifts are coveted. Although station houses result in a slight reduction in autonomy, this is seen to be a small trade-off.

Darryl and Derek, assigned to a twenty-four-hour car, comment on various strategies they have adopted to circumvent dispatch requests for units to remain in service:

Darryl: There's times, right at the end of a shift, and the scanner goes off and I'm going, "Goddamn!" And there's like a shortness of breath call in downtown Oakland at some project or something. Stupid call, right off the bat. And fifteen minutes before you get off duty is not a time to run a call because it basically takes us an hour to run a call. And not that we don't like overtime, but when it's time to go home, I can go home. I'd rather go home. I work my overtime when I want to, not at their convenience.

And so we had this call and I said, I go, "You don't wanna run the call?" And he said, "No." So I flagged this bum down, "Come over here!" And I said, "You want your blood pressure taken?" "Oh, sure!" "You want an EKG?" "Oh yeah, yeah, take my blood pressure and EKG." So I said, "Fine." Put out, "We've just been flagged over by a pedestrian downtown and won't be available!" So, we put ourselves out on this call and waited for the other unit to get dispatched to this call. They get to the call. And then we putzed around with this guy and say, "Yeah, you don't want to go to the hospital?" "Well, no, never did." [laughter] Well, we know that— "Here, sign here, bye." [laughter] And just left. Made up a patient. Didn't have to run the call and got off on time! So, you have to milk it. Milk it, like a cow. The system. Because we do what we want, hunh, Dooks?

Derek: To a point.

Darryl: To a point. We're our own bosses. To a point. [laughter] We had our supervisor here earlier, but he just wanted us to clean up our mess in the station house here.

Darryl undermines the dispatcher's authority by fabricating a patient. What he sees as an abusive act on the part of the dispatchers opens the door for him and his partner to retaliate. In turn, they force another unit to respond to a "bullshit" call. While solidarity generally exists among medic units, there is also an underlying attitude of self-preservation. Here Darryl and Derek undercut the dispatchers' orders by involving another crew.

In a humorous commentary on the lack of common sense among dispatchers, Lars tells a story of a seemingly lost ambulance and of the dispatchers' blind reliance on their technological gadgetry:

Lars: The first system was this thing, the automatic vehicle locator [AVL]. They were still having all these bugs with it. One day, you hear them asking a unit for their 10-20 and they're all like, "Oh, we're on Jackson Street in Hayward." They're like, "Well, negative, we show your ambulance, well, we show your ambulance in the bay." And they're like, "Well, we're not in the bay." "Well, that's where we show your unit." I mean, the dispatchers were insisting that this ambulance was out in the bay, because that's where it was showing—out in the bay. So, "Well, we show your unit out there." [laughter] "You're right, you're right, you caught us, man, we're sailing! "

Mark G.: Chitty Chitty Bang Bang.

Lars: Right, we've got fins, it's amphibious, and we're out here fishing. "We'll bring it back up on land." Yuh. That's the AVL.

Lars's story underscores the reluctance of the dispatchers to accept the word of the medics. The dispatcher chooses to trust the equipment over the field personnel despite what is obviously erroneous information.

Many medics express grave distrust of dispatch, viewing it as a bottomless well of improper information, echoing Tom B.'s comment: "You see the nature of the dispatch, you can't trust that!" Stories frequently mention calls that turn out to be far more serious than was indicated when the call was initially dispatched. But Bill V. points out that dispatch is not the only group to blame for the poor information that medics receive while responding to a call:

Bill V.: Because a person dials 911, they talk to a fire dispatcher or a cop dispatcher and they talk to a fire dispatcher and then they talk to our dispatcher and then they talk to us. It's the same game we used to play in Cub Scouts. You know, you have fifteen kids in the Cub Scout troop all lined up and the den mother gives a little phrase to one Cub Scout in his ear, and he passes it along, and it starts off as spinal meningitis and it ends up as smilin' baby Jesus! You know, it's the same thing. It's funny.

Bill draws attention to the multiple transmissions required before the call is dispatched and the degeneration in the signal that this causes. Not all dispatch systems work in the same manner, although most do rely on a central clearinghouse for calls.[12] In recent years, highly publicized examples of mishandled emergency calls have been examined in the press and on television.[13] While the entire EMS system is generally painted with one large brush, these failings in dispatch receive the most scrutiny.

Although several paramedics told stories which involved dispatch laxity, oversight, or other mishandling of calls, Melinda told the most clear-cut of these stories, in which the accusatory finger points directly at the dispatchers:

Melinda: We got a Code 2 once for hemorrhaging, and thought, you know, "Great, somebody's bleeding out," or something. So we said, "Confirm Code 2." They're like, "Fine." Come back a little while later and tell us that our patient is bleeding from the chest and abdomen, and we say, "Confirm Code 2," they say, "Yes." We keep going, we get there right behind the cops and there are people running around, "He's dying! Go upstairs!" You know, we go upstairs. There's this guy stabbed in the chest. Dead. That was our Code 2 fatal stabbing to the heart.

Despite Melinda's persistent queries concerning the status of the call, the dispatchers continue to give it low priority. While all of the indications are that the call should receive a Code 3 priority, they steadfastly maintain their original position. As a result, the patient is already dead by the time Melinda and her partner arrive.

Field medics resoundingly criticize dispatchers and the entire communications enterprise. Dispatchers are considered to be poorly trained, unattuned to the demands of the medics' work environment, and unwilling to use common sense. Medics express persistent distrust of the information they receive about calls and tell stories which support their misgivings. Dispatchers are seen as being vested with far too much power, and their persistent intrusion into the front seat of the ambulance—the medics' "living room"—takes on the attributes of nagging. For their part, dispatchers assail the paramedics for what they perceive to be laziness and a pervasive unwillingness to honor their requests.

Management and dispatch are subject to many of the same criticisms that other first responders and medical personnel face in paramedic storytelling. The attitudes of the medics towards their managers reveal serious organizational problems. Paramedics have a great deal of autonomy in their work, which they value highly, believing that their training and performance justify this independence. They willingly censure other medics for below par performance or any action which reflects poorly on the group. They are also quick to react to anyone who abridges their freedom or otherwise infringes on their autonomy. Field supervisors, the most persistent clear intrusion of management into the medics' work environment, are often the object of scorn. Dispatchers, perhaps because they cannot take revenge on medics, are even more commonly ridiculed than supervisors. Perceived as uncaring, disembodied voices emanating from an anonymous control room in corporate headquarters, the dispatchers become a metaphoric stand-in for the company and its administration. Like management, they are are seen as being too much concerned about maintaining a high call volume and quick call turnover, with no human element coming into play.

# CONCLUSION

People tell stories constantly. We tell each other stories about what we did over the weekend, about our vacations, about the great deal we got on a used car. We tell stories to our fellow workers about work experiences.[1] Paramedics are no different. As is true with everyone else, paramedics' motivations for storytelling are numerous. Indeed, it would be impossible to determine all the uses of storytelling and misleading to suggest that a storytelling session serves only one purpose — such events have a number of simultaneous functions. When asked directly why they tell stories, nearly all paramedics cite the entertainment component. Humorous situations, strange happenings, and surprising incongruities all appear in the stories, and listening to them offers a diversion from the tedium of paperwork and of sitting at post, from awareness of the poverty of the inner city, and from the stress of an ongoing parade of patients.

Storytelling frequently occurs as a response to geographical sites or occupational encounters. For instance, after a call for a minor auto accident, a medic may choose to tell the story of a far more serious wreck. The story thus acts as a commentary not only on the accident just encountered but on his or her entire experience of dealing with accidents. At other times, a medic's memory will be jogged by the medical complaint of a current patient (smells often trigger these memories), and he or she will narrate a call of a more critical nature. Medics also tell stories as a response to interactions with other emergency responders. A negative experience with an uncooperative firefighter may prompt a medic to tell of a similar, earlier encounter. The story thus acts as a rhetorical device, providing additional evidence of the incompetence of a perceived competitor.

Storytelling is more than an elaborate response to an event—it is itself a form of interaction. For medics, storytelling most frequently takes place between partners in the front seat of the ambulance.[2] In fact, storytelling constitutes part of the process of becoming partners. As Mark G. mentions, getting a new partner means having a chance to tell one's old stories again and to hear the partner's stories as well. Listening to these stories, the partners assess each other. Alternately assuming the role of narrator and audience, they simulate the turn-taking that occurs in their work, with one medic driving and the other caring for the patient. Not all partners get along, however, and in these cases stories can reveal the friction and even contribute to a mutual dislike. Regardless of whether or not partners get along, they spend so much time together that they inevitably become well versed in each other's stories. This narrative overlap becomes apparent when groups of medics get together and swap stories.

Since there are neither station houses nor a main facility in Alameda County, medics only interact with other crews at the emergency room loading zones of area hospitals. Here they have the opportunity to talk to coworkers and tell each other stories. One medic may take center stage, assuming the role of narrator and telling several stories, with only occasional comments offered by the audience. Sometimes, a medic will cut his or her partner off and finish the story. At other times, the two partners take turns narrating a call. More commonly, however, medics respond to the first narrator's story with stories of their own. If one describes a horrible car accident, another may tell of a grisly train wreck, with yet another recounting an even more terrible airplane crash. In these situations, there is a distinct sense of competition, each medic trying to outdo the "cool call" narrative of the next. During such competitions, the phenomenon of narrative ownership becomes apparent. Although a medic may narrate a call run by another who is not present, attempting to narrate the "cool call" of a medic who is present will usually result in protest. An exception to this may be a medic who narrates his or her partner's call. One also encounters, in these situations, the phenomenon of "narrative chicken." If one medic relates a story of bending the rules slightly to avoid transporting an offensive patient, another may tell of a somewhat more flagrant violation of the rules. The game thus augments the brinksmanship of "cool call" sessions, while adding to it the dangerous element of having transgressed company policy.

Telling stories plays a significant role in the medics' presentation of self. In their stories, they emerge as authorities, able to handle the most difficult situations with surprising composure. Despite chaotic scenes, bumbling firefighters, misinformed police, dangerous patients, failing equipment, incompetent nurses, and overzealous physicians, the medics are able to save their patients. Commonly, they present themselves as skilled experts in prehospital care; even when they make mistakes, their patients quickly recover and the gaffe is laughed away. At the scenes of terrible carnage, the medics are the only ones able to stomach the sights and smells that assault them, shrugging it all off with a sarcastic quip. In their stories, they are unafraid to enter dangerous neighborhoods, and are able to beat back assailants; this presentation of self as sarcastic superhero is often mirrored in the bravado of the storytelling.

But another presentation of self exists alongside this image of the cool, in-control medical authority who literally laughs at death—that of the compassionate, sympathetic, and caring healer willing to take extraordinary risks to save any life, who celebrates the patients' recovery and cries over their suffering. So, while medics present themselves as being inured to human misery, they simultaneously present themselves as empathetic. Different storytelling situations provoke different presentations of self. Although the two images—cool authority and empathetic healer—are apparently contradictory, most medics seem to have internalized both. Medics are, in fact, masters of contradiction, deriding in their stories many of their patients, even though they have treated these same people with all of their skill and energy.

Storytelling can also be seen as an informal mode of debriefing. One of the most touted developments in Emergency Medical Services is Critical Incident Stress Debriefing (CISD), a formal interaction in which medics discuss aspects of the work among themselves, narrating their personal experiences with a particularly difficult call, discussing their feelings about the deaths of their patients. But, because attending CISD is considered a sign of weakness, many medics are reluctant to request it. In its place, cohort storytelling acts as a much-needed outlet for expression of the emotions that arise from seeing people suffer or die. Storytelling, thus, can serve as a form of continuous CISD.

By narrating a call, a medic structures the scene, imposes a chronology on the events, and provides an ending. This last aspect is an important element of medic storytelling. Frank Kermode suggests that the human will to narrate is part of our need to provide a beginning and an end to the middle ground that we inhabit.[3] It is their ability to order the ruthless onslaught of time, the endless procession of one call after another, that allows medics to find meaning in what could easily be seen as a meaningless parade of patients. Medics' interactions with their patients are open-ended; except when their patients die at the scene or on the way to the hospital, there is rarely resolution. Once patients have been delivered to the hospital, the medic almost never learns the ultimate outcome. Did they survive? Or did they die on the operating table? While "reality" television programs such as *Rescue 911* reunite the medic with the patient long after the call, in real life medics seldom experience such closure. Storytelling may provide an "end" to the interaction.

Among medics, storytelling can act as a form of resistance. Although patients are treated with a great deal of professionalism on scene, medics can describe them callously in stories, deriding them for being uneducated, unaware, and undeserving. In this sense, the storytelling becomes an arena for expressing what Santino dubs "outlaw emotions."[4] Medics also use this mode to express resistance to authority. Even though they enjoy a great deal of autonomy in their work, they are still closely watched by hospital personnel, field supervisors, other emergency responders, and company review boards. Feeling that these groups are challenging their abilities, the medics respond in their stories. When a certain situation—such as the intransigence of a haughty nurse—provokes narration, it is usually in the form of a stinging critique. Although the medics may not be able to exact any real vengeance on their tormentors, they can exact narrative revenge. Ultimately, the frequent appeal to storytelling as a form of resistance to the company and to the medical establishment suggests a need for fundamental reform in management style as well as for a more meaningful dialogue with physicians and nurses concerning the role of paramedics as experts in prehospital care.

Medics' stories also constitute a significant part of their elaborate, ongoing, sometimes contradictory commentary on American society. In their stories, they address many of the social issues facing contemporary America, including drug abuse, crime, violence, teenage pregnancy, alcoholism, child abuse, homelessness, neglect of the elderly, and racism. They not only comment on these issues but also suggest remedies. Since they do not necessarily agree on solutions to these problems, storytelling sessions at times involve heated debates over what the best approaches would be. In these cases, stories are used as example and counterexample. Despite the disagreements, it would probably be wise for policy makers to heed the medics' frontline accounts, as there are few groups in a better position to evaluate the efficacy of certain programs or to offer ideas for solutions to social problems.

Every medic tells stories in his or her own way. Some, like Lars, have mastered a wry, sardonic attitude, and have turned the odd juxtaposition into an art form. In Lars's stories, the banal becomes horrific, while the horrible becomes banal. Others, like Darryl, tell stories at a frenetic pace, adopting the stance of the "adrenaline jockey," or, like Tony, infuse their stories with bemused incredulity. Bill L., for instance, tells more measured stories, but adds wickedly funny twists at the end. Some, such as Tom B., may place emphasis on medical treatments, or, like Lisa, on locations. In some cases, medics adopt a self-deprecating stance, while at other times they imbue their stories with great emotion. Gallows humor is often a significant element. Perhaps the only prohibited storytelling style is that of the self-congratulatory, condescending "hero"; self-aggrandizement is universally disparaged, and those who adopt that stance are immediately mocked by their cohorts.

Even though each medic develops an individual style, there is a certain amount of overlap, partly attributable to a conscious co-option of the stylistic devices of those considered to be good storytellers. For example, a medic who likes Lars's dry presentation might begin to tell his or her stories with the same kind of acerbic wit. Partners frequently have markedly similar styles, probably a result of their repeated inter-actions and the adjustments of their styles to audience response.[5] This alignment of personal style allows groups of partners to establish a cooperative storytelling style.

Expectations concerning what constitutes a good story also lead to certain common stylistic features. With few exceptions, such as stories about pediatric deaths, medics expect each other to adopt a slightly ironic tone. Any replication of the "official story" presented at the emergency room would probably be considered boring, with its excessive attention to medical treatment and monotone delivery; medics generally expect some comment on the patient's condition, as well as a characterization of locale. They also use jargon, peppering their stories with street slang, medical terminology, and radio codes. The presence of these terms makes the stories accessible only to other members of the group; unless one has spent time on the streets, in hospitals, and communicating with dispatchers, the stories are all but unintelligible. The use of specialized language, although not necessarily a conscious narrative ploy, signals that the storyteller is part of the group and excludes uninitiated listeners.

Among the most intriguing elements of story content are the surprising metaphors that medics frequently employ. Often, they place scenes of horrible trauma in the realm of the comically mundane. Brains resemble bubblegum, skulls look like salad bowls, and burn victims smell like toast. In other stories, medics dwell on the surprising anatomical incongruities which result from violent accidents. Hearts pitter-patter down the street, eyeballs dangle like keys at the end of the optic nerve, and intestines hang from trees. As in the David Letterman routines in which objects are pushed from the tops of high buildings or crushed between the plates of a ten-ton press, the humor derives from the unexpected results of the event. Often, storytellers reduce the victims to their component parts, thus eliminating the concept of a whole person; the victim is simply "teeth, hair, and eyeballs all over the desert."

The medics' stories also refer to the fictive world of motion pictures. Thus, the site of a medical emergency is "the scene," well-known motion pictures are mentioned time and again, and the descriptions of emergencies are "like something out of a horror movie." Perhaps these references act as a much-needed distancing device. By comparing the events to the world of film, the medics lessen the scene's impact — it becomes "unreal." This narrative ploy also allows the medic to act as a spectator at a horror film; as one paramedic says, the calls are "real *Night of the Living Dead* shit." Filmgoers know that the monster is not going to reach through the fourth wall of the movie screen and that blood is not going to splatter their clothes. Or perhaps the narrative device of the film offers the medic a chance to tell a story about the other side, as there is no inviolate window between the medic and the horror show. They enter that otherwise inaccessible diegetic space and return to tell about it. Like the actor on the movie screen, the medic emerges as larger than life.

Paramedics' stories bring into the open sights that are ordinarily kept hidden: bodies are opened up, organs are exposed in startling ways, skin is stripped away or disintegrates. What was once out of sight now commands center stage. In other stories, aspects of city life that are usually out of view, such as prostitution, drug use, assault, and murder, appear repeatedly as the focus of the narrative. Deviant behaviors occurring in bedrooms, tenements, and back hallways are illuminated by the glaring light of raucous stories. In these accounts, actions that were intended to be secret go awry, and what should have been a private performance becomes a public event, accompanied by screaming sirens, flashing lights, screeching ambulances, and the spectacle of an emergency response. As part of their work, medics come into frequent contact with those who have been marginalized—

intentionally kept out of view by society's biases—and, in the medics' stories of attempted and successful suicides, psychologically unstable patients, transsexuals, victims of domestic abuse, and the horrifically obese, these people emerge as subjects for everyone to hear about.

A distinction exists between the real world in which the paramedics work (and tell stories) and the world conjured up in their stories.[6] Although the streets and neighborhoods stay the same, the medics' interaction with the physical environment differs according to whether they are on or off duty. They refer to their work as a form of tourism or exploration, akin to visiting a foreign land, but they do not consider the job to be an innocuous foray. Instead, their presentation of the work environment includes a degree of danger. The medics are visiting parts of the city where, in Mary's words, "you wouldn't even think to go for a thousand dollars!" The perceived boundaries between "safe" and "dangerous" that govern their movement when they are not at work are crossed in the ambulance on a daily basis. By crossing these boundaries, the medics become, in their own eyes, more than urban tourists—they become urban warriors. (Certainly the term "paramedic," with its slightly militaristic overtones, and the uniform of jumpsuit and combat boots encourage this perception of the job.) Thus, for the paramedics, there are three distinct versions of the same environment: nonwork interactions with the physical world, on-the-job encounters with that world, and fictive representations of it in their stories.

The majority of medics' stories are told among themselves, and this tradition is an integral part of their work culture. Stories provide an opportunity for the medics to explore and organize events, release some of the emotional impact of dealing with gruesome accidents or untimely deaths, and position themselves in the world of emergency providers. For the outsider, these narratives offer a glimpse into a chaotic, albeit fictive, world hidden beneath the shiny veneer of social order. In this world, where the weirdest calls always come at three o'clock in the morning, the medics are the competent guides, able to extract themselves from dangerous situations, while simultaneously providing expert care to their sometimes undeserving patients.

# NOTES

## Preface

1. Tedlock 1972.

## Introduction

1. Abrahams 1968.
2. More and more literature has begun addressing ambiguity and contradiction in work organizations. See, for example, Gregory 1983; Martin and Siehl 1983; Meyerson 1990; Nickerson 1990; Martin 1992; Hatch and Ehrlich 1993; Alvesson 1993.
3. Allaire and Firsirotu 1984: 193. See also Silverman 1970. The work of Ouchi (1981) and Peters and Waterman (1982) were instrumental in popularizing this approach. For examples of other studies of culture in work organizations, see Barley 1983; Kanter and Stein 1979; Kotter and Heskett 1992; Pettigrew 1979; Schein 1990. Trice and Bayer (1993) provide an excellent overview of theoretical perspectives on work culture.
4. In a recent reappraisal of this trend in management literature, Allaire and Firsirotu note that, while these concepts have gained in popularity, there is little agreement either on what these phenomena are or how to interpret them (1984: 194).
5. For anthropological approaches to culture, see Benedict 1960; Geertz 1973a and 1973b; Goodenough 1971. Allaire and Firsirotu (1984) provide an excellent summary of major anthropological theory and illustrate how it can be used in relation to the study of occupational culture. See also Georges 1969; Smircich and Calás 1987.
6. Those interested in seeing and listening to storytelling performances should view the companion documentary, *Talking Trauma: Storytelling Among Paramedics* (Tangherlini 1994b). It provides far greater detail concerning kinesthetic and paralinguistic aspects of performance than the edited transcripts reprinted here.

7. Stahl 1977; Robinson 1981. Terkel's *Working* (1972) is perhaps the best-known study of personal experience narratives concerning occupations.

8. Labov and Waletzky 1967.

9. Fluids and medications are often delivered intravenously to patients; starting the intravenous line is one of the paramedics' main skills and one which distinguishes them from the less extensively trained emergency medical technicians (EMTs).

10. Lester (1986) discusses the socialization of new members of organizations. The new medic can be seen in this context as a lay ethnographer (Louis 1990). When new paramedics begin to tell stories, the others apparently evaluate whether or not the narrated experience is worth being told or, more accurately, worth listening to. As the paramedic gains experience, earlier narratives may be discarded or reworked to fit into the collective expressive culture. For the role of storytelling in developing community, see Dégh 1969; Fine 1988; Lindow and Tangherlini 1995. See also Jansen 1959 concerning the concepts of esoteric and exoteric in folklore study.

11. Once again, this performative setting cannot be generalized for all EMS systems. In the system studied, the paramedics have no fixed stations but are deployed flexibly throughout the entire area of coverage. Thus, a paramedic unit can, and often does, spend an entire shift without seeing any other paramedics. Not surprisingly, when several units have dropped off patients at the same hospital, there is a tendency for the medics to linger and discuss "calls."

12. Robinson 1981: 64.

13. In a classic formulation of this, C. W. von Sydow suggested the concept of "active" and "passive" tradition bearers (1932). In a study of Danish legend tradition, I have reformulated von Sydow's proposition, suggesting that it is more accurate to refer to active and passive "tradition participants" and recognizing that there is an entire continuum of more and less active participation (Tangherlini 1994a: 30–33).

14. In 1989, 10.6 percent of the population of Alameda County and 18.8 percent of the population of Oakland lived below the poverty level (Slater and Hall 1995: 830–32).

15. Washington, D.C. seems currently to have a lock on the title (*New York Times* Staff 1991).

## Chapter One

1. The slightly polemical *Omaha Orange: A Popular History of EMS in America* attempts to chronicle the meandering path of EMS development over the past thirty years, but gets inextricably tangled in the web of contradictions that characterize the development of EMS and the emergence of paramedicine

(Post 1992). Excellent studies of the work of emergency medical responders can be found in Metz 1981 and Mannon 1992. A photographic documentary of emergency medicine popular among paramedics is Reiter 1977. McCarl (1985) provides an excellent glimpse into the related world of firefighters. A good chronological overview of the development of EMS and paramedicine can be gleaned from reading reports on the status of emergency medicine from the past twenty years; for example, see Curry 1965; Rockwood et al. 1976; Romano et al. 1978; and Gonsalves 1988. Cook's bibliography (1978) also provides reasonable coverage of the early years of ambulance services. Cady (1992) offers an overview of service providers in the largest cities in the United States. The California Codes define in great detail the current parameters of EMS in California (State of California 1990).

2. U.S. Department of Health, Education and Welfare Survey 1971. While the survey showed substantial variations by state, funeral homes were major providers of ambulance transport in every state surveyed. Other providers of emergency medical transport noted in the survey included police departments, fire departments, public health departments, hospital-based services, and private ambulance companies. See also Chaiken and Gladstone 1974; Cady 1992. An early view of the need for coherent, well-organized ambulance services appears in Cadmus and Ketner 1965.

3. In the 1971 survey, 87 percent of the ambulances carried oxygen, 81 percent sterile gauze, 77 percent adhesive tape, 65 percent splints, 54 percent wound dressings, 43 percent suction devices, and 30 percent backboards (US DHEW 1971: 7). Only 56 percent of the ambulances carried radio equipment (US DHEW 1971: 9). All of this equipment is currently required on ambulances. The majority of ambulances—55 percent—were either hearses or station wagons (US DHEW 1971: 6).

4. The five provisions of the bill authorizing the establishment of emergency medical transportation and service programs read as follows: "The Secretary is authorized to make grants to States, political subdivisions, regional arrangements, and other public or nonprofit agencies, organizations, and institutions, or combinations thereof, for special projects—(1) to plan and develop in a region, State, or political subdivision medical emergency transportation programs; (2) to provide for the establishment and improvement of emergency medical transportation systems...to insure prompt, effective, emergency medical care...;(3) to develop programs providing for the operative use of equipment and personnel of any of the several uniformed services for appropriate emergency medical transportation assistance to civilian accident victims; (4) to research, design, and demonstrate advances in various methods of, and equipment for, medical emergency transportation and communication; and

(5) to develop and operate training programs, and train medical emergency transportation service personnel" (U.S. House of Representatives 1972: 4–5). This last provision in particular provided the impetus and the funds for the development of advanced EMT training and a subsequent gradation of training levels among EMTs. The paramedics, EMT-Ps, now represent the highest rung on this ladder. For a historical perspective on the early years of paramedic training, see Staroscik and Cayten 1976.

5. Ornato et al. 1983. There continues to be debate over the usefulness of paramedics, with some physicians expressing doubts about the effectiveness of paramedic care in optimizing patient outcomes, particularly in the case of traumatic cardiac arrest (Aprahamian et al. 1985).

6. The *New York Times* reported on one such case in which lesser-trained EMTs left a woman for dead in her apartment. A doctor from the medical examiner's office later discovered her to be alive (James 1993a and 1993b). Newspapers in other parts of the country incorrectly reported that the offending medical personnel were paramedics. See, for example, Associated Press (1993) and Gazette News Service (1993).

7. Various outcome studies support Tom's assertions concerning the skill of paramedics relative to that of other medical personnel in the prehospital environment. Mattera (1994) supports Tom's view that physicians on scene are not necessarily helpful; and Lewis, Stang, and Warren note that "EMT-Ps perform as effectively as physicians in diagnosis and care of acute cardiovascular emergencies, including endotracheal intubation" (1984: 200).

8. See, for example, Curry 1992.

9. Page 1984.

10. At times, medics decide not to make base contact, despite protocols and, as Palmer and Gonsoulin put it, "play doc," an action they interpret as deviant behavior (1990).

## Chapter Two

1. Also related to this phenomenon is the symbolic value of uniforms, alluded to by Kathryn. Kaiser notes that "a well-regimented appearance is expected in protective organizations, because such an image is viewed as a sign of efficiency and competence" (1990: 374). Joseph, in his study of the semiotics of uniforms, focuses on the reception of uniforms and clothing, noting that "the uniform is the legitimating emblem of membership within an organisation" (1986: 2). What is missing in many of the studies on the semiotics of clothing is how the wearers themselves perceive a change in self by donning a symbol-laden type of clothing such as a uniform. Certainly, in the numerous representations of "superheroes" in popular culture, there can be no mistaking

the special protective nature of uniforms, which guard the hero from the violent attacks of dangerous villains.

2. Moxibustion—the application of burning heat to acupressure points—is common in Chinese healing traditions.

3. It is difficult to determine whether the idea of paramedics being associated with legal authorities occurs to the medics as a way to justify their anxieties or is a notion held by the patients and the general community. Comments that I heard while on scene suggest that the paramedics are indeed associated in many people's minds with the "white establishment."

4. In none of the stories I collected did I find paramedics referring to their patients with racial epithets, a situation which contrasts significantly with Mark Fuhrman's storytelling and his frequent use of such derogatory terms (*Los Angeles Times* Staff 1995). While it is certainly possible that such stories exist, I did not hear or record any.

5. Peter D. Kramer, in an article in *The New York Times Magazine,* examines a similar attitude he encounters while saving a young man from a drowning. Despite saving the boy, Kramer and the two others who assist in the save, all white, are shunned by a crowd consisting of African Americans (1995: 15).

6. Public Enemy, on their album *Fear of a Black Planet,* released a song entitled "911 (is a joke)," which includes, in its refrain, the words, "911 is a joke in your town" (1990).

7. Dreifuss 1989. Dennis Bolt, vice president of American Medical Response, West, notes that only 15 percent of the sixty-seven thousand callers a year are actually reporting situations that require emergency care (Ronningen 1994).

8. Gabriel offers a similar analysis of stories from both the catering industry and the military, noting, "even if not true, people act as if they believe them and will often espouse them with considerable fervor" (1991: 870). For other discussions of truthfulness and believability, particularly in regard to legend, see Tangherlini 1990.

9. Humor and laughter among paramedics are complex phenomena. Linstead (1985) examines the role of humor in organizational culture. Morreall (1983) offers a thorough and sophisticated overview of theories of laughter, among them the theory that people laugh at people to whom they feel superior. For theoretical discussions of humor and laughter, see Apte 1985; Coser 1960; Dundes 1985 and 1987; Goldstein and McGhee 1972; Grotjahn 1966 (1957); Gruner 1978; Holland 1982; Piddington 1963; and Singer 1968. Moser-Rath (1972–1973) and Obrdlik (1982) provide analyses of the phenomenon of gallows humor. See also Dundes and Hauschild 1983. Bennet (1991) provides examples of general medical humor. Freud's theories of humor have informed much of the research in this area. In discussing humor, he notes: "Its fending

off of the possibility of suffering places it among the great series of methods which the human mind has constructed to evade the compulsion to suffer" (1927: 163).

10. The contract for Alameda County stipulated an eight-minute response time from the time of dispatch, in four regions, for 90 percent of the calls. Recently, the standard has been relaxed to a ten-minute response time. During an emergency, eight minutes can seem like a considerably long time. For perceptions of elapsed time on scene, see Jurkovich et al. 1987.

11. During my fieldwork, I noticed that burritos were one of the foods of choice among paramedics, partly because of the ubiquity of small stands and lunch wagons vending Mexican food, and also because of their low cost, their portability, and the ease with which they can be eaten as "hand food."

12. In Alameda County, paramedics respond alone to Code 2 calls, while the fire department also responds to all Code 3 calls. In the case of calls resulting from a crime, the police respond as well.

13. Gabriel suggests that some stories do not act as a means of venting built-up anxieties, but actually produce anxiety themselves, thus helping people prepare for the worst; when the worst eventually happens, it is not so threatening (1991: 869). Stories, thus, serve to inure the medics to dangerous, difficult, or threatening situations.

14. Abravanel (1983) discusses the use of stories as a means for mediating organizational ambiguity. For discussions of ambiguity in organizations, see Meyerson 1990; Hatch and Ehrlich 1993.

15. Clover, in her work on the horror film, notes a similar tendency to dwell on the violent opening of bodies and uncovering of otherwise hidden body parts (1992: 32). In a discussion of *The Texas Chainsaw Massacre,* she says that "the slasher evinces a fascination with flesh or meat itself as that which is hidden from view." This fascination with the "opened body" also seems to inform many paramedic stories. For a discussion of the "opened body" in the context of medical discourse, see Foucault 1963.

## Chapter Three

1. On August 31,1986, an Aeromexico jet collided with a smaller aircraft over Cerritos, California. Sixty-four people were killed in the jetliner, all three people in the smaller plane died, and fifteen were killed on the ground in the ensuing fires. Sixteen houses were destroyed (Thackrey 1986: 1, 4). See also Churm and Frammolino 1986; Frammolino and Jones 1986; Decker and Stein 1986.

2. Decker and Stein cite an off-duty Orange County policeman who said, "I was first on scene. When I saw the explosion, I knew they'd need help" (Septem-

ber 1, 1986: 19). Often, emergency personnel claim to be "the first on scene" at major accidents or disasters. One medic, mocking other medics' stories of the Loma Prieta earthquake, laughingly began a story with "Yeah, man, we were first on scene." Stopping short, he said, "Man, if all of the people who were first on scene really were first on scene it would have looked like a fucking convention."

3. In 1993, the year of this study, paramedics in Alameda county responded to nearly thirteen thousand vehicle accidents. Among the injured victims, slightly fewer than five hundred sustained major injuries, while one hundred six lost their lives (CHP 1994). For an interesting parallel discussion on the type of events that qualify as unusual enough to become part of a person's long-term story repertoire, see Jones 1976: 304.

4. Recaro is the name brand of a seat manufacturer renowned for making after-market seats for racing cars.

5. In recent literary and historical criticism, there has been an increased focus on the "writing of the body" (Laqueur and Gallagher 1987).

6. For work on CISD, see Rubin 1990; Mitchell 1983, 1988a and 1988b; Robinson and Mitchell 1993.

7. At the same time, the stories have similarities to the military story examined by Gabriel, which, he suggests, "resists the familiar interpretation of being a safety valve for anxiety." Instead, the story "generate[s] additional degrees of discomfort," and forces the medics into remembering and thus into a position of greater caution. Indeed, as Gabriel suggests, medic stories may in large part be seen not as an outlet for anxiety as a "dysfunctional by-product of mental processes, but, following the tradition established by McDougall and Freud, as a warning signal in situations of real danger which alerts, protects, and reduces the severity of potential trauma." Thus, for the medics as for Gabriel's navy recruits, "[a]nxiety, produced and reproduced through alarmist gossip and horror stories, ensures that the recruits are constantly prepared for the worst; and when the worst happens, the shock is somewhat diluted, the magnitude of the injury reduced" (1991: 869).

8. Perhaps the use of humor here parallels what Viktor Frankl wrote about life in the Nazi concentration camps: "[H]umor, more than anything else in the human make-up, can afford an aloofness and an ability to rise above any situation, if only for a few seconds" (quoted in Morreall 1983: 104). Morreall notes that "the more well developed a person's sense of humor, the wider the range of situations in which he can achieve the necessary distance to laugh" (1983: 104). While most people do not find the scenes of fatal auto accidents funny, paramedics have developed the ability to find humorous incongruities in such situations, which enables them to laugh.

9. The use of the term "gallows humor" is slightly incorrect in relation to paramedics, since it generally refers to the humor used by people who are facing
their own deaths. However, there seems to be a resemblance between the
medics' humor and real gallows humor. Morreall (1983: 104–105) notes this
similarity in his examination of theories of laughter. See also Freud (1927) and
A. Freud (1936) concerning emotional defense mechanisms. The humor may
in large part help the paramedics in their "debriefing" after difficult incidents.
One of the goals of debriefing is to allow a person to regain critical distance
from the traumatic event. In the world of paramedicine there is an increasing
focus on Critical Incident Stress Debriefings (CISD), pioneered by Jeffrey
Mitchell and the EMS services in Maryland in 1974 (Mitchell 1988b). Mitchell
suggests that medics responding to fewer than two hundred or more than
six hundred calls had significantly higher stress levels than their cohorts who
responded to between two and six hundred (1984: 53). Cydulka et al. (1989),
however, suggest that number of calls per shift has no significant correlation
to level of stress. Medics at Regional ran, on average, at least eight hundred
calls per year.

10. In 1991, there were two hundred forty-one accidents at railroad grade cross-
ings (the site of most accidents involving trains), resulting in twenty-nine fatalities and eighty-nine injuries (Fay 1993: 167).

11. Peloquin includes a discussion of the depersonalizing effects of medical personnel referring to patients by the ailing body part; such metaphoric references are absent from the paramedic stories (1993: 833–34).

12. Dernocoeur and Eastman (1992) were unable to report any conclusive findings on the status of women in EMS.

13. Despite the infrequency of airplane crashes, the professional EMS journals
frequently include articles on such disasters. For example, see Nordberg 1992
and Sundberg 1992. In 1991, a total of two hundred forty-nine general and
commercial aviation accidents resulted in a hundred fifty fatalities and fifty-
six serious injuries in California (Fay 1993: 171).

14. Ironically several months after the completion of this study, I was told that
Darryl had been suspended and eventually fired for alleged use of metham-
phetamine, having been turned in by his partner, Derek.

15. In a newspaper account of the Cerritos air crash, Thackrey notes that the
passengers in the small plane were decapitated (1986: 4). This suggests that
Bill V.'s observation on the instantaneous decapitation of such victims may
not be as unlikely as it sounds.

16. The Loma Prieta earthquake rolled through the San Francisco Bay Area on
October 17, 1989, at 5:04 P.M. There was a total of sixty-five casualties. Reeder
(1989) provides several other paramedic accounts of the quake response.

See Dimitrakopoulus and Murphy (1990) and Ward, Eck, and Sanguino (1990) for stories of the freeway collapse told by nurses.

17. On October 21, 1991, a wildfire raged out of control in the Oakland and Berkeley hills. Newspaper accounts report that 2,810 homes were destroyed and 25 people killed (Paddock 1993)

18. Garza 1995.

19. On October 14, 1987, an eighteen-month-old girl, Jessica McClure (nicknamed Baby Jessica), fell down an abandoned twenty-two-foot well in the back yard of her parents' house. After numerous attempts to rescue her, she was eventually freed by paramedic O'Donnell (Belkin 1995: 20).

20. Belkin 1995.

21. Ibid., 38.

## Chapter Four

1. In San Francisco, 911 ambulance service is provided by the Paramedic Division of the Department of Public Health. In 1997, the service was transferred to the fire department.

2. Bill V. makes this connection himself. The first story concerns an airplane victim whose body is mauled by a bear. See also Conrad (1994) for a discussion of similar cases, albeit less dramatically and humorously presented.

3. According to the Division of Labor Statistics and Research, in 1991, of the 2,624 reported nonfatal disabling injuries among health technologists and technicians (a group which includes paramedics and EMTs), 860, or nearly one-third, were back and spine injuries (State of California 1992).

4. Elders was forced to step down as surgeon general on December 10, 1994 after her answer to a question at a United Nations conference (December 1, 1994) was misconstrued as a suggestion that masturbation should be taught in the public schools as a reasonable strategy to help reduce the spread of AIDS (Jehl 1994). The remark provoked a furor, particularly among the conservative Republicans in Congress. Jehl reports that Elders "intended to relate that masturbation is a natural part of human sexuality" (1994: A30).

5. See Kirksey et al. 1995. One of the case studies they cite is similar to Lars's story.

6. An interesting element in this story is the mention of the "penile inversion." Laqueur (1990) suggests that in earlier conceptions of the differences between male and female, the female sex organs were seen to be an inside-out (or inverted) version of the male sex organs. In this story, the person's sex is changed by the inversion of the penis. But, from the paramedics' point of view, the change is not complete. Rather than supporting the interpretation of the female body as an inside-out male body, the paramedics suggest that

this attempted adherence to a "one-sex model" is what makes the call weird, as it resists the "two-sex model" that proposes an essential difference between the male and female bodies.

7. Sigmund Freud (1918) was perhaps the first to articulate the theory of male castration anxiety.

8. See, for example, Dresser 1994.

9. Ibid.

10. Ibid., 237.

11. Several studies have examined the level of anxiety concerning AIDS among paramedics and other emergency medical personnel. See, for example, Royse and Birge 1987; Stewart 1988; Matin and Lester 1990.

12. Despite the macho, homophobic attitude surfacing in some stories, several medics were openly gay, and there was no widespread expression of homophobia among straight medics directed at their gay colleagues, perhaps because of the Bay Area's cultural climate of acceptance. See Becknell 1994.

13. Paramedics have a strong fear of contracting AIDS (Cydulka et al. 1991).

## Chapter Five

1. Originally started in the early 1960s, the cost-cutting measures of the Reagan years increased dramatically the rate at which patients were deinstitutionalized, while funds for intermediate care facilities were markedly reduced. See Bachrach 1981; Braddock 1985; Lerman 1981; Rutman 1981.

2. Numerous studies have examined the close link between deinstitutionalization and homelessness (Funderberg et al. 1987; Dear and Wolch 1987; Johnson 1990). Lerman (1981: 58) provides figures for California showing the dramatic reduction in institutionalized patient populations, from 37,490 in 1959 to 5,715 in 1977, with a projected population of 2,890 in 1985. In 1990, there were 257 institutionalized patients in Alameda County (Slater and Hall 1995: 50); by 1994, that number had dropped to 128 (State of California 1995: 68). In 1995, the total patient population in the state was 4,135 (State of California 1995: 68).

3. In a discussion of deinstitutionalization and a North Carolina policy of "outpatient commitment," Scheid-Cook (1988) explores what she labels "mediatory myths," stories that bridge contradictions within an organization's ideology (1988: 160).

4. See Braddock 1985; Johnson 1990; Dear and Wolch 1987.

5. The homeless population in Oakland in 1992 was counted at 2,260. For the entire county, the number is slightly above 3,000 (Slater and Hall 1995: 830–32).

6. See Jurkovich et al. 1985; Selnow, Myers and Hayes 1983; Sullivan 1986. Here Lisa also plays the game of "narrative chicken," since she admits to breaking company rules.

7. This type of economic subterfuge is quite common in medic storytelling, and at times emerges as a form of revenge on either the company or the hospitals. Paul Shirley, chief operating officer of American Medical Response, mentions that 40 percent of all the bills sent out by the company for emergency transport go unpaid (Hoge 1993). Company officials also cite the cost of responding to nonemergency situations, setting that figure at $1.5 million (Ronningen 1994). Telling stories about breaking the rules contributes to the game of "narrative chicken" as mentioned above.

8. I was present when the 5150 bolted from police custody and Darryl apprehended him. As in his story, Darryl single-handedly chased the suspect and tackled him. A swarm of police, however, quickly appeared and managed to restrain the patient. Over the course of the afternoon, I was able to record Darryl retelling the event six different times. The narrative was remarkably stable, and always included a derisive reference to the police officer's poor physical conditioning.

9. Gargoyles is a brand name of sunglasses.

10. At the end of the film, a man considered to be psychologically unstable because of his rantings about a monster on the wing of an airplane is taken away by an ambulance crew. A paramedic crew member turns to him and asks if he wants to see something "really scary." From the opening sequence of the film, the audience knows that the paramedic proceeds to turn into a monster (Landis et al. 1983).

11. Verhoeven, director, 1990.

12. Romero, director, 1968.

## Chapter Six

1. A "present breech" birth is less dangerous than other types of breech births.

2. The various tubes used for collecting blood are coded with different colored tops.

3. On May 21, at 4421 Gilbert Street in Oakland, an enraged man stabbed to death his wife, Nicole Azzalina, and his three-year-old son, Warren Hoffman. He was shot and killed by police (Walker and Vasquez 1992; Harris and Kieffman 1992). While Lisa does not have total recall of the specifics of the call, she is remarkably close. Her confusion of the mother's name with the child's name is interesting.

## Chapter Seven

1. In an odd refiguration of this phenomenon, the *Journal of Emergency Medical Services* (*JEMS*) produces a yearly calendar. Some of the photographs in the calendar are quite graphic.
2. For a discussion of abuse of the elderly and paramedic response to such abuse, see Fitch 1986.
3. The terms "emic" and "etic" are derived from the study of linguistics. Emic categories are those suggested by participants in the tradition, and they may or may not correspond to the etic categories used by scholars. See Pike 1954.

## Chapter Eight

1. Patton and Komar were two field supervisors considered to be examples of "company men."
2. See Santino 1978 and 1990.
3. Santino mentions the differences between stories told by subordinates and superordinates, noting that "superordinates' stories tend to celebrate the superordinates in terms of skills and ability" (1978: 147).
4. Powers and Taigman (1992) discuss the differences between punitive "quality assurance" programs and more progressive "quality improvement" programs.
5. The California Health and Safety Codes make clear the release from liability of "good samaritans" (State of California 1990). The efficacy of bystander CPR has been proven in various outcome studies (Guzy, Pearce and Greenfield 1983; Stueven et al. 1986).
6. Garza (1994) discusses the change from ambulance companies being small, family-run enterprises to being large corporations and the implications of this change for the work environment. See also Garza 1990.
7. For examples of these attitudes, see Knight 1995 and 1996. In an *ABC World News* report, John Martin explores the practice of overcharging among private ambulance companies (1995).
8. This slogan, which means "Work makes one free," was painted over the gate to the Auschwitz concentration camp. See also Dundes and Hauschild 1983.
9. Since Melinda is Jewish, the comparison is all the more alarming.
10. The work of dispatchers is detailed in Clawson and Dernocoeur 1988. See also Clawson 1989; Clawson and Haiert 1990.
11. There is considerable literature concerning stress among air traffic controllers. For example, see Higgins, Lategola and Melton 1978. Weaver (1987) addresses stress among emergency dispatchers.

12. Hitchens and Rudd (1993) make a case for emergency medical dispatch, rather than police, being the first on-line responder in the 911 system. Goldfarb (1993) addresses some of the problems of dispatch reliability.

13. For a discussion of some of these incidents, see Nordberg 1995.

## Conclusion

1. Martin and Powers 1983. See also Jones 1991; Mitroff and Kilmann 1976; Vance 1991.

2. Occasionally, a ride-along—an intern, a physician, a journalist, or a folklorist—swells the audience to two.

3. Kermode 1967. For a similar type of relationship—one that also has an arbitrary beginning and ending—see Davis's 1959 study of cabdrivers and their customers.

4. Santino characterizes work dissatisfaction and other negative evaluations of the work environment as "outlaw emotions," a term borrowed from a description of the blues (1978: 154, 181). See also Santino 1990.

5. Georges 1979.

6. Young (1987) distinguishes between what she calls "taleworlds" and "storyrealms" to describe the world inside the story and the world external to the story.

# GLOSSARY

The following information is based on discussions with paramedics and on Anderson, Anderson, and Glanze (1994) and LeSage, Derr, and Tardiff (1991).

**ACLS:** Advanced cardiac life support.

**Activated charcoal:** Given to counteract the effects of certain poisons (often referred to simply as "charcoal").

**Airway bag:** A large bag containing equipment for intubating patients and managing their airways (mouth, nose, larynx, trachea).

**Alco:** Alameda County. Also an abbreviation for the Alameda County sheriff's department dispatch, which clears medical communications channels for the paramedics.

**Allied:** An ambulance company that at one time provided 911 service for Oakland and which merged with Regional Ambulance.

**Alupent:** Drug often administered by medics for patients suffering from asthma or chronic obstructive pulmonary disease (COPD).

**A/O times four:** Often said "A and O," A/O is an abbreviation for "alert and oriented." "Times four" means that the patient is aware of the environment regarding his or her own name, the place and time, and either the event or the identity of other people.

**Asystole (flatline):** Heart failure characterized by loss of all electrical and mechanical function in the heart.

**Atropine:** An antispasmodic and anticholinergic drug that helps increase the impulse conductivity through the heart muscle.

**Auto-ped:** An automobile accident involving a pedestrian.

**Backboard:** A board used to immobilize patients who are suspected of having back or neck injuries.

**Bag:** To resuscitate a patient using a bag-valve-mask device.

**Bag-valve-mask resuscitator:** A piece of equipment used to ventilate patients who have stopped breathing (preferred to mouth-to-mouth resuscitation).

**Barn:** Alameda County Deployment Center.

**Bleed out:** To hemorrhage.

**BP:** Blood pressure. These readings are given as systolic (pressure during a heart contraction) over diastolic (minimum pressure between heart contractions).

**Bradycardia:** A condition in which the heart beats at a rate of fewer than sixty beats per minute.

**Brevity code:** Numeric code used in radio transmissions for conciseness or to deter easy interpretation of communications. Examples are:

**10-4:** "Affirmative." Acknowledges receipt of a radio transmission.

**10-7:** Arrival at hospital.

**10-55:** A person who is dead (often pronounced "10-5-5").

**11-99:** Paramedic in distress.

**5150:** A person under psychiatric hold. The number (pronounced 51-50) comes from the California Welfare and Institutions Code and is printed at the top of the form used by the police to put somebody under psychiatric surveillance. In Alameda County, these forms are green and often referred to as "green sheets."

**Call:** Response to a medical emergency (also referred to as a "run").

**Call (a patient):** To pronounce a patient dead.

**CISD:** Critical incident stress debriefing; a formalized, psychological counseling program to assist paramedics in dealing with the emotional aftermath of difficult calls.

**Code:** A person in cardiac arrest (apparently an abbreviation of the term "Code Blue"); can also be used as a verb.

**Code 2:** A generally noncritical response in which an ambulance goes to a call or to the hospital without using warning lights or siren. Dispatchers decide whether to request medics Code 2 or Code 3. Once on scene, the medics, in consultation with the base hospital, decide whether to proceed to the hospital Code 2 or Code 3.

**Code 3:** A critical response in which an ambulance going to a call or to the hospital uses warning lights and siren.

**Code 4:** A message to dispatchers that the crew has arrived on scene and all is in order.

**Code 7:** Paramedics' request for permission to stop for a meal (as in "picking up a Code 7").

**Code 12:** Notice that the paramedics are responding with the firefighters.

**Code 100:** Paramedics' request for permission to use the toilet.

**Code Blue:** A person in cardiac arrest.

**Contraindication:** A factor that prohibits the administration of a certain drug.

**CPR:** Cardiopulmonary resuscitation, consisting of artificial respiration and external cardiac massage.

**Crash:** A verb referring to the sudden deterioration of a patient's condition.

**Crash cart:** A small cart, found in emergency rooms, which has a defibrillator and other equipment used in treating cardiac arrest patients.

**C-spine:** A series of Velcro straps and a plastic neck brace used to immobilize a patient's head on a backboard; keeps the neck from moving if there is possible neck or back injury.

**Defibrillator:** A machine used to deliver an electric shock to a patient who is in cardiac distress. Certain rhythms can be restored to normal by defibrillation.

**Deficit:** Any deficiency or deviation from what is considered normal.

**Depletion, in:** A situation in which there are not enough ambulance units in the field to cover the anticipated number of calls. The system can become depleted if ambulances are slow in clearing from hospitals after runs, if crews are late in getting their ambulances into service at the beginning of a shift, or if there has been an unexpectedly large number of calls for ambulance assistance.

**Detail:** A paramedic's request to run a personal errand.

**Drug bag:** A small locked plastic bag in which narcotics and other drugs that are either controlled substances or have a high resale value are carried. These bags must be checked out at the beginning of every shift and checked in with an accounting of all used doses at the end of every shift.

**Dystonic reaction:** A condition marked by severe, irregular muscle spasms that contort the body.

**Edema:** Abnormal accumulation of fluids in the interstitial spaces.

**EKG:** Electrocardiogram; a recording of the electric activity in the heart. Paramedics generally work with three-lead (a lead is an electrode) EKGs, although there is mounting pressure to let them use the more advanced twelve-lead system.

**EMT:** Emergency medical technician; someone who is trained only in basic life support (BLS) and generally takes care of patient transfers.

**Epinephrine (epi):** A commonly used drug administered in cases of cardiac arrest or severe allergic reactions.

**ER:** Emergency room.

**ETA:** Estimated time of arrival.

**ETOH:** Alcohol. Paramedics often refer to patients who have ingested alcohol as having "ETOH on board."

**External pacing:** Electrical stimulation of the heart by use of a defibrillator using timed discharges over a sustained period.

**Fibrillation:** Random or abnormal contraction of the heart resulting in disruption of its normal rhythm.

**Field orders:** Treatment instructions received by paramedics over the radio.

**Flatline:** See asystole.

**Flex car:** A twelve-hour ambulance shift that begins before three in the afternoon.

**Float:** A paramedic not assigned to any one shift but available for a twelve-hour assignment in a particular twenty-four-hour period.

**GPS:** Global positioning satellite, a system which allows dispatchers to locate ambulances with a high degree of accuracy. It replaced the earlier AVL (automatic vehicle locator) system.

**GSW:** Gunshot wound.

**High-flow oxygen:** Delivery of oxygen, through a mask, at a consistent pressure regardless of changes in the patient's respiration.

**ICU:** Intensive care unit.

**Intraosseous infusion (IO):** Injection of blood, bone marrow, or fluids into the bone marrow rather than a vein.

**Intubate ("tube"):** To insert a breathing tube into a patient's trachea to provide a clear airway and facilitate breathing.

**IV:** Intravenous line; an apparatus that allows direct delivery of fluids and drugs into the patient's bloodstream.

**Jump (a call):** To respond to a call dispatched to another unit. When an interesting call is dispatched, paramedics on other units may radio to the dispatch center that they are closer to the scene and therefore responding.

**Jump bag:** A large bag containing equipment for work on cardiac patients.

**Lasix:** A diuretic that is prescribed for hypertension, renal failure, and edema.

**Lidocaine:** Used in the treatment of ventricular fibrillation, ventricular tachycardia, and preventricular contractions.

**Life Pack 5:** A portable defibrillation unit. A more modern model is the Life Pack 10.

**Line:** An intravenous line. "Starting a line" means inserting an intravenous line on a patient; "dripping a line" means preparing one in anticipation of use.

**MAST pants (or trousers):** Military antishock trousers; now also an abbreviation for medical antishock trousers. Inflatable pants that are used to boost patients' blood pressure.

**Medcom:** Medical communications; to speak directly with a base hospital, the paramedics request a medcom channel from the Alameda County sheriff's department dispatch.

**Meperidine:** A narcotic painkiller also known by the brand name Demerol.

**MICN:** Mobile intensive care nurse; they generally manage the radio at the base hospital.

**Monitor:** Heart monitor, or EKG. The paramedics' defibrillators have a heart monitor built in.

**Morphine (sulfate):** A drug administered to patients suffering from severe pain due to injury; also used to treat pulmonary edema.

**NG (nasogastric) tube:** A tube threaded through the nose into the stomach.

**Naso-canulla:** A flexible tube, inserted into the nasal passages, for the delivery of oxygen.

**OR:** Operating room.

**Pacing:** Artificial electronic stimulation of a heart rhythm.

**PCR:** Patient call report; paramedics are required to fill out this form for each patient treated.

**Plasmanate:** An intravenous solution used to treat shock due to blood loss; a more correct term is plasma volume expander.

**Pleural decompression:** Removal of pressure on the lungs caused by air in the pleural cavity.

**Protocol:** A written plan detailing the specific procedures to be followed for providing care.

**Pulmonary edema:** A buildup of fluid in the lungs.

**Push (a drug):** To administer a drug, generally through an intravenous line.

**PVC:** Premature ventricular contraction. Frequent, multifocal PVCs suggest the onset of severe cardiac distress, including ventricular tachycardia or fibrillation.

**QA:** Quality assurance; a board which reviews the performance of paramedics, generally in cases when possible errors in treatment were made. The name was changed to QET (Quality, Education, and Training) as part of the company's attempt to alter the culture of the review process, but paramedics still use the term "QA."

**Red top:** A color-coded blood collection tube with a red rubber stopper.

**Rig:** Paramedics' term for an ambulance.

**Ringer's (lactated Ringer's):** Ringer's lactate solution, a fluid and electrolyte replenisher.

**Run:** See "call."

**Saline:** A solution containing sodium, introduced intravenously; it has either the same, higher, or lower salinity as blood, depending on its use.

**Stage:** To wait for the police to secure the scene of an emergency. Generally, firefighters and ambulance personnel "stage" when called to aid at the scene of a dangerous crime.

**Stat:** Situation requiring immediate attention. Also used in the phrase "stat seizures," shorthand for status epilepticus, a state characterized by uninterrupted seizures.

**Strike car:** An ambulance shift that begins after six in the evening.

**Sugar (D-50):** A drug administered to diabetics suffering from severe hypoglycemia and showing altered mental status.

**Tachycardia (sinus tach):** A condition in which the heart beats at a rate greater than one hundred beats per minute.

**Tiered response:** A system whereby EMTs respond first to medical emergencies; after evaluating the patient, they request paramedic assistance.

**Trapezius pinch:** A technique used to rouse unconscious patients.

**Trauma activation (or activation):** A patient with certain indications, such as penetrating injuries above the elbow or knee, paralysis, or two or more bone fractures. Trauma activations are transported Code 3 to the nearest designated trauma center.

**Trauma center:** A specially equipped hospital with operating rooms and surgeons available around the clock. Highland, Children's and Eden hospitals are designated trauma centers in Alameda County, and patients fitting the criteria of a trauma activation are transported Code 3 to one of these.

**Trendelenburg's position:** A position in which the head is low and the body and legs are high; often used to increase the flow of blood to the brain in cases of shock.

**Triage:** A classification according to the gravity of injuries and urgency of treatment.

**Tube:** See intubate.

**Unit:** Paramedics' term for ambulance.

**Ventilate:** To provide the lungs with air.

**Vitals (vital signs):** A patient's pulse, respiratory rate, and blood pressure.

**Work (a patient):** To treat a patient.

# WORKS CITED

Abrahams, Roger D. 1968. "Introductory Remarks to a Rhetorical Theory of Folklore." *Journal of American Folklore* 81: 143–58.

Abravanel, H. 1983. "Mediatory Myths in the Service of Organizational Ideology." In *Organizational Symbolism,* edited by L. R. Pondy, P. J. Frost, G. Morgan, and T. Dandridge, 273–93. Greenwich, CT: JAI Press.

Allaire, Yves, and Mihaela E. Firsirotu. 1984. "Theories of Organizational Culture." *Organizational Studies* 5: 193–226.

Alvesson, Mats. 1993. *Cultural Perspectives on Organizations.* Cambridge: Cambridge University Press.

Anderson, Kenneth N., Lois E. Anderson, and Walter D. Glanze, ed. 1994. *Mosby's Medical, Nursing, and Allied Health Dictionary.* 4th ed. St. Louis: Mosby-Year Book.

Aprahamian, C., J. C. Darin, B. M. Thompson, J. R. Mateer, and J. F. Tucker. 1985. "Traumatic Cardiac Arrest: Scope of Paramedic Services." *Annals of Emergency Medicine* 14: 583–86.

Apte, Mahadev. 1985. *Humor and Laughter: An Anthropological Approach.* Ithaca: Cornell University Press.

Associated Press. 1993. "N.Y. Paramedics Who Said Live Woman Was Dead Face Discipline." *Chicago Tribune* (September 5): A10.

Bachrach, Leona L. 1981. "Deinstitutionalization: Developmental and Theoretical Perspective." In *Planning for Deinstitutionalization: A Review of Principles, Methods and Applications,* edited by Irvin D. Rutman, 5–22. Rockville, MD: The Project.

Barley, Stephen R. 1983. "Semiotics and the Study of Occupational and Organizational Culture." *Administrative Science Quarterly* 23: 393–413.

Becknell, John M. 1994. "Gays in EMS: Strengthening the EMS Team." *JEMS* 19(8): 94–100.

Belkin, Lisa. 1995. "Death on the CNN Curve." *New York Times Magazine* (July 23): 18–23, 32, 38, 41, 44.

Benedict, Ruth. 1960. *Patterns of Culture.* New York: Mentor Books.

Bennet, Howard J., ed. 1991. *The Best of Medical Humor*. Philadelphia: Hanley and Belfur.

Braddock, David L. 1985. *Deinstitutionalization in the Eighties: 1985 Public Forum on Deinstitutionalization*. Chicago: Institute for the Study of Developmental Disabilities.

Bucher, Rue. 1988. "On the Natural History of Health Care Occupations." *Work and Occupations* 15: 131–47.

Cadmus, Robert R., and John H. Ketner. 1965. *Organizing Ambulance Services in the Public Interest*. Chapel Hill: University of North Carolina Press.

Cady, Geoffrey A. 1992. "EMS in the United States: A Survey of Providers in the 200 Most Populous Cities." *JEMS* 17(1): 75–78, 82–92.

Chaiken, Jan M., and Robert J. Gladstone. 1974. *Some Trends in the Delivery of Ambulance Services*. Santa Monica: The RAND Corporation.

CHP (California Highway Patrol). 1994. *Annual Report of Fatal and Injury Motor Vehicle Traffic Collisions*. Sacramento: California Highway Patrol.

Churm, Steven R., and Ralph Frammolino. 1986. "Cerritos Crash: View from Ground Zero." *Los Angeles Times* (September 8): A1.

Clawson, Jeffrey J. 1989. "Emergency Medical Dispatch." In *EMS Medical Director's Handbook*, edited by Alexander Kuehl. St. Louis: Mosby-Year Book.

Clawson, Jeffrey J., and Kate B. Dernocoeur. 1988. *Principles of Emergency Medical Dispatch*. Englewood Cliffs: Prentice Hall.

Clawson, Jeffrey J., and Scott A. Haiert. 1990."Dispatch Life Support: Establishing Standards that Work." *JEMS* 15(7): 82–84, 86–88.

Clover, Carol J. 1992. *Men, Women and Chainsaws. Gender in the Modern Horror Film*. Princeton: Princeton University Press.

Conrad, Lily. 1994. "The Maul of the Wild." *Emergency Medical Services* 23(3): 71–72, 76.

Cook, Joseph Lee. 1978. *Ambulance Services: A Selected Bibliography*. Monticello: Council of Planning Librarians.

Coser, Rose Laub. 1960. "Laughter Among Colleagues: A Study of the Social Functions of Humor Among the Staff of a Mental Hospital." *Psychiatry* 23: 81–95.

Curry, G. J. 1965. "Immediate Care and Transport of the Injured, History and Development." In *Immediate Care and Transport of the Injured*, edited by G. J. Curry, 8–16. Springfield, IL: C. C. Thomas.

Curry, Jill L. 1992. "Oil on Troubled Waters: Unlicensed Assistance Personnel in the Emergency Department." *Journal of Emergency Nursing* 18(5): 428–31.

Cydulka, R. K., J. J. Matthews, M. Born, A. Moy, and M. Parker. 1991. "Paramedics' Knowledge Base and Attitudes Towards AIDS and Hepatitis." *Journal of Emergency Medicine* 9: 37–43.

Cydulka, R. K., J. Lyons, A. My, K. Shay, J. Hammer, and J. Mathews. 1989."A Follow-up Report of Occupational Stress in Urban EMT-Paramedics." *Annals of Emergency Medicine* 18: 1151–56.

Davis, Fred. 1959. "The Cabdriver and His Fare: Facets of a Fleeting Relationship." *American Journal of Speech* 65: 158–65.

Dear, Michael J., and Jennifer R. Wolch. 1987. *Landscapes of Despair: From Deinstitutionalization to Homelessness.* Princeton: Princeton University Press.

Decker, Cathleen, and George Stein. 1986. "Sledgehammer from the Sky Hits Cerritos; Terror and Death." *Los Angeles Times* (September 1): A1.

Dégh, Linda. 1969. *Folktales and Society. Storytelling in a Hungarian Peasant Community,* translated by Emily M. Schossberger. Bloomington: Indiana University Press.

Dernocoeur, Kate B., and James N. Eastman, Jr. 1992. "Have We Really Come a Long Way? Women in EMS Survey Results." *JEMS* 17(2): 18–19.

Dimitrakopoulas, Christine, and Patricia Ann Murphy. 1990. "Recollections of Two Emergency Nurses Responding to the Collapsed Cypress Structure After the 1989 Bay Area Earthquake." *Journal of Emergency Nursing* 16(4): 56A-60A.

Dreifuss, R. 1989. "911 Misuse." *Emergency Medical Services* 18(7): 43–45.

Dresser, Norine. 1994. "The Case of the Missing Gerbil." *Western Folklore* 53: 229–42.

Dundes, Alan. 1985. "Game of the Name: A Quadriplegic Sick Joke Cycle." *Names*: 289–92.

———. 1987. *Cracking Jokes. Studies of Sick Humor Cycles and Stereotypes.* Berkeley: Ten Speed Press.

Dundes, Alan, and Thomas Hauschild. 1983. "Auschwitz Jokes." *Western Folklore* 42: 249–60.

Fay, James S., ed. 1993. *California Almanac.* 6th ed. Santa Barbara: Pacific Data Resources.

Fine, Gary Alan. 1988. "Letting off Steam? Redefining a Restaurant's Work Environment." In *Inside Organizations: Understanding the Human Dimension,* edited by Michael Owen Jones, Michael Dane Moore, and Richard Christopher Snyder, 119–27. Newbury Park: Sage Publications.

Fitch, Jay. 1986. "Stopping Elderly Abuse." *JEMS* 11(4): 50–53.

Foucault, Michel. 1963. *Naissance de la Clinique.* Paris: Presses Universitaires de France.

Frammolino, Ralph, and Jack Jones. 1986. "Kin of Missing in Cerritos Feel 'Wrenching Grief.'" *Los Angeles Times* (September 2): A1.

Freud, Anna. 1936. *The Ego and the Mechanisms of Defense.* New York: International Universities Press.

Freud, Sigmund. 1918. "Anal Eroticism and the Castration Complex." In *The Standard Edition of the Complete Psychological Works of Sigmund Freud,* translated by James Strachey. Vol. 18: 1–64. London: Hogarth Press, 1986.

———. 1927. "Humour." In *The Standard Edition of the Complete Psychological Works of Sigmund Freud,* translated by James Strachey. Vol. 21: 161–66. London: Hogarth Press, 1986.

Funderberg, Richard G., Lou Evon, James M. Thomas, and Anthony Carbo. 1987. *California's Homeless: Part of a Nation's Shame.* Sacramento: California State Employees' Association.

Gabriel, Yiannis. 1988. *Working Lives in Catering.* London: Routledge.

———. 1991. "Turning Facts into Stories and Stories into Facts: A Hermeneutic Exploration of Organizational Folklore." *Human Relations* 44: 857–75.

Garza, Marion Angell. 1990. "Changing the Complexion of EMS." *JEMS* 15(8): S4-S6, S8.

———. 1994. "From Mom and Pop to Big Business: The Ambulance Industry Consolidates." *JEMS* 19(4): 44–45.

———. 1995. "After the Bomb: Oklahoma City Rescuers Talk About Their Experiences." *JEMS* 20(6): 40–41, 84–88.

Gazette News Service. 1993. "Paramedics Botched Job, State Says." *Phoenix Gazette* (September 4): A2.

Geertz, Clifford. 1973a. "Thick Description: Toward an Interpretive Theory of Culture." In *The Interpretation of Cultures.* New York: Basic Books.

———. 1973b. *The Interpretation of Cultures.* New York: Basic Books.

Georges, Robert A. 1969. "Toward an Understanding of Storytelling Events." *Journal of American Folklore* 82: 313–28.

———. 1979. "Feedback and Response in Storytelling." *Western Folklore* 38: 104–11.

Goldfarb, Bruce. 1993. "Dispatch: In Apple Pie Order?" *JEMS* 18(5): 61, 64–66.

Goldstein, Jeffrey H., and Paul E. McGhee, ed. 1972. *The Psychology of Humor: Theoretical Perspectives and Empirical Issues.* New York: Academic Press.

Gonsalves, Danny. 1988. "Historical Background of Emergency Medical Services in the United States." *Emergency Care Quarterly* 4: 73–82.

Goodenough, Ward H. 1971. *Culture, Language and Society.* Reading, MA: Addison-Wesley.

Gregory, Kathleen L. 1983. "Native-view Paradigms: Multiple Cultures and Culture Conflicts in Organizations." *Administrative Science Quarterly* 28: 359–76.

Grotjahn, Martin. 1966(1957). *Beyond Laughter: Humor and the Subconscious.* New York: McGraw-Hill.

Gruner, Charles. 1978. *Understanding Laughter: The Workings of Wit and Humor.* Chicago: Nelson Hall.

Guzy, P. M., M. L. Pearce, and S. Greenfield. 1983. "The Survival Benefit of Bystander Cardiopulmonary Resuscitation in a Paramedic Served Metropolitan Area." *American Journal of Public Health* 73: 766–69.

Harris, Harry, and Sandy Kieffman. 1992. "Stabbing Victim Was Not Allowed Restraining Order." *Oakland Tribune* (May 23): A3, A5.

Hatch, M. J., and S. B. Ehrlich. 1993. "Where There Is Smoke: Spontaneous Humor as an Indicator of Paradox and Ambiguity in Organizations." *Organization Studies* 14: 505–26.

Higgins, E. A., M. T. Lategola, and C. E. Melton. 1978. *Three Reports Relevant to Stress in Aviation Personnel.* Washington D. C.: Dept. of Transportation, Federal Aviation Administration, Office of Aviation Medicine.

Hitchens, John, and Joe Rudd. 1993. " '9–1–1 Emergency . . .': Putting EMS Dispatch First Online." *JEMS* 18(5): 62–63.

Hoge, Patrick. 1993. "Battles Raging Statewide to Control Ambulance Services." *Sacramento Bee* (July 24): B1.

Holland, Norman Norwood. 1982. *Laughing: A Psychology of Humor.* Ithaca: Cornell University Press.

James, George. 1993a. "Ruled Dead by Medical Workers, a Brooklyn Woman, 40, Is Alive." *New York Times* (June 16): A1.

———. 1993b. "State to Investigate Case of Woman Left for Dead." *New York Times* (June 17): B2.

Jansen, William Hugh. 1959. "The Esoteric-Exoteric Factor in Folklore." *Fabula* 2: 205–11.

Jehl, Douglas. 1994. "Surgeon General Forced to Resign by White House." *New York Times* (December 10): A1, A30.

Johnson, Ann Braden. 1990. *Out of Bedlam: The Truth About Deinstitutionalization.* New York: Basic Books.

Jones, Michael Owen. 1976. "Doing What, with Which, and to Whom? The Relationship of Case History Accounts to Curing." In *American Folk Medicine: A Symposium,* edited by Wayland Hand, 301–14. Berkeley: University of California Press.

———. 1991. "What if Stories Don't Tally with the Culture?" *Journal of Organizational Change Management* 4(3): 27–34.

Joseph, Nathan. 1986. *Uniforms and Nonuniforms: Communication through Clothing.* Contributions in Sociology 61. New York: Greenwood Press.

Jurkovich, G. J., D. Campbell, J. Padrta, and A. Luterman. 1987. "Paramedic Perception of Elapsed Field Time." *Journal of Trauma* 27: 892–97.

Jurkovich, G. J., R. Chapman, A. Luterman, M. L. Ramenofsky, and P. William Curreri. 1985. "The Senior Citizens' Use and Misuse of the EMS." *Journal of Trauma* 25(7): 696.

Kaiser, Susan B. 1990. *The Social Psychology of Clothing: Symbolic Appearances in Context.* 2nd ed. New York: Macmillan.

Kanter, Rosabeth Moss, and Barry A. Stein, ed. 1979. *Life in Organizations.* New York: Basic Books, Inc.

Kermode, Frank. 1967. *The Sense of an Ending: Studies in the Theory of Fiction.* Oxford: Oxford University Press.

Kirksey, Kenn M., Mary Holt-Ashley, Kathryn Williamson, and Ricardo Omar Garza. 1995. "Autoerotic Asphyxia in Adolescents." *Journal of Emergency Nursing* 21(1): 81–83.

Knight, Jonathan. 1995. "Paramedics Wary of EMS Overhaul." *Synapse* (October 12): 1, 8.

———. 1996. "Riding with the Paramedics." *Synapse* (January 4): 1, 8.

Kotter, John P., and James L. Heskett. 1992. *Corporate Culture and Performance.* New York: The Free Press.

Kramer, Peter D. 1995. "A Rescue without Cheers." *New York Times Magazine* (July 16): 15.

Labov, William, and Joshua Welletzky. 1967. "Narrative Analysis: Oral Versions of Personal Experience." In *Essays on the Verbal and Visual Arts,* edited by June Helm, 12–44. Proceedings of the 1966 Annual Meeting of the American Ethnological Society.

Landis, John, Joe Dante, Steven Spielberg, and George Miller, dir. 1983. *Twilight Zone: The Movie.* Burbank: Warner Bros.

Laqueur, Thomas W. 1990. *Making Sex: Body and Gender from the Greeks to Freud.* Cambridge: Harvard University Press.

Laqueur, Thomas W., and Catherine Gallagher, ed. 1987. *The Making of the Modern Body.* Berkeley: University of California Press.

Lerman, Paul. 1981. *Deinstitutionalization: A Cross-Problem Analysis.* Rockville, MD: USDHEW.

LeSage, Paul, Paula Derr, and Jon Tardiff. 1991. *EMS Field Guide.* 7th ed. Fort Washington, PA: Rhône-Poulenc.

Lester, R. E. 1986. *Organizational Culture, Uncertainty Reduction and the Socialization of New Organizational Members.* Communication and Information Science 3. Studies in Communication. Norwood: Ablex.

Lewis, R. P., J. M. Stang, and J. V. Warren. 1984. "The Role of Paramedics in Resuscitation of Patients with Prehospital Cardiac Arrest from Coronary Artery Disease." *American Journal of Emergency Medicine* 2: 200–203.

Lindow, John, and Timothy R. Tangherlini. 1995. "Nordic Legends and the Question of Identity. Introduction." *Scandinavian Studies* 67: 1–7.

Linstead, Steve. 1985. "Joker's Wild: The Importance of Humor in the Maintenance of Organizational Culture." *The Sociological Review* 33: 741–67.

*Los Angeles Times* Staff. 1995. "The Fuhrman Tapes." *Los Angeles Times* (August 30): A14.

Louis, Meryl. 1990. "Acculturation in the Workplace: Newcomers as Lay Ethnographers." In *Organizational Climate and Culture,* edited by Benjamin Schneider, 85–129. San Francisco: Jossey-Bass.

Mannon, James M. 1992. *Emergency Encounters. A Study of an Urban Ambulance Service.* Port Washington: Kennikat Press, 1981. Reprint, Boston: Jones and Bartlett Publishers, Inc.

Martin, Joanne. 1992. *Cultures in Organizations: Three Perspectives.* New York: Oxford University Press.

Martin, Joanne, and Caren Siehl. 1983. "Organizational Culture and Counter Culture: An Uneasy Symbiosis." *Organizational Dynamics* 12: 52–64.

Martin, Joanne, and Melanie Powers. 1983. "Organizational Stories: More Vivid and Persuasive than Quantitative Data." In *Psychological Foundations of Organizational Behavior,* edited by Barry Staw, 161–68. 2nd ed. Glenview: Scott Foresman.

Martin, John. 1995. "Your Money—Private Ambulance Companies Overcharging." *ABC World News Tonight* (March 6).

Matin, Scott A., and David Lester. 1990. "Attitudes of Emergency Medical Service Providers Towards AIDS." *Psychological Reports* 67: 1314.

Mattera, Connie J. 1994. "Physicians on Scene: Blessing or Burden?" *Journal of Emergency Nursing* 20(5): 400–403.

McCarl, Robert S. 1985. *The District of Columbia Fire Fighters' Project: A Case Study in Occupational Folklife.* Washington D.C.: Smithsonian Institution Press.

Metz, Donald L. 1981. *Running Hot: Structure and Stress in Ambulance Work.* Cambridge: Abt Books.

Meyerson, Debra E. 1990. "Uncovering Socially Undesirable Emotions: Experiences of Ambiguity in Organizations." *American Behavioral Scientist* 33: 296–307.

Mitchell, Jeffrey T. 1983. "When Disaster Strikes . . . : The Critical Stress Debriefing Process." *JEMS* 8: 30–36.

———. 1984. "The 600 Run Limit." *JEMS* 9(1): 52–54.

———. 1988a. "Stress: Development and Functions of a Critical Incident Stress Debriefing Team." *JEMS* 13(11): 43–46.

———. 1988b. "Stress: The History, Status and Future of CISD." *JEMS* 13(11): 46–47, 49–52.

Mitroff, Ian and Ralph Kilmann. 1976. "On Organizational Stories: An Approach to the Design and Analysis of Organizations Through Myth and Stories." In *The Management of Organization Design: Strategy and Implementation,* edited by Ralph Kilman, Louis Pondy, and Dennis Slevin, 189–207. New York: North Holland.

Morreall, John. 1983. *Taking Laughter Seriously*. Albany: State University of New York Press.

Moser-Rath, Elfriede. 1972–1973. "Galgenhumor wörtlich genommen." *Schweizerische Archiv für Volkskunde* 68/69: 423–32.

National Institute of Mental Health. 1986. *Role Stressors and Supports for Emergency Workers: Proceedings from a 1984 Workshop Sponsored by the National Institute of Mental Health and FEMA*. Rockville, MD: U.S. Department of Health and Human Services.

*New York Times* Staff. 1991. "U.S. Capital Sets Murder Record." *New York Times* (December 26): C7, D12.

Nickerson, Bruce. 1990. "Antagonism at Work: Them and Us, A Widget World View." *American Behavioral Scientist* 33: 308–17.

Nordberg, Marie. 1992. "Lessons from La Guardia." *Emergency Medical Services* 21(7): 52, 54–55, 68.

———. 1995. "Dispatch Disasters." *Emergency Medical Services* 24(8): 33–34, 36, 38, 40, 42, 44–47, 50–52.

Obrdlik, Antonin J. 1942. "'Gallows Humor'—A Sociological Phenomenon." *American Journal of Sociology* 47: 709–16.

Ornato, Joseph P., Edward J. Craren, Norman Nelson, and Henry D. Smith. 1983. "The Impact of Emergency Cardiac Care on the Reduction of Mortality from Myocardial Infarction." *Journal of Cardiac Rehabilitation* 3: 863–66.

Ouchi, William G. 1981. *Theory Z: How American Business Can Meet the Japanese Challenge*. Reading, MA: Addison-Wesley.

Paddock, Richard C. 1993. "Scars from Firestorm Keep Oakland on Constant Vigil." *Los Angeles Times* (November 2): A1, A21.

Page, James O. 1984. "Understanding the Fire Service." *JEMS* 9(6): 30–31, 34–37.

Palmer, C. E., and S. M. Gonsoulin. 1990. "Paramedics, Protocols and Procedures—Playing Doc as Deviant Role Behavior." *Deviant Behavior* 11(3): 207–19.

Peloquin, Suzanne M. 1993. "The Depersonalization of Patients: A Profile Gleaned from Narratives." *The American Journal of Occupational Therapy* 47: 830–37.

Peters, Thomas J., and Robert H. Waterman. 1982. *In Search of Excellence: Lessons from America's Best-Run Companies*. New York: Harper and Row.

Pettigrew, Andrew W. 1979. "On Studying Organization Cultures." *Administrative Science Quarterly* 24: 570–81.

Piddington, Ralph. 1963. *The Psychology of Laughter: A Study in Social Adaptation*. New York: Gamut Press.

Pike, Kenneth L. 1954. *Language in Relation to a Unified Theory of the Structure of Human Behavior*. Glendale, CA: Summer Institute of Linguistics.

Post, Carl. 1992. *Omaha Orange. A Popular History of EMS in America*. Boston: James and Bartlett.

Powers, Robert J., and Mike Taigman. 1992. "Debating Quality Assurance vs. Quality Improvement." *JEMS* 17(1): 65, 67–70.

Public Enemy. 1990. "911 (is a joke)." In *Fear of a Black Planet*. New York: Def-Jam Music Group.

Reeder, Lee A. 1989. "California Quake. Special Report." *JEMS* 14(11): 24–25.

Reiter, B. P. 1977. *The Saturday Night Knife and Gun Club*. Philadelphia: J. B. Lippencott Co.

Robinson, Jonathan A. 1981. "Personal Narratives Reconsidered." *Journal of American Folklore* 94: 58–85.

Robinson, R., and J. T. Mitchell. 1993. "Evaluation of Psychological Debriefing." *Journal of Traumatic Stress* 6(3): 367–82.

Rockwood, C. A., C. M. Mann, J. D. Farrington, O. P. Hampton, and R. E. Motley. 1976. "History of Emergency Medical Services in the United States." *Journal of Trauma* 16: 299–308.

Romano, T. L., S. Eisenberg, C. Fernandez-Caballero, and C. G. Cayten. 1978. "Paramedic Services: Nationwide Distribution and Management Structure." *JACEP* 7: 99–102.

Romero, George A., dir. 1968. *Night of the Living Dead*. New York: Continental.

Ronningen, Judy. 1994. "Ambulance Misuse Described. Many Alameda County Calls Not Emergencies." *San Francisco Chronicle* (October 19): A11.

Royse, D., and B. Birge. 1987. "Homophobia and Attitudes Towards AIDS Among Medical, Nursing and Paramedical Students." *Psychological Reports* 61(3): 867–70.

Rubin, Joanne Gowins. 1990. "Critical Incident Stress Debriefing: Helping the Helpers." *Journal of Emergency Nursing* 16(4): 255–58.

Rutman, Irvin D., ed. 1981. *Planning for Deinstitutionalization: A Review of Principles, Methods and Applications*. Rockville, MD: The Project.

Santino, Jack (John Francis). 1978. *The Outlaw Emotions: Workers' Narratives from Three Contemporary Occupations*. Ph.D. diss., The University of Pennsylvania, Philadelphia.

———. 1990. "The Outlaw Emotions: Narrative Expressions on the Rules and Roles of Occupational Identity." *American Behavioral Scientist* 33: 318–29.

Scheid-Cook, Teresa L. 1988. "Mitigating Organizational Contradictions: The Role of Mediatory Myths." *The Journal of Applied Behavioral Science* 24: 161–71.

Schein, Edgar H. 1990. "Organizational Culture." *American Psychologist* 45(2): 109–19.

Selnow, Gary, Dennis Myers, and Scott Hayes. 1983. "The Misinformed Public: A Study Measures Public Knowledge of Emergency Medical Services." *JEMS* 8(3): 45–48.

Silverman, David. 1970. *The Theory of Organizations*. London: Heinemann.

Singer, David L. 1968. *Aggression Arousal, Hostile Humor, Catharsis.* American Psychological Association. Journal of Personality and Social Psychology. Monograph supplement.

Slater, Courtenay, and George E. Hall, ed. 1995. *1995 County and City Extra. Annual Metro, City and County Data Book.* Lanham, MD: Bernam Press.

Smircich, L., and M. B. Calás. 1987. "Organizational Culture: A Critical Assessment." In *Handbook of Organizational Communication: An Interdisciplinary Perspective,* edited by F. M. Jablin, L. L. Putnam, K. H. Roberts and L. W. Porter, 228–63. Newbury Park, CA: Sage.

Stahl, Sandra. 1977. "The Personal Narrative as Folklore." *Journal of the Folklore Institute* 14: 9–30.

Staroscik, R., and C. G. Cayten. 1976. "Emergency Medical Technician-Paramedic Training." *JACEP* 5: 605–8.

State of California. 1990. Emergency Medical Services. In *H.&S.C.A.* [Health and Safety Code, Annotated] of the State of California. Deering's California Codes, 404–96. San Francisco: Bancroft Whitney Law Publishers.

———. 1992. *Division of Labor Statistics and Research. Work Injuries and Illnesses, 1991.* San Francisco: State Department of Industrial Relations.

———. 1995. *California Statistical Abstract.* Sacramento: California Department of Finance.

Stewart, Charles E. 1988. "AIDS and the Emergency Provider." *Emergency Medical Services* 17(3): 24, 26–27, 46.

Stueven, H., P. Troiano, B. Thompson, J. R. Mateer, E. H. Kastenson, D. Tonsfeldt, K. Hargaten, R. Kowalski, C. Aprahamian, and J. Darin. 1986. "Bystander/First Responder CPR: Ten Years Experience in a Paramedic System." *Annals of Emergency Medicine* 15: 707–10.

Sullivan, John P. 1986. "The Homeless: Responsibilities and Guidelines for EMTs and Paramedics." *JEMS* 11(11): 30–34.

Sundberg, Chuck. 1992. "When a Plane Goes Down." *Emergency Medical Services* 21(7): 42–46.

Tangherlini, Timothy R. 1990. " 'It Happened Not Too Far From Here...': A Survey of Legend Theory and Characterization." *Western Folklore* 49: 371–90.

———. 1994a. *Interpreting Legend: Danish Storytellers and Their Repertoires.* Milman Parry Studies in Oral Tradition. New York: Garland Publishing, Inc.

———, dir. 1994b. *Talking Trauma: Storytelling among Paramedics.* Los Angeles: Traumatic Productions.

Tedlock, Dennis. 1972. *Finding the Center.* New York: Dial Press.

Terkel, Studs. 1972. *Working.* Chicago: Avon Printing.

Thackrey, Ted, Jr. 1986. "70 Die as Planes Collide in Air." *Los Angeles Times* (September 1): A1, A4.

Trice, Harrison M., and Janice M. Bayer. 1993. *The Cultures of Work Organizations.* Englewood Cliffs, N.J.: Prentice-Hall.

U.S. Department of Health, Education, and Welfare (USDHEW). 1971. *Digest of Surveys Conducted 1965 to 1971—Ambulance Services and Emergency Departments, May 1971.* Rockville, MD: USDHEW.

U.S. House of Representatives. 1972. Committee on Interstate and Foreign Commerce. *Emergency Medical Services Act of 1972. Parts 1 and 2.* Washington D.C.: U.S. Government Printing Office.

Vance, Charles M. 1991. "Formalizing Storytelling in Organizations: A Key Agenda for the Design of Training." *Journal of Organizational Change Management* 4(3): 52–58.

Verhoeven, Paul, dir. 1990. *Total Recall.* Los Angeles: Carolco Pictures, Inc.

von Sydow, Carl W. 1932. Om traditionsspridning. *Scandia* 5. Reprinted as "On the Spread of Tradition" in *Carl W. von Sydow, Selected Papers on Folklore,* 11–43. Copenhagen: Rosenkilde and Bagger.

Walker, Thai, and Daniel Vasquez. 1992. "Cop Kills Man After Alleged Double Murder." *Oakland Tribune* (May 22): A3.

Ward, Patrick M., Catherine A. Eck, and Thomas F. Sanguino. 1990. "Emergency Nursing at the Epicenter: The Loma Prieta Earthquake." *Journal of Emergency Nursing* 16(4): 49A-55A.

Weaver, William C., Jr. 1987. "Stress and the EMS Dispatcher." *Emergency Medical Services* 16(7): 18, 20, 23, 25–26.

Young, Katherine Galloway. 1987. *Taleworlds and Storyrealms. The Phenomenology of Narrative.* Dordrecht and Boston: Nijhoff.

Printed in the United States
4673

9 781578 060436